Praise for *PhD Thesis by Publication in Social*

'Margaret Merga is a trailblazer in the wor
In this easy-to-read book, she has shared her experiences of doing a TBP and
the invaluable knowledge she has gained to support current and future
researchers who are pursuing this approach. This book offers practical
guidance on TBP using scholarly literature and real-world examples. Merga
writes in a personable and relatable style, thoughtfully guiding the reader
through the book with the warmth and ease of a conversation. She covers
every possible topic of interest for those considering undertaking a TBP.
Merga does not sugar coat the choice of undertaking a TBP as she outlines
potential risks, while also acknowledging the incredible potential of TBP for
both those who wish to stay in academia and for those with plans beyond.
The most striking aspect of this book is Merga's unwavering sense of
compassion for the research student. Her words are genuine, reflective and
heartfelt. In every chapter, there is underlying advice and support reminding
students to prioritise self-care, especially when undertaking a TBP. This book
stands as a testament to Merga's continued outstanding contribution to the
TBP discussion.'
**Natasha Kitano, Language & Learning Educator, Queensland University of
Technology, Australia**

'Dr Margaret Merga has developed a valuable resource for any doctoral
researcher in the social sciences who hopes to pursue the Thesis by
Publication (TBP) pathway. Written in accessible language and drawing on a
perfect balance of research and experience, this volume offers clear actionable
guidance on navigating some of the most pressing challenges for doctoral
researchers engaging in scholarly publishing, such as how to practically
negotiate author order, and how to effectively communicate to audiences
beyond academia. I highly recommend this must-have resource!'
**Associate Professor Shannon Mason, Department of Education, Nagasaki
University, Japan**

'This book is a fantastic and very timely resource, as more and more students
pursue theses by or with publication in the humanities and social science
disciplines. Margaret Merga weaves together tremendous personal
experience and research understanding to offer an eminently useful,
accessible, and down-to-earth text. The book fills key gaps in the existing
advice literature through its concrete examples and frank discussions around
navigating things like journal article revisions, high-risk research, or
unsupportive or unclear institutional policies. Merga offers practical advice

while acknowledging complexity and variation across contexts. I will be recommending this book to my students wholeheartedly!'
Dr Katrina McChesney, Senior Lecturer, University of Waikato, New Zealand

'Despite its increased popularity, the Thesis by Publication (TBP) is still an unsettled genre with wildly differing rules and expectations across institutional environments. PhD candidates and supervisors alike desperately need common sense guidance on how to write a doctoral thesis with multiple scholarly outputs, sometimes with multiple authors. Using her own experience to illustrate some of the dilemmas that arise when writing a TBP, Dr Merga takes the reader through the entire process: from understanding what the genre is, to writing the articles, putting the thesis together, and getting across the finish line. Written in clear, accessible language, *PhD Thesis by Publication in Social Science Research* should be essential reading for anyone considering writing, supervising, or evaluating a TBP.'
Dr Lynn P. Nygaard, author and workshop leader for academic writing at doctoral level, Peace Research Institute Oslo, Norway

'Reading this book feels like having a great discussion with a knowledgeable colleague. Drawing together research and lived experience, Margaret offers advice regarding the technical and academic elements of TBP, as well as the interpersonal challenges of navigating academic culture. Not afraid to address the pitfalls and ethical minefields students must be aware of, this work is refreshingly accessible as it unpacks and demystifies diffuse and ambiguous policy and practice. As an early-career academic supervisor, reading this book has deepened my understanding of TBP and it will be a valuable reference while supporting future TBP students during their higher degree candidature.'
Dr Kay Oddone, Course Director, Master of Education (Teacher Librarianship), School of Information & Communication Studies, Charles Sturt University, Australia

'If you are a doctoral student considering a Thesis by Publication, this book is for you. If you are supervising a doctoral student who is completing a Thesis by Publication, this book is essential reading. Margaret Merga's research in this field is unparalleled, and the *PhD Thesis by Publication in Social Science Research* is an accessible, transparent and brilliant contribution that demystifies this approach to completing a PhD. Reading this book is like reading the thoughts and reflections of a generous colleague who has been there and done that. However, this book has great significance beyond the

Thesis by Publication; it is a must-read for any doctoral students and early career researchers who are learning to navigate the complex world of publishing in academia.'
Dr Patrick O'Keeffe, Senior Lecturer, Social Work and Human Services Cluster, RMIT University, Australia

'This book is an invaluable resource for anyone considering a PhD thesis by publication (TBP) in the social sciences. Dr Margaret Merga is a leading international researcher on the emergence of the TBP, and this highly accessible and engaging book is packed with research-informed advice for PhD candidates, supervisors, and those involved in policy and curricular development of PhD programs. As an early adopter of this thesis format in her institutional context both as a student and a supervisor, she brings research insights to life with practical experience, presenting examples and concrete strategies that will be helpful for all involved in the TBP process. The book is particularly strong at guiding novices through the journal publication process, placing a key emphasis on ethics and authorship to help navigate the pressures and pitfalls of the current academic publishing industry. In addition, it includes a timely chapter on communicating beyond the academy, highlighting this skill as an integral part of becoming a researcher. In all, an essential guide for understanding the complexities of completing a TBP.'
Dr Kristin Solli, Associate Professor, Oslo Metropolitan University, Norway, co-author of *Strategies for Writing a Thesis by Publication in the Social Sciences and Humanities*

'Margaret Merga's *PhD Thesis by Publication in Social Science Research* is an accessible guide for research students exploring this pathway. In addition to highlighting the many benefits of undertaking this approach, Margaret provides practical advice on navigating university policy and supervisory dynamics. What I loved most in these discussions was her open and candid approach which worked to demystify the various complexities involved. The excellent guidance and illustrative examples for choosing journals, understanding publication impact, and responding to reviewer feedback (or not!), make this book an essential companion for research students!'
Barbra Zupan, Associate Professor and Academic Lead (Graduate Coursework), School of Graduate Research, CQUniversity, Australia

PhD Thesis by Publication in Social Science Research

Every purchase of a Facet book helps to fund CILIP's advocacy, awareness and accreditation programmes for information professionals.

PhD Thesis by Publication in Social Science Research

A Practical Guide

Margaret K. Merga

facet publishing

Published by Facet Publishing
c/o Woburn House, 20–24 Tavistock Square, London WC1H 9HQ
www.facetpublishing.co.uk

Facet Publishing is wholly owned by CILIP: the Library and Information
Association.

British Library Cataloguing in Publication Data
A catalogue record for this book is available from the British Library.

ISBN 978-1-78330-819-4 (paperback)
ISBN 978-1-78330-820-0 (hardback)
ISBN 978-1-78330-821-7 (PDF)
ISBN 978-1-78330-822-4 (EPUB)

First published 2025

The manufacturer's authorised representative in the EU for product safety is
Logos Europe, 9 rue Nicolas Poussin, 17000 La Rochelle, France
(contact@logoseurope.eu, www.logoseurope.eu).

Typeset from author's files by Flagholme Publishing Services in
10/13 pt Palatino Linotype and Open Sans.
Printed and made in Great Britain by CPI Group (UK) Ltd, Croydon, CR0 4YY.

Contents

Figures and Tables

Tables

About the Author

Dr Margaret Kristin Merga has published more than a hundred peer-reviewed journal articles and seven books on literacy, libraries, research methods, higher education and research communications. Her 2022 book *School Libraries Supporting Literacy and Wellbeing* highlights her research on the relationship between libraries, reading and wellbeing, and her 2023 book *Creating an Australian School Literacy Policy* details how to design and implement a whole school literacy policy. Her other 2023 book *Creating a Reading Culture in Primary and Secondary Schools* explores building a whole school reading culture, including detailed content on the research in this area, as well as practical advice on how to evaluate such initiatives.

Margaret's interdisciplinary research in the social sciences has been cited more than 4,500 times and translated into many languages. Committed to sharing research knowledge beyond academia so that a wide range of stakeholders can use her research findings in practical ways, her work has been featured in the media, and she has won numerous awards for public engagement and made many appearances as an international keynote speaker (see her LinkedIn profile). She is also actively involved in higher education policy work, as touched upon in her 2024 article for the London School of Economics Impact Blog 'Is your thesis by publication policy hostile to students?', and in creating evaluation tools for education workplaces such as the Copyright Agency-funded 2025 *Evaluation to fuel advocacy for writer visits in Australian schools: Open-source impact resource*.

At the time of writing this book, she was working as an Associate Professor in Education at the University of Notre Dame Australia (UNDA). As of October 2025, she works as Lead Consultant at Merga Consulting on a range of projects with schools, universities, professional associations and government departments, often related to innovation evaluation, libraries and literacy.

Across her academic career she has played a key role in researcher development of staff and postgraduate students, most recently delivering the

Method of the Month research methods and communication training seminars, and also revitalising and teaching the EDUC5000 Research Methods in Education course at UNDA.

Acknowledgements

I would like to thank Andrew James and the team at Facet for their ongoing support for my work and the excellent publishing experience that they consistently provide. Special thanks to Michelle Lau for her masterful production management and excellent communications skills, while moving this book to the finish line, and to Julie Rowbotham, a genius legend whose editorial eye is second to none.

I'm really lucky in that I have been fortunate enough over the years to work with amazing academics who are experts in this field. I need to particularly thank Associate Professors Shannon Mason and Julia Morris for leading or being part of our numerous thesis by publication and research communication related projects. While I cite a lot of their work in this book, I also strongly suggest that you look up their individual profiles as they do excellent work in this field, as well as in their other research interests. Shannon Mason also runs a fantastic website which is a useful resource in their space. You can learn more about this here: https://thesisbypublication.com.

I need to thank the doctoral students and staff who regularly attended the Method of the Month (MOM) seminars that I ran at the University of Notre Dame Australia in 2024 and 2025. You were excellent participants and after every session I felt increasingly motivated to get this book out. Particular thanks to Patrick Hampton, my line manager at the time who gave me time and support to develop this research development series.

I would also like to acknowledge the members of the Australia/New Zealand branch of the Supervisor Development Reading Group led by the lovely Natasha Kitano. As a group we had many productive conversations in this space that inspired some of my work on this book, and I really appreciated the opportunity for this warm and supportive collegial exchange.

This book talks a bit about the notion of academic upbringing during a PhD, and I would like to sincerely thank Dr Natasha Teakle (formerly Natasha Ayers) for being the most significant positive influence on my researcher identity formed during my own thesis by publication journey. Your generosity, strong research methodology skills, ethical outlook and commitment to knowledge mobilisation shaped my understanding of what it means to be a researcher, and while I appreciated this at the time, I didn't fully grasp the significance of what you were giving me. Years later I'm still enjoying the benefits of your early guidance. I also need to thank my principal supervisor Associate Professor Brian Moon for allowing me to pursue a TBP.

I would like to thank Gabriel (Gabe) and Samuel Merga for their encouragement, kindness and patience. Also, thanks Gabe for being the first reader (yet again); I always appreciate your feedback.

I would also like to thank the book endorsers for their early comments on and support for this book, listed in alphabetical order by last name: Natasha Kitano, Associate Professor Shannon Mason, Dr Katrina McChesney, Dr Lynn P. Nygaard, Dr Kay Oddone, Dr Patrick O'Keeffe, Dr Kristin Solli, and Associate Professor Barbra Zupan. I really appreciated you generously taking the time out from your very busy work schedules to provide your thoughtful, expert feedback.

Finally, I dedicate this work to all doctoral students past and present (especially my own!); so many of you make a huge contribution that may be poorly remunerated and appreciated within and beyond your institutions.

Abbreviations

3MT	Three Minute Thesis
AQF	Australian Qualifications Framework
BERA	British Educational Research Association
COPE	Committee on Publication Ethics
DORA	San Francisco Declaration on Research Assessment
EAL	English as an additional language
EC	Equal contributor
ECR	Early career researcher
ECU	Edith Cowan University
EFL	English foreign language
EQF	European Qualifications Framework
FET	Feedback Expectation Tool
GDPR	General Data Protection Regulation
HASS	Humanities and social sciences
HDR	Higher Degree by Research
HREC	Human Research Ethics Committee
ICMJE	International Committee of Medical Journal Editors
ISLWP	*International School Library Workforce Project*
KMb	Knowledge mobilisation
LIS	Library and information science
MOM	Method of the month
NHMRC	National Health and Medical Research Council
ORCID	Open Researcher and Contributor ID
PhD	Doctor of Philosophy
PID	Persistent identifier
RBR	Recreational book reading
RfP	Reading for pleasure
RQ	Research questions
SLP	School library professional
SO	Scholarly output

STEM	Science, technology, engineering, and mathematics
TBP	Thesis by publication
TEQSA	Tertiary Education Quality and Standards Agency
TWP	Thesis with publications
UK	United Kingdom
UNDA	The University of Notre Dame Australia
UNESCO	United Nations Educational, Scientific and Cultural Organization
US	United States (of America)
WASABR	*West Australian Study in Adolescent Book Reading*

Introduction

As one of the first to undertake a thesis by publication (TBP) at my university, I found myself becoming an early and ongoing advocate for this approach (with qualifications explored further herein!). The next step in this pathway for me was the writing of this book.

So who is it for?

It might be for you if you are:

- trying to decide if a TBP is for you, getting your head around how it compares to the traditional monograph PhD thesis journey to figure out if it's worth the extra work;
- determined to go with a TBP, and you're reading this book to figure out what this is going to involve, and what 'succeeding' even looks like;
- already on the journey, and you're wondering if what you're experiencing is 'normal', and maybe how to make a bumpy process smoother;
- supervising a TBP for the first time, or you're looking to build your capacity in supervising this kind of thesis.

Life doesn't stop for a PhD, and TBP students can find themselves balancing complex work, caring, and other commitments, while in some cases also dealing with the challenges of studying as an external or distance student (McChesney et al., 2024). A recent report from Australia contends that 'the average PhD candidate is 37 years old, often with significant work experience and financial responsibilities like families and mortgages' (Universities Australia, 2024, p. 4). Taking time to weigh up your options makes total sense given that you need to make the PhD experience viable for your own unique individual circumstances, with potential benefits and risks both known and considered. While this book won't tell you exactly what to do, and how to do it, it will let you into some of the tacit TBP knowledge and provide a range of considerations, options and possibilities that you can draw upon across your journey. As such, it's more a knowledgeable friend than a dictator of practice.

First, let's agree on what a TBP even is. For the purposes of this book, a TBP is a thesis including published or accepted scholarly outputs (SOs) produced *during the period of doctoral study* along with other binding material (explored in detail in this book). Let's not confuse it with the *retrospective* PhD by Publication, a route usually taken by academics who have *prior* peer-reviewed SOs to gain a PhD in recognition for the impact of their existing work on knowledge in their field (Campbell, 2022). Along with PhD folio thesis and the PhD thesis by exegesis among others (Deakin University, 2021; Razoumova & Hooley, 2024), there are a growing number of ways that PhD students can meet the requirements of a doctoral degree (as explored in more detail later in this book).

The TBP has been a norm for longer in science, technology, engineering and mathematics (STEM) than it has been in humanities and social sciences (HASS) (Christianson et al., 2015; Paltridge & Starfield, 2023). However, we are catching up; in the UK, Australia, and many other countries, there is increasing pressure for PhD students in HASS, including education and library research, to publish during candidature, and to use those publications as part of their PhD thesis to avoid duplicating their labour, and to ensure that research findings are disseminated as rapidly and widely as possible.

So why this book?

> In 2012 I made the decision to attempt to achieve thesis by publication (TBP) to report on my PhD research project, the *West Australian Study in Adolescent Book Reading* (WASABR). The WASABR investigated adolescents' attitudes toward, and frequency of engagement in recreational book reading, as well as how key social influences, such as teachers and parents, can support the practice effectively. My thesis was one of the first TBPs produced in the School of Education at my institution, Edith Cowan University (ECU).
>
> (Merga, 2015, p. 291)

When I started my TBP in 2012 it wasn't really a 'thing' yet in my School, or at my university, so I spent a fair bit of time convincing everyone (including my supervisors) that the decision was the right one for me. In this book, I draw on my own experiences and the substantial body of research I've conducted or contributed to on TBP and academic research communication that is interwoven throughout this book.

Also, you'll note that I used the words 'attempt to achieve' a TBP in the above quote: this is because 'before my work was accepted, it felt like a gamble to invest so much time on this approach, despite the potential benefits' (Merga, 2015, p. 295). While all PhD journeys have a notable risk of non-completion (Kis et al., 2022), as I explore in this book, chasing a TBP, particularly at a university with a restrictive policy, offers its own unique challenges.

While most TBP policies make no mention of the risks of this approach (Mason et al., 2024a), doing a TBP can be a high-risk, high-reward gamble, though the risk is lower depending on a range of variables discussed throughout this book, which include but are not limited to the flexibility of the university TBP policy, the experience and cohesion of the supervisory team, the speed of peer review, and the individual abilities and characteristics of the TBP student.

While research on TBP is growing, current TBP students are still complaining about the lack of an accessible, reader-friendly book that explains some of the tricky issues and concepts in a straightforward manner, informed by research but with practical implications foregrounded. Furthermore, differences across fields, contexts and supervisory groups can lead to some confusion around norms in this space. In some contexts, such as the UK, there may be 'a fragmented policy landscape in which there is a notable lack of consistent and coherent policy and guidance across institutions' (Robinson, 2023, p. 140), so not all TBP students will necessarily be able to access the level of guidance they need at their institution.

I also need to add that while what counts as *social science research* widely varies depending on context, for the purposes of this book I'm using a broad and inclusive conceptualisation of the term aligning with the view that it relates to 'research on and knowledge about society: its institutions and structures, its histories and its people' (Academy of the Social Sciences in Australia, 2021, p. 6):

WHAT IS 'SOCIAL'?
Social in this context refers to events, objects, rules, patterns and other things that emerge spontaneously or by design when humans interact in groups . . . Think friendship, families, religion, language, politics, schools and hospitals, legislation, markets, armed forces and elections. Or traffic rules, slavery, poverty, crime, corruption, cooperation, justice, homelessness, activism, social media, consumerism, and so on. Social scientists define social systems as comprising biological, political, economic and cultural components. A social system can be as small as a family or a football team, and as big as a group of nations. (p. 6)

While a lot of my research focuses on education and library and information sciences aspects of social sciences research, I have published in social sciences beyond these areas (see Appendix), so I am confident in grounding this work in the norms I have encountered through this experience. My own research, and the work of my research students, is often interdisciplinary within and beyond the social sciences, with relevance for both researchers and professionals, and publication plans from these research projects often consider dissemination across disciplines as applicable. This is also responsive to an overall turn towards embracing interdisciplinarity in doctoral research in some contexts, as captured in a recent systematic review of doctoral education (McKenna & van Schalkwyk, 2024).

As a researcher committed to knowledge mobilisation (KMb) (e.g. Merga, 2021a), I decided to write a book that instead of focusing on more abstract and philosophical aspects of the TBP, focuses on both the extant research and the practical aspects of doing this kind of thesis, aligned with the burning pragmatic questions that current and prospective students may have. I've got some suggestions for you, but this is not a paint-by-numbers doctoral advice book that offers one-size-fits-all solutions (Kamler & Thomson, 2008). Indeed, it may raise more questions than it answers for you as you explore which parts are helpful, and which parts do not apply to your own unique situation.

Rather than breaking down how to compose the perfect academic sentence, this guide is far more focused on the things which we don't really talk about, but which preoccupy PhD students nonetheless.

For example, you may want to know:

- How do we figure out author order on my publications (without bloodshed)?
- How can I reduce my chances of getting rejected by journals?
- How long is the TBP journey probably going to take?
- How can I make sure my work gets read outside academia?
- Are there potential wellbeing risks that I should consider?
- What's the deal with predatory journals and conferences, and how can I avoid them?

Consideration of these kinds of practical questions can be found within this book. I hope that you'll find that while the TBP approach involves some unique challenges, drawing on the knowledge in this book can help students to anticipate and overcome these challenges where possible, even if their supervisors have limited knowledge of TBP. I frequently include real-world examples, as well as drawing on the research.

The book starts with an overview of the basic concepts in Chapter 1, before quickly moving on to deeper detail on the kinds of personal and institutional supports that can help to sustain your success across the TBP journey. In Chapter 2, I delve deeper into the practicalities, from finding the right supervisory team, to planning for quality publications that meet ethics requirements from early stages of candidature. We then move into the practicalities of navigating journal article publication in Chapter 3, with a focus on maximising the chances of journal article acceptance and avoiding desk rejection. Chapter 4 explores a neglected area that will impact on most TBP students – the complex challenge of negotiating authorship within the power imbalance of the student/supervisor relationship, while Chapter 5 helps readers to be responsive to a common criticism of the TBP – the lack of cohesion in the thesis. Chapter 6 provides clear advice on how to deal with the challenges of journal article revisions, including practical wording that you can consider to respectfully say no to unwarranted revisions. Chapter 7 will help you to move your research findings beyond academia so that they can resonate with diverse audiences and ideally lead to real-world change, while keeping you across possible risks you may face during this process. Finally, I use the conclusion section to talk more about what I'd like to see happening in this space going forward (hopefully inspiring you to undertake some of this research!).

I hope that you enjoy this book, and find it a useful read.

## CHAPTER 1

What is a Thesis by Publication?

Let's start by further clarifying what a TBP actually is (at least for the purposes of this book, given that there's some ambiguity around this), briefly touched upon in the Introduction. We need to consider this in relation to what a PhD is, while also pinning down how key terms such as 'scholarly output' will be conceptualised and why. Not for the last time I will point out that the way I frame these concepts is responsive to *the overall research*, not your own unique situation. There may be significant differences in your context that you need to keep in mind/familiarise yourself with.

We will then look at some of the advantages and disadvantages of the approach, considering how it might be structured, and what kinds of personal attributes might make you best suited to this approach. Finally, we will pragmatically consider how long it should probably take, blowing up some current myths on the way, and the kinds of policies that your institution may have that can help you get to the finish line successfully. Even if you look like a best-fit candidate for a TBP, if your university has a hostile policy you need to carefully consider whether this is the right choice for you.

What is a PhD?

When we're thinking about defining a TBP, we need to consider what a PhD is, given that a TBP is the examined text that is used to justify this award.

A PhD (short for Doctor of Philosophy) is a flagship qualification typically sitting at the pinnacle of academic attainment (Shrestha, 2023). It has been contended that possession of a doctoral qualification such as a PhD is 'evidence of a successful attempt to make a knowledge claim and acquisition of research skills and capabilities including much tacit knowledge of the culture of the academy' (Rigby & Jones, 2020, p. 1388).

If this is the case, it means that getting a PhD is not just about proving what you've learned in relation to your topic, it's about demonstrating a degree of mastery over a tacit and therefore somewhat hidden 'cultural' skill set. One of the key reasons that I decided to write this book was to attempt to make visible this 'tacit' skill set in relation to the TBP journey, to even the playing field for PhD students who do not have universities or supervisory teams that are well equipped to prepare them in this endeavour. What this means for you is that from the outset of your PhD journey, it is almost a given that you will need to be intrepid in identifying and aligning with hidden cultural norms, which can be a bumpy process, so be patient with yourself. Furthermore, as I explore to some extent in other sections in this book, some of these aspects of the culture can be toxic and contradictory, so learning how to deal with and mediate those aspects may be one of the most challenging features of your PhD journey.

So how do you show that you've achieved this goal? Any pathway to a PhD needs to tangibly satisfy these knowledge contribution and skill demonstration requirements (Inouye & Bengtsen, 2023). Traditionally, this was achieved through examination of a thesis as a monograph: 'a single long form document typically containing literature review, methods, and results chapters' (p. 224). This chunk of knowledge would then go on to live out its remaining days among 'numerous unpublished PhD theses gaining dust in library archives' (Silverwood, 2023, p. 153), though it is now often uploaded to an online institutional repository.

Along with traditionally producing this mandatory dusty orphan, while a PhD by any route must allow for reaching 'equivalence of doctorateness' (Christianson et al., 2015, p. 6), what constitutes this doctorateness is known to be ambiguous and elusive (Campbell, 2022). It can be contended that this is commonly tied to demonstrating the ability to devise and manage high-quality research with a notable degree of *autonomy*, and in alignment with accepted ethical standards (Evans et al., 2018). However, in some contexts such as the UK, 'from the initial adoption of the research doctorate in the UK in 1917, it was left up to individual universities to define the standards of their doctoral awards' (Taylor & Whisker, 2025, p. 156), and while more recent developments have moved towards standardisation and uniformity, 'that process is not complete' (p. 157). As such, ambiguity remains both within and across some contexts that must be acknowledged when attempting to define a PhD. This means that a TBP, like any other PhD journey, needs to fit what counts as doctoral rigour in the context where it is being undertaken, and this can vary quite a lot. Furthermore, what counts as quality research is also really contentious and the subject of much debate (Rigby & Jones, 2020).

Even within the same university, Department (or whatever level or strata your institution is using), and supervisory team, students can take very different journeys towards a doctorate that involve different levels of attainment and autonomy. For example, Student A in the supervisory team may be on a project funded by a grant won by their supervisor, who has *already* developed the project design; Student A will be the one who conducts and writes up the project with considerable support from the supervisory team. Student B might have the same supervisory team, but be designing their own self-devised, unfunded project with high autonomy.

Are both of the students demonstrating the same level of attainment? I would argue probably not, but that the degree of difference in complexity will very much depend on the nature of supervision, and how much autonomy is fostered and permitted.

I draw on Bloom's Taxonomy here, which presents a hierarchy of categories in relation to complexity of knowledge and skills required. For example, being able to simply remember basic facts and concepts is a lot easier than having to analyse and draw connections across different ideas. I use the Taxonomy not because I think that it is an infallible and perfect framework; rather, I just want to show that the journey to the PhD may involve *different levels* of skill and knowledge, and to illustrate that this is really an issue when it comes to pinning down 'doctorateness'. For those who are not familiar with this Taxonomy, Vanderbilt University Centre for Teaching (n.d.) has kindly shared this visual (Figure 1) with Creative Commons licensing to give you a brief overview.

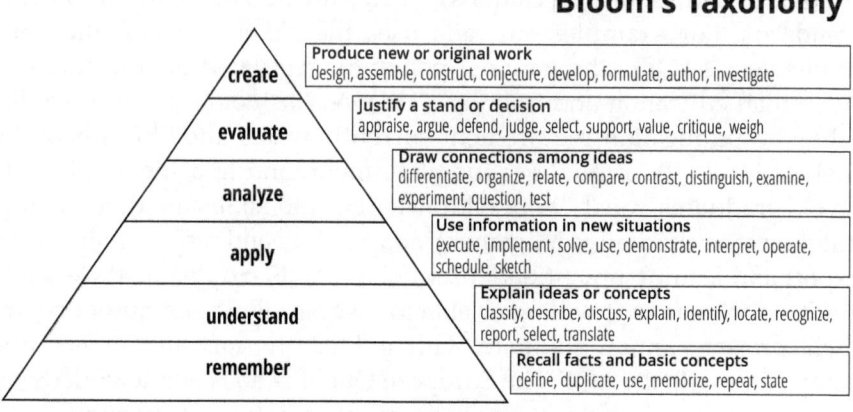

(CC BY Vanderbilt University Center for Teaching)

Figure 1 *Bloom's Taxonomy*

In this instance, depending on the level of support from the supervisory team, as Student A's work around project design has already been done by the supervisor, it is possible that across their PhD they could only rise as high as *analyse* or *evaluate*, depending on the level of autonomy they are encouraged and enabled to adopt on the project beyond the point of design.

In contrast, Student B may find themselves at the pinnacle of this taxonomy (*create*) from day one, requiring a very different level of skill and ability.

My point here is simply to illustrate that even at a local level within the same supervisory team, there is not necessarily equivalence around skill or effort demonstrated during the PhD; there will be many differences. If Student A is discouraged from working with autonomy and reaching the upper pinnacles of this taxonomy because this work has been done by their supervisor to ensure that funder milestones are being met, at the end of the PhD journey, it is reasonable to expect Student B to be far more equipped to autonomously conduct research than Student A. However, if after winning the grant and recruiting Student A, the supervisory team takes a big step back from the higher order decision-making on the project, encouraging Student A to increasingly move into that position so that they are not merely functioning as a Research Assistant, at the end of the PhD journey, these two students might be expected to have reached a more similar level of research skill attainment, though Student B will still probably have contributed more to their project.

While in academia we don't really talk much about the vast differences in skill and knowledge demand between PhD projects that are possible, we do have some regulations supporting a high autonomy requirement. In some countries the expectations of a PhD are backed up by nationwide standards. For example, Australia uses the Australian Qualifications Framework (AQF), 'the national policy for regulated qualifications in Australian education and training' (TEQSA, 2023, para. 1). In Australia, while no publication requirement currently exists, the PhD sits at the highest level (10) of qualification attainment, and to achieve this AQF level, graduates must 'apply knowledge and skills to demonstrate autonomy, authoritative judgement, adaptability and responsibility as an expert and leading practitioner or scholar' (AQF, n.d., para. 4). As such, students who are not willing or able to assume significant autonomy on their project cannot graduate with a PhD in Australia in genuine compliance with the AQF. The European Qualifications Framework (EQF) is primarily devised to support mobility and related recognition of qualifications within Europe (Australian Government, 2016). While the AQF and EQF have many fundamental differences, they share commonality in placing the PhD at the highest level on their qualification scale, and in expecting demonstrable autonomy from these graduate students. The top of the EQF scale is level eight, in relation to responsibility and autonomy. Expectations are that graduates 'demonstrate substantial authority, innovation, autonomy, scholarly and professional integrity and sustained commitment to the development of new ideas or processes at the forefront of work or study contexts including research' (Europass, n.d., para. 9).

Of course, ambiguity about AQF and EQF attainment remains, and many of us know at least one student who got over the line on a PhD primarily due to excessive supervisory intervention. However, as I explore further later in this book, it's in your best interests to progressively build your autonomy and magnitude of contribution across your TBP journey where possible, not only because it can make you compliant with these Frameworks where applicable. Practically identifying what needs to be done to achieve a PhD in your context will involve referring to such Frameworks, reading institutional policy, attending any induction sessions, and using your supervisory team as a key source of knowledge. For example, when I take on a new PhD student, I provide them with links to key current documents, and we have an early conversation about what a PhD is at my university. We also discuss what doing a PhD will mean for them, and what they are hoping to get out of the experience. Increasingly, these conversations seem to centre on making a substantial impact on real-world problems. While a PhD has been traditionally concerned with making a novel knowledge contribution to a field of *academic* research, on a practical level, as I explore further in this book, I don't want to suggest that that is all that it does, or indeed that this is the primary motivation of PhD students. A PhD can be much more.

What is a TBP?

As soon as I heard about the TBP as part of my Graduate Research School training during my PhD journey, I knew that it was what I wanted to do. It's great that I had a really huge level of personal enthusiasm to pursue this approach, because I certainly wasn't getting support from all quarters, given that it was relatively new with my School, and therefore triggered some understandable trepidation in those concerned with my completion. I was lucky enough to be exposed to high-quality TBP training, which gave me confidence to pursue this approach (and helped me complete well within the expected time frame), and a key part of this training involved getting my head around what a TBP actually is.

There is no standard nomenclature for a TBP. It is known by many names, including but not limited to PhD by Publication and Publication-Based Thesis (Sammon et al., 2024), though recent research found that in 41% of cases, it is not given a distinct name at all (Mason et al., 2024a). Similarly, though it is no longer a new form of thesis in many contexts, a TBP is not universally accepted 'or approached in a homogeneous way' (Mason et al., 2024a, p. 1). Generally, a TBP refers to 'a collection of research papers, preferably published in well-regarded, peer-reviewed journals' or other scholarly outputs (SOs) (explained further in the next section), and it will also typically have binding text, 'such as an introductory chapter and/or discussion section, which bring together the ideas explored in the papers into a cohesive whole' (Merga, 2015, p. 291).

As such, the SOs contribute to the thesis, but are part of a whole that may also include an introduction, linking content, a separate discussion, and many other possible elements as explored further subsequently. Given that a TBP includes this binding text and content, not only SOs, perhaps the best name for TBP is actually thesis *with* publication(s) (TWP) (Merga, 2014a). As I explore further in this book, the role of the text in addition to the SOs can be really important, though often neglected in discussion of TBP. In the UK,

> there is general consensus that inclusion of published material in the body of work submitted for examination is acceptable, but not sufficient to merit a doctoral award: in addition the work presented needs to be coherent and to demonstrate explicitly the candidate's individual contribution to knowledge.
>
> (Christianson et al., 2015, p. 5)

It's also worth noting here that while TBP may invoke an image of a plurality of publications, in some cases there may only be one publication in the whole TBP and it can still work as a TBP (depending on the policy in play, as I explore further subsequently).

As briefly touched on previously, TBP is also not the same as a PhD by prior publication, though they are often conflated and confused. Most of the questions I receive about TBP from international prospective TBP students are actually about the PhD by prior publication. As I've noted previously, this

> differs mainly from the TBP in that it is a retrospective award consisting predominantly of peer-reviewed articles that have already been published prior to candidature (Davies & Rolfe, 2009), whereas in the TBP, all publications are written during candidature, and are directly relevant to the doctoral research questions.
>
> (Merga, 2015, p. 292)

This means that in many conceptualisations of a TBP, you cannot use your prior SOs as significant components of your TBP.

Due to the lack of consistency about what a TBP is, you must be guided by your institution's TBP policy and related examination guidelines. As noted by Inouye and Bengtsen (2023), 'the precise requirements differ across institutions and even departments' within institutions (p. 225). Advocates who encourage students to familiarise themselves with extant published TBPs from across institutions should always qualify this with the need to be responsive to *current institution specific norms and policies*. As an obvious example, if you choose to model your TBP structure on a thesis that includes three SOs, but your TBP requires at least four to be compliant with your university's regulations, this won't end well for you. I'll return to this in the section titled 'Hostile policy red flags'. While I provide a brief description of what a TBP is here, what a TBP really is for you will depend on your institutional policy, which may change during your PhD studies, so it's really important to remain across any evolutions in expectations.

How long should it take?

It's often contended that a TBP is a lengthier option than the traditional alternative, but is this supported by the current research?

Given that 'depending on the country and discipline, it takes about 3 to 6 years for a doctoral candidate to fulfil all requirements for the doctoral degree, including submitting a comprehensive dissertation of 100 to 400 pages and to graduate' (Asanov et al., 2024, p. 2390), anything that potentially slows this process further needs to be weighed up on merits.

Our analysis of survey data from 246 doctoral graduates from Australian universities found that

> most full-time candidates who selected the TBP mode were close to the 4-year time frame for completion, and around two thirds of respondents felt that their completion was shorter or around the time expected of them . . . Without capacity to compare length of candidature of the TBP to that of the traditional model, it cannot be stated if this is better or worse in terms of timely completion, however it can be concluded that it is certainly possible for students to complete a TBP on or close to the four-year period, in line with institutional expectations.
>
> (Mason et al., 2024b, p. 255)

As such, while it is possible that a TBP can take longer than a traditional thesis, it is certainly not a given that this is the case.

I think it's also important to note here that there is not necessarily a problematic relationship between the number of SOs that you publish and the length of your doctoral candidature, again suggesting that a TBP won't *necessarily* take longer than a traditional PhD journey, even when you try to publish a lot. Research found that

> doctoral candidates who published four or more journal articles during their candidature (i.e., the highest category of research productivity tested in this paper) also completed their degree in the shortest time (≤3.99 FTE years), exhibiting a mean of 3.76 FTE years.
>
> (Churchill et al., 2021, p. 703)

While there are many possible explanations for these findings that I won't be delving into in detail, these data challenge the conceptualisation of the TBP path as necessarily being longer, and the contention that higher SO productivity is necessarily risky for completion.

What is a scholarly output?

Many different kinds of SOs can be included in a TBP, and I'll be referring to these diverse publications as SOs throughout as a global term inclusive of all of these scholarly outputs, though I'll most frequently be talking about specifics in relation to peer-reviewed journal articles, given their preponderance.

What counts as an SO for the purposes of a TBP can vary widely across institutions. You will need to consult your own university's policy to make sure that your SO choices are compliant, and you don't wind up submitting a thesis that gets rejected by your own institution before even being read by an examiner. If you don't have a policy, if this scope is vague or absent, or if you are currently involved in writing or revising policy, take the following into account.

According to recent international research, SOs in TBPs included journal articles, edited book chapters, books, conference proceedings, non-written outputs, and non-peer-reviewed outputs (Mason et al., 2024b). In our earlier analysis of 165 TBPs from the HASS fields, we found that 'a considerable proportion of candidates, almost one fifth, who included conference proceedings and conference papers in the TBP', perhaps acknowledging 'the importance of dissemination of research findings to wider audiences' (Mason & Merga, 2018a, p. 148). With my own TBP I played it safe by sticking with journal articles. Despite presenting at conferences during my PhD journey, I never gave permission for my papers to be published in conference proceedings to avoid *duplicate publication* (see Chapter 2, which includes content on self-plagiarism), given that I was always planning to write them up as academic journal articles. This was also dictated by my desire to get work in academia using my publications as a foot in the door, and the fact that in education, journal articles in respected journals have a higher perceived value than published conference proceedings.

Regardless of the SO type that you choose, reputability matters. While reputability is a multifaceted construct, in academia peer review can be a key component in determining the direct reputability of an SO publisher. Though clearly in some contexts it's fine to include work that hasn't been peer-reviewed (Mason et al., 2024b), including at least some publications that have been through the rigour of peer review at a well-regarded journal may have a positive influence on your thesis examiners, among other obvious benefits. While there are a lot of issues with peer review, some of which I explore in my recent publication (Merga, 2024a), acceptance after peer review is taken to mean 'that field experts have deemed that the content of a journal article is reliable and ethically produced, making a fitting contribution to the body of research knowledge' (p. 683).

So what is quality or adequate peer review?

There are numerous types of peer review; if you look closer at them, you'll notice that there are many names at play for the same thing. For the purposes of this book, I'm going to go with Wiley's (2025a) nomenclature just to keep it simple (hopefully). While there are also other kinds of peer-review models, you'll most typically see single anonymised, double anonymised, and open peer review, so I'll focus on these here (Wiley, 2025a).

There has certainly been a trend towards the open type in recent times but, at least in the fields where I typically publish, double anonymised remains predominant.

Table 1 *Common kinds of peer review*

Type of peer review	What's involved
Single anonymised	'Reviewer identity is not made visible to author, author identity is visible to reviewer, reviewer and author identity is visible to (decision-making) editor.'
Double anonymised	'Reviewer identity is not made visible to author, author identity is not made visible to reviewer, reviewer and author identity is visible to (decision-making) editor.'
Open	'Reviewer identity is visible to author, author identity is visible to reviewer, reviewer and author identity is visible to (decision-making) editor.'

(Adapted from Wiley, 2025a)

However, just because an SO looks, at face value, like an academic journal article, it cannot be assumed that it actually is viewed as legitimate in the academic publishing world, and there may be substantial questions around the rigour of its peer-review process, if it even (genuinely) has one:

> . . . there may be a tendency for journal articles to be broadly viewed as 'safe' sources for students and library clients to draw upon, however the rise of 'predatory' journals negates the validity of this premise. The notion of 'predatory' publishing was introduced by academic librarian Jeffrey Beall, establishing a contentious 'divide between "legitimate" and pseudo publishing practices' (Mertkan et al., 2021, p. 470). Predatory journals can be conceptualized as journals that deprioritise research quality through an absent or marginal peer-reviewing process for fee-paying authors, sometimes also associated with misleading information including fake affiliations and editorial boards (Perlin et al., 2018), and they may lack rigorous methodological standards and ethical approval (Grudniewicz et al., 2019). Solicitation coupled with high fees is also a common part of this model . . .
>
> . . .extreme examples of predatory journal articles meet the criteria for disinformation, in that it can be argued that they have 'explicit intent to manipulate or deceive others' (American Psychological Association, 2023, p. 7) through mimicking a peer-reviewed output. This leads readers to 'wrongly believe such publications are legitimate scientific journals', with '9/11 conspiracy theorists' regularly citing 'an article in a predatory journal as evidence in support of their views', with other highly questionable outputs including 'a study of ancient Martian management practices' (Pyne, 2017, p. 137). However, it is a mistake to assume that articles in predatory journals will always be so easy to recognize (Walters, 2022).
>
> (Merga, 2024a, pp. 683–684)

This space is even more complex than it was when I undertook my PhD back in 2012. Where students lock their work into predatory journals, they are taking a potentially very costly path that can impact on the perceived reputability of their TBP. It may also go directly against your university's policy.

For example, at my former university, our *Guideline: Authorship, Peer Review, and Dissemination of Research* includes the following statements (look for something similar in your policies):

> 6.4 . . . Researchers are responsible for ensuring the University is not affiliated in the dissemination of research in low quality or predatory journals, books, or conferences. (University of Notre Dame Australia, 2024, p. 6)

10.5 Researchers are responsible for exercising due diligence to ensure that research is disseminated through trusted academic outlets and publishers that meet best practice expectations for the discipline. In line with their responsibilities under The Code, researchers must actively avoid publishing with, or providing editorial services for, predatory publishers. (p. 9)

11.2.6 Predatory publisher refers to journal, book, or conference publishers with intentional or non-intentional practices below acceptable standards for academic publishing. Examples include but are not limited to inadequate peer review processes, lack of transparency in article costs, manuscripts are accepted and published with little or no review, or information in or about the outlets are misleading or false. Further information can be found at Think Check Submit. (p. 10)

There's ambiguity about the specific Code that is 'The Code' in this quote, as this document mentions multiple internal and external Codes without explicitly determining one as 'The Code', but you get the basic picture.

So how can you play it safe when it comes to identifying reputable journals? As it is so difficult in many cases to determine whether a journal is predatory or not without advanced knowledge (indeed, many experienced scholars still struggle with this), *please do not submit any of your PhD work to a journal* until you have confirmed with your supervisory team and/or your academic library team that it is a reputable journal. If you check with your supervisory team and still have doubts (because yes, many senior scholars, perhaps even your supervisors, still publish either knowingly or unknowingly in these journals), please seek additional advice from your academic library team (Mertkan et al., 2021). There are also many online resources and checklists devised to help novice researchers detect predatory journals such as Think Check Submit (2023), though there's no universally accepted list or website where you can check a journal, with attempts to create and maintain these lists controversial and sometimes vigorously contested, given that journals are unsurprisingly not terribly keen to be deemed predatory, whether or not this contention is legitimate (Merga, 2024a). While not without controversy, Cabells' *Predatory Reports* (2025) are favoured by some, but access is not free, so if your university doesn't subscribe, they will be of no use to you.

The emergence of hijacked journals just makes it harder for students seeking to publish in a reputable journal (Parray et al., 2024). These are 'fake scientific publications that mimic the appearance of legitimate journals, exploiting their metadata and accepting papers for publication by using mirror images of reputable journals' (p. 2). This is not always a straightforward false impersonation:

> Usually, hijacked journals mirror legitimate journals without permission from the original journal; at rare times, however, publishers will buy rights to a legitimate journal but continue the publication under considerably less stringent publishing protocols and without clearly noting to the reader the change in ownership or publication standards (sometimes known as 'cloned' journals). Scholars can be duped into publishing in hijacked journals – many of which require fees – by offers of fast publication and indexing in databases such as Scopus; being indexed in such databases is viewed by many universities and governments as a mark of legitimacy.
>
> (Retraction Watch, 2025a, para. 2)

This means that it is now possible to submit a paper to a hijacked journal that looks the same, and has the same name, as a legitimate journal; unsurprisingly, given the resemblance, these journals 'attract more manuscripts' than predatory journals not using the same impersonation tactics (p. 4). This is why you need to involve your supervisors at the stage of submission as more experienced academics might be more likely to spot anomalies in URLs and other telltale features. There's also a list being maintained on the Retraction Watch (2025a) website that provides useful information if you think you might be submitting to a hijacked journal.

If only 'legitimate' journal publishers could make life easier by not running their own exploitative model. You'll find as your experience in academia increases that one of the biggest issues is that the so-called legitimate academic publishing environment is so incredibly sketchy that it's kind of hard to distinguish from the predatory models. In 2024 I had to explain legitimate academic publishing to a group of postgraduate students as part of a research methods course I was coordinating and, as might be imagined, they left thinking that academics have somewhat of a cult mindset. While we are ostensibly remunerated for our labour on journal articles by our institutions through our academic salaries, I don't know any research-active academic who does not put in a vast volume of additional personal overtime that is unpaid on this work. We then submit our articles to academic publishers, sometimes having to pay a processing fee, and/or an open-access publication fee. We do not get paid a single cent by the publisher:

> Imagine being an expert in your field, and working for months – maybe years – on a cutting-edge research project. And then imagine sending that research to a publisher who pays you nothing for your work. Instead, they charge you an

enormous fee for the privilege of having it appear in their journal. No one would go along with that kind of racket, right? Unfortunately, that's the entire business model of academic publishing.

(Scicluna, 2024, para. 2)

You won't be surprised to hear that their profits are extraordinary given this model, generating billions in revenue (Scicluna, 2024). As such, it's pretty rich that we frame predatory journals as the more exploitative option when ironically they can be cheaper to publish in than 'legitimate publishers', who have faced class action for denying peer reviewers payment, among other claims (see Scarcella, 2024). However, given the quality control issues around peer review associated with predatory journals, we are stuck with things as they are for the time being unless we academic peasants revolt en masse and journals lose their free flow of content and reviewer labour.

Beware; it's not just predatory journals looking to dupe you. While I was undertaking my PhD I worked as a SOAR Ambassador and Mentor (Booth et al., 2016), which was basically a paid research consultancy where one day a week I made myself available to support my peers on their research journey. During that time, a number of my peers were approached by vanity publishers who attempted to stroke their egos with regards to their achievements in order to secure payment for thesis publication as a book. Unsolicited emails from vanity publishers agilely dodging the spam folder claimed that the student's work was truly groundbreaking, offering to publish the work for a fee, leading to much agonising over whether or not to proceed with the opportunity.

There may be field-specific differences in this, but personally I would never pay for anyone to publish a book that I've written. It's bad enough that we often have to pay for open-access journal article publication; we certainly shouldn't be paying for people to publish an entire book that we've written. Please take care during your PhD journey as there are plenty of scammers proliferating in that space who are becoming increasingly adept at manipulating a vulnerable and inexperienced target group.

In addition to predatory journals and vanity book publishers, we also have predatory conferences that you are strongly advised not to submit to. I receive invitations to be part of these conferences at least weekly if not daily, and in some instances have difficulty determining the difference between these invitations and the legitimate keynote invitations that I also receive. Again, you need to check with your supervisory team before submitting to conferences, and you can also use online resources to evaluate their reputability. For example, the Australian Government's Tertiary Education Quality and Standards Agency (TEQSA) has released an A–Z resource that can be used as a guide, which also acknowledges that while 'there is no single checklist for determining if a conference is predatory', 'reputable conferences share some common qualities and features' (TEQSA, 2024). I've linked to this resource in the reference list.

Ideally you are working in a context where beyond reputability, there are no limitations on your choices, so you can choose reputable SO outlets in consultation with your supervisors that are most appropriate for your field and project. However, in reality, your university and/or your supervisory team will probably expect you to meet certain *criteria for impact*. Your supervisors will advise you about any limitations related to impact relevant at your university, as well as the best metrics to consult for your field and institution (if applicable). You may find yourself locating what you believe to be the perfect journal for your work, and you may confirm that it is a legitimate journal only to speak with your supervisors and have them tell you that it is too low-impact. If you are new to academia, this may seem quite mystifying. By the end of your PhD you may have a stronger understanding of the kind of forces that dictate SO decision-making in higher education, and how academics are forced to be responsive to them in some contexts far more than others (Merga et al., 2025); we are not all identically constrained.

Some universities demand a certain specified quality level of SOs for career progression. For example, an Australian university document on academic promotion specified the following under 'evidence for quality' related to 'research outputs': % of pubs in Q1 journals/conferences university presses (or equivalent lines with scholarly commercial presses using peer review) (University of Newcastle, 2021, p. 9). Similarly, at another Australian university, their *Practice and evidence guide for research* supporting staff to reach academic levels C, D and E (Senior Lecturer, Associate Professor and Professor) includes mentions of Q1 outputs as 'evidence demonstrating impact of practice' in all three cases, as: 'Data and/or documentation demonstrating the proportion of articles published in Q1 journals or discipline equivalent' (Royal Melbourne Institute of Technology, 2019, p. 13).

This aforementioned Q1 status is one of many ways that journal impact is determined, though you should only use it if your supervisors think that it is applicable to you (your field(s) may be more reliant on other measures). Q1 refers to quartile rank:

> Quartile rankings are calculated for each journal in each subject category according to which quartile of the journal occupies in the impact factor

distribution of that subject category. Q1 denotes the top 25% of the impact factor distribution, Q2 the middle-high position (between top 25 and top 50%), Q3 the middle-low position (top 50 to top 75%) and Q4 the lowest position (bottom 25% of the impact factor distribution).

(Miranda & Garcia-Carpintero, 2019, p. 480)

Quartile rankings are deemed useful because what is a 'good' number of citations will wildly vary across fields: 'Due to incomparability across different research areas field-normalized JIFs (journal impact factors) such as JIF quartiles have been introduced and increasingly adopted in research evaluation', as 'citation counts of publications from different fields should not be directly compared with each other, as there are large differences in the citation density, i.e. the average number of citations per publication, among fields' (Miranda & Garcia-Carpintero, 2019, p. 480). So how different are we talking? Patience et al. (2017) found that 'the number of citations per paper vary by several orders of magnitude and are highest in multidisciplinary sciences, general internal medicine, and biochemistry and lowest in literature, poetry, and dance' (p. 1).

Also, working in the social sciences, assuming you use them, you can't just get your quartile rankings from anywhere. For example, Web of Science generated quartile rankings are felt to be an unreliable option given that 'coverage of the humanities, social sciences, business, and even mathematics are poorer than they are for natural sciences and health sciences' (Patience et al., 2017, p. 20), so at the universities where I have worked, we have mostly relied on Scopus generated quartiles, which are also not perfect.

Finally, some fields, institutions and contexts are turning away from the use of JIF; the San Francisco Declaration on Research Assessment (known as the DORA) describes the many notable limitations of relying on JIF. Their recommendations emphasise 'the need to eliminate the use of journal-based metrics', such as JIF, 'in funding, appointment, and promotion considerations', and 'the need to assess research on its own merits rather than on the basis of the journal in which the research is published' (DORA, n.d., para. 4).

I'll talk more about journal impact in relation to journal selection in Chapter 3 on navigating journal article publication, so you can jump straight to this section if you wish.

Why you should do a TBP

There are many reasons why it can help to have sound reasons to attempt a TBP. For instance, you may need to justify your decision to others; not all environments are equally supportive and knowledgeable about the TBP, so if you can articulate its benefits, it may help you to advocate for the opportunity to attempt this mode.

You may also need to periodically remind yourself of these benefits when you are feeling a bit low during the journey, and are perhaps questioning your life choices!

Luckily, as I briefly cover in this section, there are plenty of solid reasons to choose a TBP. While we need more research in this area, to date some of the possible benefits include the following.

Landing that academic job

Doing a TBP can enhance students' prospects of future academic employment (Cash, 2023; Mason et al., 2022; Xu et al., 2024), and as a related point, boost your post-PhD workload allocation for research in academia. From my own personal experience, while I've spoken to colleagues who had to fight to get 40% of their workload allocated to research early in their career, I was offered this in my first post-PhD academic role as I had already proven my value in this regard, and others have been offered even more. Doing a TBP is a golden opportunity to prove that you can succeed in one of the most challenging aspects of the academic role, making you an attractive prospective employee. You may never have time to devote yourself to a single research project ever again if you move into academia post-PhD, and the limited time for research you may encounter as an early career researcher (ECR) beyond your PhD (if you move into this) can absolutely inhibit your capacity to establish your research, and yourself as a researcher, at that point (Laudel & Gläser, 2008). A TBP is an opportunity to set yourself up as a researcher, with publications under your belt.

Looking good at examination

SOs can be peer-reviewed quality indicators within the thesis that have met disciplinary standards (Guerin, 2016; Merga, Mason & Morris, 2020), also appealing to examiners where publications are in well-regarded journals (Mullins & Killey, 2002; Sharmini et al., 2015). Your publications could be used to actually attract examiners; 'if the student has been undertaking a PhD by publication, it is likely that the examiner will have been exposed to a student's published work, and this may encourage them to accept the invitation to examine the thesis' (Robins & Kanowski, 2008, p. 13).

Tapping into external expert feedback and joining the party

Peer review can provide high-quality feedback from beyond the supervisory team, contributing a fresh perspective that can enable students to enhance the quality of their research (Merga, 2015; Merga, Mason & Morris, 2020). Publication also allows TBP students to be 'active participants in international publication and peer dialogue' (Kamler, 2008, p. 292), and thus valued knowledge contributors influencing their research knowledge fields.

Learning the ropes of academic publication, writing and work

Let's face it, a person is going to write very few theses across their lifespan. Developing mastery of reusable academic publishing and text production skills for the creation of SOs (e.g. journal articles) is a better investment of time (Mason et al., 2020a; Merga & Mason, 2021a; O'Keeffe, 2022). Completing a TBP can also lead to a more realistic understanding of what it means to be an academic researcher compared with creating the traditional monograph (O'Keeffe, 2022); before committing to being an academic, it's useful to know whether you can handle being occasionally excoriated in peer review.

Efficiency, time saving, originality and freshness

Publishing as you go on a TBP could be time-saving if you were committed to doing SOs anyway, as published work does not need to be rewritten to be included in the thesis (Christianson et al., 2015; O'Keeffe, 2020). TBP also enables you to share findings while they are fresh and current; for example, sample or data age can contribute to desk rejection in some cases (Stolowy, 2017), and waiting until post-PhD to begin to publish means trying to publish older data. This also removes the pressure to publish PhD findings post-PhD; Cash (2023) contended that 'it made a huge difference to complete my degree and immediately to move on to other new projects without the need to publish and disseminate my research still hanging over my head' (p. 154). While many students avoid the TBP and seek to publish later, some academic journals will not accept work from published dissertations, or will only accept them if they are 'a significantly advanced version' (Klein & Müller, 2022, p. 544).

Boosting your university's productivity and meeting requirements

SOs with TBP student authors can make up a notable portion of a School or Faculty's overall outputs (Robins & Kanowski, 2008). The publications in your TBP increase overall SOs for your institution, which will benefit from this increased 'productivity' during the PhD (Christianson et al., 2015; Frick, 2019). This optimised return on investment (Connoway & Malherbe, 2024) can potentially be leveraged by you during your PhD when applying for additional internal funding at your university, such as for conference travel, or for a job post-PhD.

At some universities, publication of a set number of articles is an institutional requirement prior to the doctoral thesis being sent for external examination (Oboirien, 2024) or prior to degree conferral (Arrieta et al., 2024; Hidayat et al., 2024), making a TBP a logical choice in these contexts to avoid duplication of labour. Sometimes this is a nationwide mandate. For example, the Philippine Qualifications Framework (PQF) requires that graduate students publish 'a research work in an internationally or nationally refereed and indexed journal or have a juried creative work outlet' (Arrieta et al., 2024, p. 40). It is very interesting to note that the introduction of a similar PhD publication requirement in Kazakhstan led to substantial growth in publication volume, but also a decline in publication quality (Kuzhabekova, 2025). Some nations and institutions that previously had this requirement instituted have since backflipped, also (at least in part) due to concerns about the impact of the policy on research quality (Hemant, 2022; Niazi, 2022). I hope that we can see more research in this area to better understand the impact of such policies across contexts.

Managing and maintaining momentum

Completing a TBP can help you maintain momentum across the life of the project, breaking down the whole into a series of achievable published goals (Guerin, 2016; Robins & Kanowski, 2008). Personally, I found tackling my PhD in smaller bites as SOs prevented me from being overwhelmed by the immensity of a monograph, and each time an article was accepted for publication, I found it incredibly motivating, inching closer to the finish line. However, as I explore further in this book, the labour of constructing a cohesive thesis remains on a TBP.

Scholarly impact and knowledge mobilisation

Sharing your PhD study beyond a traditional monograph thesis can enhance the prospects of the research being read in general, given the typically low citation rate of the traditional form (Kousha & Thelwall,

2020; Larivière et al., 2008). TBP requires the production of higher-calibre SOs more likely to contribute to the extant knowledge in a field; dissertations are often purposefully excluded from literature reviews due to their perceived lower-quality status (Taylor et al., 2014). TBP also potentially enhances the prospects of the research reaching relevant stakeholders in industry and the professions, perhaps influencing your employability prospects beyond academia (Shrestha, 2023).

Finding a voice, defending perspectives

Given the dominance of academic authors from higher-income countries in many journals (e.g. Mason, Merga et al., 2021), a TBP constitutes an opportunity for scholars from lower-income contexts to focus on generating SOs that are responsive to local concerns and issues with unique relevance currently marginal or missing in the academic literature (Connoway & Malherbe, 2024).

Experiencing peer review during doctoral candidature can also help you to learn how to effectively and critically challenge popular ideas (Merga, 2015). Personally, I knew from the outset that undertaking a TBP predicated on the ongoing value of recreational book reading was not going to be well received by reviewers who viewed this interest as horribly outdated and irrelevant. The irony that many adult academics much older than me were more determined that books are 'done' than the children I spoke with did not escape me; my research went against the scramble to dismiss 'dated' texts to be 'future focused', and this was a constant arm-wrestle in peer review. I noted that 'from my first publication I was frequently challenged by external journal reviewers to argue for the legitimacy of focusing on a text type that some within my profession viewed as outdated' (p. 295). This taught me to anticipate their arguments and make a stronger case for the value of my research, preparing research-supported points I then drew on in future communication with both scholarly and professional audiences. As such, while having to defend a legitimate perspective can be frustrating, it can also help you to address any perceived chinks in the armour of your rationale.

Some of these reasons are a little bit shady

Clearly, some of these points are *highly problematic* realities, and while this book does not focus on addressing the forces that led us to this point, or delving deeply into related criticism, I do need to acknowledge this early and clearly.

For example, the notion of the TBP as facilitating optimal return on investment for institutions (Connoway & Malherbe, 2024) while being a legitimate point reflecting current reality in many academic contexts, is also a result of the concerning trend towards neoliberal rationalisation in higher education, and where not all academics are positioned fairly and equally for TBP attainment. Huang (2021) devised the concept of '*neoliberal publication habitus*', where 'the market logic for getting doctoral writing published has been structured internally as a collective habitus in the international Chinese doctoral students' (p. 757):

> Once embodied, the neoliberal publication habitus on the one hand generates the strategies to maximise the individual profits from doctoral writing, such as choosing to undertake a PhD by publication, writing for publication outside a doctoral thesis, and getting published in co-authorship. On the other hand, the embodiment of the neoliberal publication habitus produces the symbolic violence of shame and regret in international Chinese doctoral students with 'zero' publications. (p. 757)

This is particularly concerning given that the playing field was not level to start with, with native English speakers publishing in English language journals already in a position of relative advantage. However, nonetheless, it remains a reality that the quality and quantity of SOs produced by affiliated staff and students shape university funding in some contexts (Huang, 2021).

Despite spending much of my academic life chasing good metrics to ensure my job security (Merga et al., 2025), and being partly motivated to do a TBP to support this goal, I don't mean to suggest that this is how it should be. O'Keeffe (2020) relatably described how doing this kind of PhD inculcated him in norms that led to him losing sight of his original motivation for even doing a PhD:

> I didn't start a PhD to emerge with a good h-index; I had hoped that I might somehow contribute to how Australian society can be understood and, in particular, draw attention to how an economically rationalist policy shift has been made possible. I had hoped to fulfil the potential that I had in scholarly work, to pursue a career in work that I valued and enjoyed. Yet, when assessing my own employment prospects towards the end of my candidature, I had largely forgotten about these ambitions, when facing the bright and disorienting lights of publication outputs, h-index and citation counts. (pp. 297–298)

For those new to academic metrics, the h-index and related citation counts referred to here are ways researchers endeavour to quantify their impact (Rousseau & Daraio, 2025):

> In the neoliberal environment of contemporary academia, an individual's research rankings and outputs can shape their career security and progression. When applying for ongoing employment and promotional opportunities, academics may benchmark their performance against that of superior colleagues to demonstrate their performance in relation to their discipline. The h-index and citation rates are commonly used to quantify the value of an academic's work, and they can be used comparatively for benchmarking purposes.
>
> (Merga, Mat Roni & Mason, 2020, p. 2505)

As we explore further in our 2020 article, and as has also been noted by others (e.g. Light et al., 2025), the h-index is a pretty questionable metric, but as it is still commonly used as an achievement indicator in many fields, we still keep an eye on how this metric evolves; the h-index is a kind of nonsensical buoy that we cling to, bobbing in the choppy waters of academic prestige.

So just how nonsensical is it? Person X could publish two papers, cited more than a million times each. They can still only have an h-index of two. Person Y could publish three papers, each cited exactly three times. Due to the formula, Person Y has the higher h-index of three despite being barely cited in comparison. As such, though this is an extreme example to illustrate the point, there are plenty of issues with making decisions on merit purely based on 'citation-based indicators'; for example, 'they are often related to visibility and not necessarily originality', they can be manipulated, there is serious linguistic bias at play, among many other valid concerns (Rousseau & Daraio, 2025, p. 3). Regardless, they are still widely used and valued, and I include them in grant applications and other contexts where I need to argue for impact alongside a range of other qualitative and quantitative indicators, many of which I outline in Chapter 7.

In the process of becoming part of the academic machinery, and beginning to internalise its priorities, a red flag is waved around the possible consequences. This is one of the many reasons that this book includes an entire chapter devoted to KMb (Chapter 7). I held onto it as a parallel priority both during my doctoral candidature and for substantial periods of my academic career, though this added great pressure at times, given that KMb-related labour was poorly recognised in the workload models I typically operated under (Merga, 2021a). Your TBP will help your metrics, but it can and arguably should be much more than a metric-harvesting exercise, and being able to show real-world impact beyond metrics can also offer notable benefits.

Am I a TBP kind of person?

Weighing up the possibilities and risks of TBP for you can involve an element of introspection where we look at the alignment between our own strengths and capabilities and what is demanded by the venture.

Given that the TBP is relatively new, we are still very much in the early stages of learning about the kinds of personal characteristics that support success. In 2018, we carried out a study led by Shannon Mason that captured the views and experiences of 246 recent Australian TBP graduates. One of the things that we sought to capture was their perception of the skills and personal attributes they felt supported them to succeed at TBP. We saw *skills* as something that could be learned both at the outset and throughout the journey, whereas we conceptualised *attributes* as being more fixed, 'personal qualities that may be more challenging to influence' (Merga et al., 2019, p. 272).

Bear in mind that as I will constantly reiterate, I am not suggesting that your skills and attributes should all be perfect on day one as the TBP is a doctoral apprenticeship, and you can have the best skills and attributes in the world and still fall short if your TBP takes place in an extremely unfavourable environment. This section does not seek to put the responsibility for TBP success onto the student; rather, it invites consideration of a single facet that can support success. Also, these skills and attributes are derived from limited research in this space and may not be applicable to all contexts, and this book is designed to boost your knowledge of some of the key related areas. To help you gauge whether you are perhaps a TBP kind of person, here are some of the skills and attributes you might need to have or develop as applicable/possible:

1   **Collaboration and interpersonal skills.** You're good at managing up, and can manage supervisors and delegate specific supervisory and related project tasks to them where a clear power imbalance exists. You are comfortable with networking and leadership and can grasp and be responsive to the often-complex dynamics at play in academic environments. You have enough confidence to advocate for yourself and your project. You clearly communicate and negotiate expectations of your research team (usually your supervisors and any other applicable individuals adding value to your project) and associated milestones and deadlines.

2   **Academic reading and writing.** You have confidence in your current levels of written academic expression, and you have external affirmation that this confidence is warranted. You are determined to commit to lifelong improvement and refinement in this skill area. You can adjust your academic writing style to communicate with different academic audiences. You edit your work rigorously and seek academic writing support as needed. You invest significant time in reading broadly and deeply within your research area.

3   **Publication journey negotiation.** You have some understanding of the publication journey and your role in facilitating it as project leader on a TBP. You are developing realistic expectations of the amount of time and work that this can take. You know how to assess journals for alignment and quality, and how to familiarise yourself with, and respond to, their author guidelines and related submission requirements. You don't assume that this is your supervisor's responsibility unless this has been directly communicated to you. You have confidence in your ability to liaise clearly and effectively with publication staff (e.g. journal editors, peer reviewers, etc.).

4   **Dealing with peer review and feedback.** You can handle rejection in a healthy and regulated manner, and deal with constant scrutiny and examination of aspects of your thesis (SOs) by supervisors, editors and peer reviewers. As explored in greater detail later in this book, sometimes peer-reviewer feedback can be brutal and contradictory, which can exacerbate anxiety levels, and you have (or are developing) strategies for dealing with confronting episodes without sacrificing your wellbeing.

5   **Organisation, planning and time management.** You have 'high-level organisation, planning, and time management skills' (p. 276); when things don't proceed as you might ideally want them to, you proactively identify and address the issues as far as possible within your control. No one has to nag you about time management, because you're already ahead of the game, and watching the clock to stay that way.

6   **Information technology (IT) proficiency.** You are not daunted by the need to gain rapid functional knowledge of a wide array of new systems and applications, and you actively fill in gaps in your proficiency as required. You can judiciously select from available IT tools to support your research and publication needs in consultation with your supervisory team.

7   **Resilience and patience.** You'll need vast quantities of resilience and patience, and not just for dealing with peer review and feedback. Across the phases of the project, there are plenty of opportunities for unanticipated barriers and hurdles to arise, even in carefully designed projects; just ask any Higher Degree by Research (HDR) student or researcher who planned to collect data from human subjects in 2021 if they planned for a global pandemic. Personally, I switch from a controlling style to a flexible style—there is no point in getting down over the things you can't control. Control what you can, but when things get out of control, switch it up, reduce your scope if needed, just make sure you are ethics and policy compliant. Scaling down your project to be responsive to unanticipated limitations doesn't make your project worthless.

8   **Determination, focus and passion.** From a supervisory perspective, at the outset of the project when my PhD students are selecting their area of focus, they usually have multiple competing projects in mind, often with comparable merits in terms of meeting a research gap and real-world need. At that point, I advise them to select the project that they are most passionate about, and that they feel the most urgency to deliver. Given the challenges of the TBP, determination, focus and passion will all be needed to sustain commitment to a project that will be a significant drain on your time and potentially also on your emotions and sense of wellbeing. PhD attrition is high (Kis et al., 2022), and choosing the project that you want to do, that you can remain invested in despite foreseeable and unanticipated setbacks, is one thing you can do to tip the odds in your favour.

9   **Independence and assertiveness.** You ideally need to be able to transition into a high autonomy orientation towards your work in order to meet the qualification requirements of the PhD. If the idea of being independent, assertive and autonomous seems terrifying, a TBP might not be for you. If you are so dependent on the input of your supervisory team that the sickness of one of your supervisors would mean that you would have to completely stop working on your project, you could also have a serious problem. As soon as practicable, you need to shift into the driving seat on your TBP, with your supervisors coaching and supporting from the passenger seats. I do need to be clear again here though, that not all supervisory teams and institutions will be equally supportive of you developing high autonomy, and given the power imbalance, if you struggle here it's not necessarily on you.

10 **Introspection, adaptability and openness to self-improvement.** If you are not willing to embrace change and self-improvement, the TBP might be an extremely challenging experience. Are you highly resistant to advice and feedback? If so, this could hold you back in terms of growing your knowledge and skills for research project management, and also make it very challenging for you to move through peer review. You also can't really think like this as a researcher, as it can manifest in unfortunate ways. For example, if you go into your project already certain of what you will find, there's no point in undertaking your research, and you will struggle to convince people of its merits.

(Partly adapted from (Merga et al., 2019, pp. 274–278))

Sometimes mature-age students feel reluctant to embark on a PhD, but I don't think this should hold you back as older students are often outstanding. Related to the previous points, I also want to stress that *sense of purpose born from experience* seems to be a great motivator. I really like working with mature-age PhD students who have developed expertise in their fields, often coming in with a skill set that includes project and time management, and a well-developed communicative capacity. Running TBP promotion sessions with these kinds of candidates, and working with them in a supervisory capacity, I've noticed the following general traits in those who thrive during candidature. While we need far more research in this area, I'll dare to generalise a little here to see if this resonates with you, as I do think their motivations seem to be common in some cases. These professionals can enjoy an opportunity to investigate that thing they are obsessed with/knowledgeable about from a practitioner and/or leadership standpoint anyway; they are often interested in a PhD as they've honed in on a research knowledge gap with serious real-world implications encountered in the course of their professional experience. While they often have no interest at all in entering academia post-PhD, they are keen to become a (more) credible source of knowledge based on what they find and can be looking to establish a foundation of expertise to leverage to meet their current/future career and leadership goals. They want to work with an expert supervisor with genuine ongoing professional connections to their community, someone that they trust and who understands them and their priorities, even while working in academia rather than directly in the professional or industry-specific field. They may also be looking to further build transferrable outstanding project management and research methods skills, communication skills, data literacy and research skills, among many others, to bring back to their workplace and upskill others. Also, when they have already risen to the top of their professional field, they are often open to new challenges, such as mastering the complexity of academic writing or switching from an advocacy standpoint to a researcher standpoint.

What might make it harder

While this is challenging to measure, as mentioned earlier, attrition from PhD study *in general* is high (over a third) for many reasons (Kis et al., 2022), and as I explore in depth throughout this book, the TBP offers some pretty major challenges that are unique to this journey. Anecdotally, speaking with students who intended to complete the TBP, but were forced to either revert to the traditional thesis or abandon the PhD altogether, there can be many contributing factors, some of which cannot be anticipated, and therefore are completely outside your control. Among the many factors to consider when you're weighing up whether or not a TBP is the right fit for you and your circumstances, here are some of the many that are worth considering beyond the aforementioned skills and attributes.

Unsupportive environment

An unsupportive environment is going to make it really tough. Just as a fish cannot thrive (or perhaps even survive) in an aquarium in low pH water (so please take care of their water as they can't walk away), some students find themselves in an environment that becomes incrementally more acidic, not really noticing that it has become untenable until they are already seriously struggling. I've heard plenty of stories from fledgling students about unsupportive environments, and I'll touch on this in more detail in the section on hostile policy red flags, though that is only part of the issue.

Here are some of the features of an optimally supportive environment for PhD students undertaking a TBP:

- An experienced and capable supervisory team who are committed to supporting you. Sometimes the only supervisors who are suitable for your project will indicate that they are unwilling to supervise a TBP. While in some cases this can be because they have drawn upon their experience to make an accurate assessment of your capability for academic publication, helping you to avoid risk, in other instances this assessment process is flawed and thus no reflection of your capability at all. I've heard of instances where talented students who already have experience as first authors on quality peer-reviewed journal articles have been blocked from undertaking a TBP, often with limited rational explanation provided. I also want to be clear here that just because an academic has been around for a really long time does not mean that they are a great supervisor; in some cases the relationship between experience and competence is there, but in others, it simply is not. You will get a feel for whether or not your supervisor's style aligns with your own learner needs early in your journey. As long as your expectations are reasonable and realistic, you should trust your instincts if you get the feeling that the fit is not good, rather than expect your supervisors to change, as that is unlikely to end well. This noted, very few students will have the perfect supervisory team as supervisors are human too. Also, a supervisory style that suits one student may make another feel undermined. There is a lot of subjectivity at play.

- A well-resourced Graduate Research School or similar which is able to support your ongoing research training, particularly if you are using research methods that your supervisors are rusty on (which can be okay, as no one knows everything, not even your supervisors); even where research methods courses are provided as part of the degree, this may not be enough to meet students' specific needs (Bahtilla & Huang, 2024). While in some instances research training is primarily provided by the supervisor or supervisory team, a recent review notes that 'there is a clear trend towards curriculating for more structure and towards more intentional community building, sometimes in place of the traditional one-on-one or co-supervision approach but often alongside it' (McKenna & van Schalkwyk, 2024, p. 988).

- A suitably clean and quiet space in which to work, whether it be in the academic library or an allocated space within your School, Department or Faculty. Depending on your circumstances, it may be impossible for you to feasibly secure this kind of space for yourself independently, making you completely reliant on the university's provision of such a space. Ideally, this space needs to be adequately resourced with an appropriate desk, chair, and information technology devices and access as required. For TBP students with work, childcare or other caring responsibilities, the space needs to be accessible 24 hours a day, seven days a week.

- Access to writing consultants. These are particularly crucial for TBP students who are still developing their English academic reading and writing skills, and failure to provide this access can particularly impact on TBP students from linguistically diverse backgrounds where the research is expected to be communicated in English.

- Access to funding to conduct and publish research. While TBP students can scale their projects to be responsive to available funding and resourcing, there is a bare minimum that needs to be available, and sustained, to support the conduct of research of a sufficient scope and quality to justify the awarding of a PhD. In the case of a TBP, funding to support research publication may be pertinent for fields where payment of article processing fees is increasingly the norm.

- Access to the literature. This is not a given. Even at my former university at the time of writing, the University of Notre Dame Australia (UNDA) which is in a high-income context, I didn't have access to some journals via my university library licensing and subscriptions, including some journals where I have published in the past, such as the Elsevier journal *Library & Information Science Research*. Yes, I could not access my own past research at this journal via my library, research that I provided to this journal free of charge—you read this correctly. I know that there are many scholars in other contexts who have *even more limited access to the literature,* to the point that they are scraping by on pre-prints and journal articles where the authors have been able to afford open access, giving them an incomplete picture of the field. Those celebrating the potential of open science often conveniently ignore the Matthew Effect here—it can be expected that wealthy universities and individuals who can afford to pay for open access will benefit from far broader readership and related citations. These citations include from lower-income contexts where TBP students will cite the literature with little hope of ever being able to afford to publish in the journal. It's frankly a disgrace, but one that suits the wealthy.

It's certainly possible to succeed without all of these things being optimal, but if in the early days, you notice that there are environmental factors that are currently inadequate or projected to notably decline, you should closely consider whether TBP at your institution is the right way forward for you if you have other viable options.

Resistant design

Beyond environment, there are instances where a PhD project design is excellent, but a bad fit for a TBP; not all doctoral projects work incorporating a set of SOs (Inouye & Bengtsen, 2023; Robins & Kanowski,

2008), and imposing this structure is not always appropriate. For instance, Robins & Kanowski (2008) note that

> research that requires data collection over a number of seasons (e.g., some animal behavioural studies) provides less opportunity for publishing early in the research process, and probably scope for fewer articles overall, than does the research topic of the first author's thesis. (p. 6)

Policy will also influence what designs will work for you. As I'll explore further in the section on policy, if initial planning indicates your project should result in two very high-quality SOs to be incorporated in a TBP that will transform the field, but the TBP policy at your university requires *a minimum of four* SOs to go out for examination as a TBP, that is obviously not going to work for you.

Other project designs may be expected to yield five or six papers *at the end of candidature*, but if the policy requires four *accepted* SOs, this is unlikely to work with reasonable knowledge of the peer-review process, and some guidelines specify that TBP 'may not be suitable for projects where publishable results come near the end of the three years' (Kubota et al., 2021, p. 4).

Low communicative competence in academic English if needed (and low support to improve)

Where research must be shared in English, TBP students who are not yet at the level of academic English competence to comfortably and efficiently share their ideas will face challenges in this approach. Publication options in other languages can be comparably limited, given that almost 80% of indexed journals are in English, and commonly used search engines 'are biased towards manuscripts published in English-only journals' (Bahji et al., 2023, p. 10), and this linguistic bias is pervasive and often unacknowledged (Bedenlier et al., 2025).

Concerns have been raised about the 'exclusion of the non-English-speaking world from the scientific literature' (p. 6), and how scholars from outside these contexts may be underrepresented voices in their disciplines (Mason, Merga et al., 2021), but unfortunately, while there is growing awareness of these issues with the academic publishing industry (Mills & Inouye, 2021), 'it is hard to imagine all "legitimate" academic journals actively addressing the issue, as those in a position to lead change are also those benefiting from the current status quo' (Merga, 2024a, p. 686).

As briefly mentioned earlier, some countries or institutions have a publication requirement for the graduation of doctoral students. In Indonesia, where this policy exists, it has 'created new problems, particularly for students who had to adopt English as an additional language (EAL) or English foreign language (EFL)', and these language issues emerged as a key challenge in research with Indonesian EFL doctoral students seeking to publish articles in 'Scopus or WOS-indexed journals' (Hidayat et al., 2024, p. 1228).

In other contexts, novice EAL researchers have published compelling first-person accounts of the challenges they have experienced attempting to publish their work in peer-reviewed journals where they have issues with communicative competence in academic English:

> It was frustrating for me who had little experience of the review process. By then I had invested more than a year without any success. Even my teachers, who were my co-authors in this manuscript, were getting frustrated. And I could clearly sense it. We were trying our best to make the manuscript more readable but somehow, we're not able to reach the expected standard of written English that the journal was looking for.
>
> (Banerjee, 2022, p. 1453)

Accounts such as these illustrate how, for a novice researcher, this communicative skill gap coexists with other gaps in knowledge about the journal publishing process, compounding disadvantage, and the importance of the availability of high-level EAL support through university and/or journal provision.

This section *shouldn't be read* as advice that EAL students should be excluded from TBP programmes. Levels of academic English proficiency in this group will be highly varying, and target journals aren't necessarily in English anyway. Furthermore, international students can be faster and more productive completers than domestic students:

> An unexpected finding in this study was higher proportion of international (25%) than domestic (19%) students who were both research productive (four or more papers) and efficient completers . . . What is noteworthy is that in our study population 29.3% of the doctoral students did not list English as their primary language, and yet 65.7% of them published one or more papers, with an average of 3.60 papers. There was a negligible difference in the average output of papers between students who did not speak English at home and those who did, at 3.60 and 3.65 papers (per publishing student), respectively.
>
> (Churchill et al., 2021, pp. 703–704)

While more research is needed in this space, this is evidence that EAL students can achieve TBP, so EAL status should not be used to exclude students from pursuing this modality. However, where students have relatively low academic English language competency, whether they be EAL status or not, they will need early and thorough support if they are intending to publish in scholarly outlets that require highly developed academic English proficiency.

Autonomy resistant vs autonomy embracing

A PhD is a research apprenticeship, and you will be expected to learn much along the way; the learning curve is notoriously steep and challenging. Given that, as will be explored in a recurring manner throughout this book, managing a TBP project is a significant responsibility, it may be more suitable for autonomy-embracing students compared with autonomy-resistant ones.

I'm not suggesting that students should be out there managing their projects with absolutely minimal supervisory support from day one, because that sounds like a recipe for disaster in many cases. However, students who after sufficient training and regular supervisory support still need lengthy discussion before they can make any minor decision about their projects may not be well positioned to succeed in a TBP approach.

In many cases, students who start out autonomy-resistant because of cultural or gender expectations or their academic experiences up to that point make the (smooth or bumpy) transition to being autonomy-embracing. However, in other rare instances, students can reach quite an advanced stage in the doctoral degree without independently applying their reading and their learning to the project; they are constantly waiting for their supervisors to tell them exactly what to think, what to do, and how to do it. In some very rare cases, there is a sense that they are waiting for the supervisors to literally do the entire project for them.

One problem in this kind of case is the obvious one; this student will not meet the rigorous demands of the doctoral degree as defined earlier in the book, though there is no mechanism to determine whether a PhD student's work is sufficiently their own (and arguably, given recent advances in generative artificial intelligence (AI), this will be a growing issue). While there is some debate over the merits of the oral defence or viva for quality assurance (Kiley et al., 2018), it could play a role in mitigating these concerns if conducted in a manner conducive to this purpose. However, at the time of writing this book, in Australia the oral defence is not standard.

Supervisors in this context who cross the line and make the key decisions for their students may not be aware that they are moving into academic misconduct themselves if applicable (e.g. in Australia, this would be in relation to the aforementioned AQF). The march over this line is actually a crawl, perhaps breached without the supervisor fully realising that it has happened, and the overreach is often done with the best of intentions, to 'help the student'. Whether this misconduct is planned or inadvertently unfolds, the end result is the same: a student is awarded a qualification that they have not genuinely attained.

However, even if you're not bound by the AQF or similar in your country or institution, our research suggests that 'doctoral preparedness for producing research outputs for the academic community was related to high autonomy and self-driven learning which was not always dependent on supervisory support' (Merga & Mason, 2021a, p. 677). I fully understand that being autonomy-embracing may simply not be supported in your context. Where supported, it can still be incredibly scary and involve a significant mindset shift, perhaps particularly when you are not a highly confident person to begin with. This noted, it may be required in your context, and it can certainly help you to achieve a TBP as you can benefit from taking responsibility for your work and owning your project as far as reasonable and practicable. Supervisors' orientation towards you and your project can make a huge difference; supervisors who offer 'choice rather than control' in an 'autonomy-supportive environment' were linked with successful student completion as opposed to 'a controlling or impersonal motivational climate' (Brownlow et al., 2023, pp. 1617–1618).

The TBP journey may particularly encourage students to become autonomy-embracing progressively across the journey:

> I have seen students nervous and anxious with the first paper. The first paper is where the student makes the most mistakes. They are anxious, possibly suffering from imposter syndrome and feel out of their depth just like when they send the parent home from the hospital without a newborn guidebook! Yet they learn exponentially from the first paper. The second paper brings different challenges, such as how does it compete with the first paper? They are familiar with the process yet not the new data or new method. It feels the same yet different. They rely heavily on the guidance and support of the supervisor. By the time the third paper comes along, the experience of the first two papers stands to the student. They are less anxious, more confident. They take the advice of the supervisor less maybe as they can now stand over their research more, taking more ownership. From my experiences, I have seen papers thrive under the guardianship of the

candidate and believe the stronger the nurturing relationship is with the supervisor, the better the experience for the paper . . .

(Sammon et al., 2024, p. 16)

As such, this progression can be marked with each iterative SO that is produced, with the student ideally increasing their control over the work as they learn through this research apprenticeship.

A key reason that I think an autonomy-embracing student is more likely to succeed than an autonomy-resistant one is that it is unlikely that anyone is as committed to your research project as you are. Your supervisor will typically be stretched across all of their student projects, as well as their own work. If you don't feel confident in leading your project to success, there is no better equipped person for the role in most circumstances.

Wellbeing

Any kind of PhD is hard, and the challenges of completing it can negatively impact on your sense of wellbeing (Xu et al., 2020). Doing a TBP may involve a lot more rejection and critical feedback than the traditional approach, as I explore further later in the book. This may really sting for high achievers facing rejection in the academic context for the first time, potentially in conjunction with personal and professional life challenges as applicable. Other reasons that the PhD can impact on wellbeing relate to 'stressors such as work/life balance, long commutes, financial constraints, health problems, forming an identity as a scholar, issues with supervisors/committee members, and worries about securing employment in academia' (Jalongo, 2024, p. 1). While this may vary widely across contexts, doctoral students experiencing chronic illness or with a disability may find insufficient concentration on support at postgraduate level in their university; 'they may fall through the cracks of institutional policies, processes, and practices that have often been developed with undergraduate (UG) and Postgraduate Taught (PGT) students in mind' (Burford et al., 2024, p. 12).

It is important that prospective students do not underestimate the impact that the PhD journey may have on their health and wellbeing. In recent work, Taylor (2023) described the shift in our collective understanding of the wellbeing issues faced by PhD students:

In recent years, however, a significant volume of evidence . . . has emerged suggesting that doctoral candidates suffer disproportionately from low levels of wellbeing and, in a number of cases, from mental distress (depression and anxiety) and mental health issues (clinically proven depression and anxiety as well as more severe illnesses including bipolar and psychosis). (p. 611)

It is foreseeable that the SO publication journey, as outlined later in this book, may involve significant stress that certainly has the potential to exacerbate some pre-existing health conditions. If you know that you have a physical or mental health condition that is negatively affected by stress, you will need to take this into account when deciding the right path for you.

I also strongly encourage you to keep a close eye on your wellbeing as you progress through your doctoral journey; we do not know whether TBP students are more or less likely to experience negative wellbeing outcomes than those pursuing the traditional thesis, as this research has not yet been undertaken at the time of this publication. However, there are some risk factors identified in recent research that are worth bearing in mind; for instance, 'higher levels of imposter thoughts, perfectionism discrepancy, and loneliness were strong predictors of depression, anxiety, and suicidality' (Mills et al., 2024, p. 1), and the quality of your relationship with your supervisor can also be a factor at play (Poli et al., 2025). We also know that, as reviewed in Clarke et al. (2024), peer review can expose students to unique wellbeing threats, identifying the process as sometimes being 'actively hostile', and that 'research on authors' experiences of peer review has highlighted the harms of peer review for authors and particularly early career academics' as well as 'those from marginalized groups' (p. 2).

Waiting too long to decide to jump into a TBP journey could potentially compound wellbeing issues, because you may put too much pressure on yourself. Our research on factors related to students' decisions to undertake a TBP found that 36% opted into a TBP before even enrolling (Mason et al., 2020a); making an early decision to undertake a TBP may be useful for planning, but it will also help you to avoid imposing late-stage publication pressures on yourself.

Please familiarise yourself with any wellbeing-related supports available to you through your institution if applicable, as well as any external supports that you can draw on across your journey as needed. Please also be careful not to excessively identify with your PhD—*you are much more than your PhD* and inevitable scrutiny on and criticism of your PhD should not be seen as repudiation of yourself.

Hostile policy red flags

In some cases, prospective TBP students have multiple prospective institutions where they could conduct their PhD. If you find yourself in this fortunate position, I strongly encourage you to get yourself a copy of the TBP policies from the institutions that you are considering and carefully compare them to inform your choice. As I will expand upon here, this can literally shape whether or not your thesis is institutionally deemed examinable in relation to the SOs that it contains, so I cannot sufficiently stress the importance of a supportive policy.

As I've noted recently,

> while there is a growing body of research on theses by publication, there is no universal model for best practice. In developing fit for purpose policies, universities may draw heavily from extant available policies and research. Institutions may seek to develop policies that support publication in doctoral candidates, while at the same time, ensuring the thesis reflects somewhat ambiguous notions of quality relating to PhD attainment. At university level, debates during policy development and revision processes may become complicated by a lack of shared vision around the purposes of the policy, and conflicting notions of what a thesis by publication is or should be, particularly in relation to how it can best serve societal, institutional, supervisory and student goals.
>
> (Merga, 2024b, p. 2)

This ambiguity and flexibility in interpretation allows for some strange policies in this space that do not remotely align with best practice in relation to available policies and research.

At the most general level, the point of a TBP policy should be:

- to provide clear guidelines for students, supervisors and examiners on all relevant areas, particularly where a TBP differs from a traditional thesis and therefore is not covered by policy related to traditional thesis production and examination
- to encourage quality SO production within the time constraints of candidature
- to support the creation of examinable theses that meet disciplinary norms as required while meeting broader expectations related to the PhD qualification as covered earlier in this book.

It's in institutions' best interests to get these policies right, and to adjust their policies in a timely manner when the policy fails to keep abreast of student, supervisor and/or examiner needs, and evolving expectations and norms related to the TBP and how it can be enacted in different disciplines. Policies encouraging publication during the completion of research degrees and providing realistic supports and mechanisms can play a vital role in enhancing the *research excellence* of an institution, while noting that research excellence is often ambiguous and controversial, and evolving in conceptualisation and measurement (Schweiger et al., 2024). The magnitude of the contribution of research students may be substantial. Around a third or more of research outputs may be authored by doctoral candidates (Griffith University, 2019; Lariviere, 2012). Our 2020 study of 246 doctoral graduates from universities in Australia found that they 'developed over 1,200 research papers, and an average of five papers, which is a valuable contribution to university outputs', highlighting 'the value of students embarking on the TBP pathway to their institutions, as well as highlighting the contribution of these individuals to their field more broadly' (Mason et al., 2020b, p. 254).

Not all TBP policies are student-friendly, so before you proceed with a TBP, read your institution's policy *very carefully*, and ask questions if you're not sure about any of the clauses that it contains. Sometimes when I read TBP policies created by universities I am deeply mystified about their origins and motivations, as some seem to be designed to inhibit SO publication and/or thesis completion. Sometimes they make sweeping determinations that are contrary to some disciplinary norms while favouring others.

So what should you *specifically* be looking for in a TBP policy?

Low minimum number of published/accepted SOs

I accept the logic of policies including a minimum number of SOs for a TBP, bearing in mind that the P stands for publication, so without *any* form of accepted or published SO, a TBP without a P isn't really a TBP.

Where a university specifies a minimum number of SOs that must be published or accepted, it's best for you if the minimum number of published/accepted SOs for a TBP is low (i.e. one). This means that there is less pressure for you to publish at the early stages of your PhD, perhaps before you've even collected data. This is important because the student has limited control over the time it takes for their accepted work to progress to publication. In my own experience, I'm sometimes waiting for several months from formal journal acceptance to even do the copyedits on a paper, let alone see it published in the early online version or (usually even later) with issue and volume allocated.

There is no universal norm anyway. Previous research found that in the case of TBPs from HASS,, there was 'an average of 4.5 papers'. However, there was also a 'wide range of number of publications, anywhere from one to 12' (Mason & Merga, 2018a, p. 148). Policies do not have to stipulate a fixed minimum number, and often don't. According to the most recent research in this space,

> in regards to the number of publications that constitute a Thesis by Publication, more than a quarter of policies (n = 54, 28%) do not provide this information, and a further 9% explicitly state that there is no specific requirement regarding the number of publications . . . Around half of all policies state a required minimum number of publications for a Thesis by Publication, with one and three being most common. . .In some cases, a given number refers to the number of outputs to be published, while in others it refers to outputs to be included but not necessarily published . . .
>
> (Mason et al., 2024b, p. 4)

Earlier research by Jackson (2013) found that 'in regard to the actual number of included papers, the majority of universities do not stipulate a minimum' (p. 360). Given that there's no accepted norm, there is no need for there to be an arbitrary and universal (to be applied across all disciplines) minimum of accepted/published SOs in a university TBP policy.

Nonetheless, it is clearly not unusual for universities to impose a minimum, often with no or weak justification. If minimums must be applied, they must be discipline/field responsive, and there must be *clearly articulated logic* around the choice of the minimum so that revisions to the policy can consider whether this logic has remained stable or changes require an adjustment to the minimum.

It can be the case that a single rich and dense article accepted or published in a high-quality journal situated in a thesis with supporting and linking material that tells a cogent story may be better received by examiners than a PhD thesis with more than four SOs that does not have the same lucidity or quality. The emphasis should be on the thesis narrative, not the number of outputs. Mason (2018) described how having a minimum of just one published SO made the TBP an attractive, (relatively) low-risk option:

> Fortunately, my university had only one requirement for the TWP, and that was for a minimum of one paper to be published at the time of submission. Other papers were allowed to be in-press or submitted for review. This alleviated some

of the stress that may have otherwise been felt, and it appears that universities are generally accepting of publications which have not yet undergone the complete publication process. Given the realities of what can realistically be achieved in terms of multiple publications in a limited time frame, this acceptance is well justified. (p. 1237)

Furthermore, we can't avoid the fact that requiring an arbitrary number of publications, rather than a figure that is responsive to the project design, may encourage adoption of ethically questionable research practices such as *self-plagiarism*, *salami-slicing* and *duplicate publication* (Pfleegor et al., 2019). You'll learn more about what these things are in the section on initial planning in the next chapter. Though 'early planning at the outset of the research journey may attempt to ensure that there are four discrete but related areas worthy of individual publication, the results cannot be controlled, and the value of entirely predictable research must be questionable' (Merga, 2024b, p. 3). Many untoward issues can arise during candidature even in instances of high-quality project management, as any experienced supervisor would attest (e.g. international pandemics). You may plan for a minimum number of four publications, but then discover that findings related to two of the four research questions (RQs) wound up being far more interrelated than you expected, making three quality publications the more ethical choice to avoid salami slicing. Unexpected things do happen in the research space, perhaps particularly where the research is exploratory rather than confirmatory, so look for a TBP policy that is responsive to this possibility, allowing a low minimum number of SOs.

But what should be done if a student reaches examination stage on a TBP with no outputs accepted (i.e. missing the P)? For TBPs with late-stage SOs, where key research findings will not be available until quite late in candidature, this is a serious issue. Should they have to rewrite the structure of their entire thesis?

I believe that universities should seriously consider building in allowance for a thesis with *no* publication/acceptance but *components formatted for publication*, enabling students to pursue doctoral projects with a late-stage yield, and focus their writing on the production of draft SOs incorporated within a TBP (while being clear that they are not yet accepted/published). The additional advantage of allowing this approach will be that even if time runs out and a student is unable to submit SOs for peer review during candidature, it will be relatively easy for them to submit during the examination period, ensuring that their work is considered before the data becomes stale. For universities that are committed to KMb of the work of the doctoral students, allowing this kind of flexibility where the thesis still remains cohesive would be prudent. It can basically be the same as the TBP format; the only difference is that nothing has been formally accepted yet, and that can be acknowledged at the outset. Maybe we can call it a Thesis for Future Publications (a TFP).

Allow under-review content

It is perfectly acceptable to allow under-review content to appear in a TBP. In a study of 165 HASS TBPs, 35% of publications appearing in the thesis were not yet published, being either under review or not under submission (Mason & Merga, 2018a). However, some TBP policies don't permit inclusion of under-review content. Where this is the case, you can't present a thesis with a combination of accepted/published and under-review SOs.

As long as under-review content does not masquerade as published or accepted content in a TBP, this is an unrealistic and unhelpful position for a TBP policy to take. It can inhibit students from being ambitious if they can only include manuscripts that are accepted or published, as there is little incentive to prepare any manuscripts late in candidature where they are unlikely to pass through peer review in time for inclusion.

It's also unfair as the supervisor and HDR student have very little control over the length of the peer-review process (e.g. see Merga et al., 2018 for some of the many issues that may arise when navigating journal article publication). While the supervisor may have experience enabling them to advise selection of journals with a viable projected review period, these journals could be lower impact and not necessarily the best choice in terms of alignment with the desired audience(s). Furthermore, it will still only ever be a projected review period, as significant variations in review time can occur within one journal. While the supervisor can guide the best choice in the balance of quality and speed, even those most predictable journals can have unexpected and dramatic peer-review lags. Even if you are the smartest, most hardworking and best student, you may still fail to meet an arbitrary minimum due to these lags, so I would advise that you don't attempt a TBP at a university with an inflexible minimum requirement that is unrealistic for your discipline (Merga, 2024b).

This kind of policy requirement inhibits embracing risk in doctoral research for the reward of innovation. It may lead students to avoid including RQs in their projects that have the potential to yield null results, given that null papers take months longer to publish, perhaps relating to 'the increased difficulties of trying to persuade reviewers of the merits of null findings' (Button et al., 2016, p. 3). As I've noted previously, 'this limitation may lead to incomplete reporting of research findings, with only the most palatable and peer-reviewer friendly being incorporated within the thesis, and the rest concealed' (Merga, 2024b, p. 3).

One of the most mystifying aspects of this inclusion in some TBP policy is that it is not in anyone's best interests, including the university's, given that 'denying flexibility in publication status may significantly impede completion' (Merga, 2024b, p. 3). Taylor's (2023) review of the international studies done in this space suggests that the rate of failure to complete may be as high as 50%, and these and other concerning data on degree-length blowouts have 'public research sponsors across much of the globe' acting 'to improve completion times' in the last three decades (p. 608). To understand this push, readers should bear in mind that in some contexts, universities only receive government funding for PhD candidates upon completion, which is the case in Australia.

This kind of policy restriction would not have worked for me. As per Table 2 (Merga, 2015), at the time of PhD submission, my TBP included two publications under review, five formally accepted for publication, and three that had been published.

Table 2 *Journal articles in my TBP* (from Merga, 2015)

Title of publication	Research questions addressed	Publication status at time of submission
Are Western Australian adolescents keen book readers?	1.1, 1.2, 2.1, 2.2	Accepted in the *Australian Journal of Language and Literacy*
Peer group and friend influences on the social acceptability of adolescent book reading.	2.3, 3	Published in the *Journal of Adolescent and Adult Literacy*
Are teenagers really keen digital readers?	2.4	Accepted in *English in Australia*
Are avid adolescent readers social networking about books?	2.4	Accepted in *New Review of Children's Literature and Librarianship*
The influence of movie adaptations on adolescents' attitudes toward source books.	2.4	Under review
Exploring the role of parents in supporting recreational book reading beyond primary school.	3	Published in *English in Education*
What would make them read more? Insights from Western Australian adolescent readers.	3	Under review
Should Silent Reading feature in a secondary school English programme? West Australian students' perspectives on Silent Reading.	3, 4	Published in *English in Education*
"What would make you read more?" Opportunities for supporting an increase in teenagers' book reading.	4	Accepted in *Asia Pacific Journal of Education*
Western Australian adolescents' reasons for infrequent engagement in recreational book reading.	4	Accepted in *Literacy Learning: The Middle Years*

If I had had to wait for the 'under review' papers to be accepted (bearing in mind that these were written closer to the end of my candidature), this would have dramatically slowed my completion time. If I had left them out of my thesis there would have been a significant gap and partial reporting. Due to the flexibility of the policy at ECU, as a full-time student raising two young sons and working one full day a week in a research support role at ECU among other responsibilities, I was able to submit my thesis for examination two years and five months from commencement. Waiting for the last publication to slither over the line through peer review would have literally blown out this completion time by years, not months: one of these final publications took a very long time to progress for a range of reasons, some of which were totally outside of my control. Policymakers need to understand the realities of the process, and closely consider the potential impact of restrictive decisions.

The knowledge that unaccepted outputs could be incorporated in the thesis meant that I could write *many* articles, and that my university could continue to benefit from affiliated publications beyond the scope of candidature, continuing to boost institutional research productivity (Mason et al., 2020b):

> The psychological benefits for risk averse HDR students may be notable, with research finding that while most TBP candidates included at least one published output in their TBP, not all of the papers were published, which may be of comfort to doctoral candidates for whom some uncertainty around publication status of all included papers persists at the point of submission.
>
> (Mason et al., 2020b, p. 254)

Most Australian universities allow for some flexibility in publication status. Jackson's (2013) earlier review of Australian universities with PhD by Publication policies found that 'all the universities indicate that published, accepted and submitted papers may be included in the final thesis', but some do 'stipulate that a certain proportion of papers should be published, ranging from 33 to over 50%' (p. 360). As such, there is poor logical justification for denying the inclusion of under-review content.

Allow a wide variety of SOs as appropriate to disciplines

The policy needs to allow for a wide range of SO text types and they should be specified in the policy so that you don't find yourself having to battle to have non-traditional SOs accepted if this is relevant for you. I also need to be clear here that I am using the term 'text' in the very flexible sense, not limited to written forms, given the current and evolving SO types that can be meaningfully incorporated in a TBP in the social sciences. Alternatively, the policy should specify that it allows university sub-strata (such as Schools, Faculties and Departments) to make the determination of what constitutes an SO based on (potentially evolving) disciplinary norms. It is reasonable for universities to expect that TBP students clearly specify which SOs have passed through the rigour of peer review. With this qualification, there is no reason for universities to adopt a restrictive policy on the variety of discipline-supported SOs that can be included within a TBP.

Allow an easy route to thesis embargo

Once you include SOs in your thesis that are not open access under a licence allowing republication, you may find yourself in the unenviable position of having to negotiate back rights that you have signed away in order to have your TBP published (usually stored in an online institutional repository). With some academic publishers this will be straightforward, but with others it may be very complex and perhaps even impossible in some instances. If your institution requires that you publish your thesis and you cannot negotiate back these rights, the thesis either has to be placed under an embargo, or be made available with big holes where the SOs sit in the original TBP.

I'm pretty confident that policies that assign the role of wrangling IP rights from academic publishers so that SO content can be included within a published thesis are written by people who have never had to actually do that wrangling in reality. Those of us who have published multiple journal articles with different publishers are aware that while the nature of this negotiation may vary notably across publishers, it can't be assumed that this process can be easily managed by a doctoral student with no legal qualifications or background in this area, and even their supervisors may struggle to do this without support. So universities either need to provide high-level support, and ideally funds for open access for all SOs written during doctoral candidature, or they need to allow theses that contain SOs to be placed under *unlimited embargo*.

There needs to be a clear statement in the TBP policy that reads something like this:

> Failure to secure permission from academic publishers to republish SOs in the thesis is not a barrier to thesis submission. If permissions cannot be obtained, the thesis can be put under indefinite embargo if required. Contact (relevant persons and emails inserted) for more about options.

My own thesis is under indefinite embargo (follow the link in the reference for Merga, 2014a), and knowing this was an option reduced stress when dealing with notoriously challenging open access and intellectual property discussions with international publishers, particularly given that a TBP was less common at that time in my field. It also meant that I could go back after my PhD and publish big chunks of content from my unpublished introduction and discussion sections in SOs without running into issues around self-plagiarism.

Of course, indefinite embargo is not ideal because it means that the next generation of researchers will have limited access to TBP models. However, where (as can be the case) academic publishers do not allow republication, or place significant limitations on the inclusion of SOs in the thesis stored in the university repository, publishing the thesis in this form via the repository is simply not viable in terms of risk.

Give examiners a heads-up about unavoidable repetition

Some TBP policies include comments like 'repetitive passages must be avoided' in a TBP, but this is unhelpful given that there will be some *unavoidable* repetition across outputs.

For example, if your PhD reports on surveys, you can't change the demographic characteristics of your surveys, and you will need to consistently report them across SOs that present findings on different RQs and therefore are not duplicate publications. A degree of repetition is going to be inevitable, so the 'must' in this statement shows limited awareness of the realities of producing this kind of work. There are also certain features in method and background that will remain constant across publications, such as sample size. This language has to be left out or softened, particularly given that research has found that this could lead to unreasonable expectations in examiners (see Merga, Mason & Morris, 2020, p. 1252), or even better, the policy can ask examiners to be lenient and reasonable around unavoidable repetition.

Final point

If you find yourself in a position of being able to make a choice between institutions, I urge you to select an institution that will allow you to produce the most flexible TBP and free up your choices about your doctoral journey, given the implications outlined in this section. An institutional TBP policy that protects the rigour of the doctorate while also allowing for optimal flexibility and tailoring to disciplinary norms can help you to achieve your research goals and support your completion. I strongly advise against attempting a TBP at an institution that has a clearly hostile policy.

## CHAPTER 2

Getting Started and Positioning for Success

Once you've decided to go down the TBP path, ideally at a university that offers supportive resources and policies, you'll be looking to make good choices early in your candidature to optimise your chances of success. As I explore in this chapter, when things go wrong in a doctoral journey, it can often be due to factors relating to the student–supervisor relationship and expectations alignment, so I'll outline some early considerations for choosing a supervisory team. I'll also touch on some initial planning implications, how to fill training gaps to support your preparedness, and the kinds of publications you might want to produce in the early stages of your journey if so inclined, among other considerations.

Getting the right supervisory team

Different contexts use different terms for the supervisor, also known as 'advisor' or 'mentor', but referring to 'faculty members who provide various forms of support and guide doctoral students during the dissertation stage' (Kumar et al., 2023, p. 1). If you've spent any time interacting with doctoral students (regardless of whether or not they are embarking on a TBP), the supervisory relationship is often at the heart of both student success and discontent. Research suggests that the 'quality of the relationship between the student and their supervisor' is closely linked to your student experience on a PhD (Brownlow et al., 2023, p. 1617). While as I outline in this section, there is much you can do to foster this positive relationship, it's not completely within your control, so I am not suggesting that any issue in this space is your sole responsibility. Rather, I use the section to show you what could be happening on the other side of the fence to give you some insight into the supervisory experience and the research being conducted in this space, given that 'negative relationships with the supervisors can be primarily explained by the expectation gap where the two parties might prioritize different things' (Schmidt & Hansson, 2021, p. 54).

While we need far more comparative research on this, supervising a TBP could potentially be harder work for supervisors than supervising a traditional thesis, while possibly being more rewarding, particularly in relation to the career-progressing extrinsic reward of co-authorship opportunities. For example, when Mason (2018) swapped supervisory teams and moved to a TBP approach, this led to a 'higher frequency of meetings', and 'a new relationship dynamic of author/co-author' (p. 1236).

Historically, supervision of the PhD was more of a solo affair, with PhD students nurtured by a single (ideally expert) individual. Placing total reliance on a single supervisor meant that when that relationship deteriorated or materially changed (such as through the death, retirement or resignation of the supervisor during candidature), the negative impact on the student could be significant, leading universities towards embracing a team approach instead. Taylor (2023) notes that while this *collectivisation* of doctoral education can solve some issues, 'it can also cause others in so far the relationship between supervisors and students becomes more complex and potentially subject to conflict over competing intellectual perspectives, interpretations of projects, supervisory roles and supervisory styles' (p. 609). Instead of being responsive to a single supervisor, students can find themselves in a position of having input from a broader range of more senior guides. While this can be positive, I have heard many stories of TBP students working with supervisory teams where supervisor/supervisor relationships have fallen apart, placing the TBP student in the unenviable position of having to deal with contradictory feedback and passive-aggressive undertones to all supervisory interactions. As such, where a supervisory team works well together, having multiple supervisors is a valuable asset. Where it does not, it can absolutely be a hindrance, placing students in the position of having to adjudicate from a position of power imbalance to manage the relationship of more senior staff.

Prospective students often get excited about their supervisor's research fame and expertise, easily verifiable with reference to a search engine, without knowing whether or not they have the supportive and nurturing skills to facilitate doctoral supervision, as this isn't as easy to access or measure. Recent research proposed that 'the absence of care during doctoral education in neoliberalised academia – which fosters values and measurements of the market, such as individualism, comparison, and accountability – is a form of violence' (Castelao-Huerta, 2025, p. 1), and while of course there are some limitations on what you can realistically expect from academic supervisors in terms of care (i.e. they are no substitute for a trained mental health professional), *at the very least* they should show you respect and consideration, and not exploit you for their own gains to your detriment.

When I write about the 'right' supervisory team in this section, it is helpful to begin by considering which factors are associated with the best outcomes for students in the research on doctoral supervision more generally. As recently synthesised from the literature in Pyhältö et al. (2024), these include:

- having regular meetings with the supervisory team;
- receiving constructive feedback and pastoral support;
- having aligned expectations of the supervisory relationship and rules;
- receiving writing support and encouragement; and
- being supported to integrate into the research knowledge community.

All of the above 'are associated with timely completion, positive doctoral experience and employment after completing the PhD degree' (p. 555).

It's useful to know about this, as there's no one norm that you can expect, so if you find yourself failing to progress and you feel that this may be because your supervisory team isn't working, it's definitely worth taking a close look at why, with consideration of these factors potentially being a useful starting point. You can also consider models of supervision, with numerous available in the literature. For example, recent research looking at the supervision of international students in Chinese higher education contexts found three distinct types of student–supervisor relationship, 'collaborative research partnerships, boss–employee dynamics, and nominal doctoral relationships' (Dai et al., 2025, p. 71), all of which as can be imagined will offer a different student experience.

I'll now focus on some of those supervisory factors specific to the TBP student journey.

Tangibly supportive of the TBP

As a first goal, if you want to do a TBP, at the very least you will need a TBP-supportive supervisory team. You can't assume your supervisors are fine with you undertaking a TBP; you need to have the conversation and get their explicit support. Despite the fact that the TBP has been around for some time now, there can still be resistance to the TBP approach in some contexts and disciplines. O'Keeffe (2022) describes his own experience:

> Within the university where I completed my doctoral studies, the PhD by
> Publication is a relatively new way of approaching a PhD in social science. Early
> in my candidature, I attended an information session where presenters explained
> the merits of the PhD by Publication to a group of doctoral candidates. A senior
> academic was in attendance, and they appeared to view their role in proceedings
> as needing to discourage us bright young things from taking this option; out of
> concern that the PhD by Publication would lead to the ruination of doctoral
> research, and ultimately, the end of tertiary education as we know it. (p. 201)

Positioning a TBP as the less credible model is questionable given that
SOs within it have been subject to peer review; a TBP has typically
sustained far more external critique than a traditional monograph by the
time it has been submitted for examination. However, not all supervisors
agree with this logic, and not all will be willing to support a TBP.

Low or non-existent supervisory support for the TBP approach can
sometimes be related to a lack of supervisor training in supporting TBP.
Just because an institution allows submission of a TBP does not mean that
individual supervisors are knowledgeable about how to support students
to achieve this goal, as explained by a respondent in our research:

> Although as an institution TBP is strongly encouraged, there is very little support
> or information about expectations about this mode. My supervisors were also not
> familiar with this mode and I spent a lot of time seeking information and
> educating my supervision team. (Frances)
>
> (Mason, Morris & Merga, 2021, p. 63)

Once you have a team that has confirmed its willingness to support this
mode, the next goal is to get the team to provide tangible support. It has
been reported that 'strong expectations and support' from a supervisory
team can not only enable students to achieve a TBP but also motivate these
students to become similarly supportive supervisors (Merga & Mason,
2021a, p. 676).

So what do I mean by tangible support? You will talk about publication
planning early and often. You will consider implications for publication
at all stages of your TBP journey. Your supervisors will be interested in
and responsive to your needs to fill knowledge and skill gaps appropriate
to the TBP journey, referring you to training and literature as required.
They will not ghost you for long periods of time, leaving you spiralling
and second-guessing yourself. While you may feel somewhat out of your
depth leading a TBP project, you should not feel abandoned. I'll now
further explore what this tangible support looks like in greater detail.

Trustworthy, on your team, knowledgeable

Trust among the members of a research team is incredibly important for success and quality assurance in research projects, and I only work with those I can trust. For example, when I co-author with someone, where we agree to use the Vancouver Convention as an author order guideline (see Chapter 4 for more on this), I'm agreeing 'to be accountable for all aspects of the work', not just the parts that I produce (ICMJE, 2024). If someone else is analysing the data, I won't repeat the analysis unless there is a methodological reason for me to do so, so I need to have full trust in my team and their willingness to adopt a sound approach, at my own risk.

You will need to be able to trust your supervisors, and build your supervisors' trust in you. Recent research suggests that on the TBP journey, students need to be able to trust their supervisors to confidently negotiate the often challenging process of peer review, rely on the expertise of their supervisor, and have confidence that the supervisor will always act with their best interest at heart (Sammon et al., 2024). This is particularly important given the power imbalance between supervisor and student.

HDR students will be looking for supervisors who are not *prey searchers* (Lei & Hu, 2015). Our research with ECRs in both Australia and Japan found that close supervisory attention to doctoral students' publications 'was not always positive', with perception, in some cases, of 'a sense of being controlled and manipulated to secure research outputs for their supervisors' (Merga & Mason, 2021a, pp. 676–677). In my own experiences, these kinds of people may be challenging to identify, though there are also occasionally very clear red flags, such as a surprising willingness to forget that their doctoral student was even involved with their own doctoral research.

Recently, I was speaking with a prospective TBP student about his experiences and learned that his supervisor had recently shared his data at an international conference without even telling him that this presentation was taking place. While I urge you to be trusting of your supervisors where that trust has been earned, unfortunately due to the nature of the contemporary academic climate and certain actors within it, you still need to be aware that prey searchers exist, and that you may need to take steps to protect yourself in line with your institutional policies if you find yourself a target.

You really need a supervisory team that are on your team. In addition to trust, ideally you will see 'empathy, flexibility, openness and humility, personal support' and 'respect' in their treatment of you and others (Buirski, 2022, p. 1387). These qualities may be even more important in a

TBP supervisor, given the many unique challenges that students will face on this journey:

> The journey is characterized by peaks of elation when the student has a paper accepted to a conference or journal, but equally the troughs of despair when rejection letters are received. The supervisor's role during these key points is to act as either a 'coach' or a 'therapist'. They must motivate the student to ensure that they meet strict deadlines for submission (coaching) while also consoling them when critical feedback is received on their evolving work (therapy). This involves managing the student's expectations as they come to learn that rejection is an inevitable part of the road to publication, and resilience is a crucial skill to bounce back.
>
> (Sammon et al., 2024, p. 6)

While I don't really agree that a supervisor should ever be acting as a therapist, even metaphorically, as you are the driver of your project, knowing that your supervisor genuinely supports your efforts and values your project by what they do, as well as what they say, can do much to inspire you to push through the most challenging times.

While a supervisor's breadth and depth of research experience isn't everything, it can help in relation to negotiating the publication journey of SOs on the TBP. As might be expected, former TBP student research respondents 'connected the provision of assistance with the publication process to their supervisors' experience and track record of publishing' (Mason, Morris & Merga, 2021, p. 65).

Aligning expectations and maintaining focus

There needs to be clear and open communication with your supervisory team and early alignment of expectations that support the progress of the TBP. While this is easy for me to say, I understand that this is really hard to put in practice if not initiated by your supervisors; you may be the one driving the alignment of expectations and the maintenance of focus, and on the bright side, this can set you up to be an excellent project manager beyond your PhD.

Aligning expectations and maintaining focus on your project may be trickiest to enact when the supervisors themselves are drawing your focus away from your PhD. Specifically, in some instances, students also work on their supervisors' other projects. Where this is done in a manner that *does not impede* the student's progress on their own work, and the student's contribution is *explicitly recognised* and compliant with author guidelines, this can be a great learning opportunity for the student.

However, if you find yourself being constantly taken away from your own PhD labour to instead work on the research of your supervisory team, this will have a negative impact on the progress of your TBP, particularly given the time constraints involved that are explored in subsequent parts of this book. Being constantly distracted from your own project can also be a significant source of stress (Dai et al., 2025), perhaps particularly as the power imbalance between student and supervisor makes it difficult to resist these interruptions, and to advocate for time to work on your own project.

Expectations also need to be aligned around what is realistically achievable in terms of publication. This can be very challenging for a TBP student who is often a novice in this knowledge area:

> In several cases, respondents noted that the guidance was geared towards the building of publications for the supervisor themselves, rather than the candidate. In one case a supervisor 'put a bit of pressure on his PhD students to publish so he could use it toward his promotion' (Jenny), and another where the supervisor was 'more interested in her own interests [in regards to the] number of publications, and very disinterested in working on publication drafts after first draft – she once stated that the reviewers could edit the submitted paper!!' (Ying).
>
> (Mason, Morris & Merga, 2021, p. 66)

If you encounter issues in aligning these kinds of expectations, it will be valuable to speak to experienced colleagues or mentors to get some perspective around norms and what is in fact realistically achievable, given that you may not be knowledgeable enough to confidently make a judgement call in this space. While supervisors can *typically* be expected to act in your best interests, the cited research indicates that this is not universally the case, and that sometimes other factors, such as the supervisor's own publication ambitions or knowledge gaps, can get in the way.

It's also crucial that you align expectations on the basics – such as how often you will meet, and realistic timelines for supervisory feedback – as these are common points of frustration for doctoral students linked with slower completion (Lee et al., 2025). Some universities create a mandatory or recommended checklist to be discussed at an early meeting with students and supervisors (e.g. University of Bath, 2025), though these are rarely TBP specific.

Focus on feedback

As briefly raised previously, high-quality and regular feedback from supervisors is really important to help doctoral students maintain momentum and grow their knowledge and skills. This noted, they won't be your only source of feedback on your TBP journey, given that you will also get feedback from peer reviewers assessing your SOs, as well as potentially receiving feedback from peers, colleagues and perhaps broader groups of scholars if you are able to share your work in forums such as conferences and online networks. Indeed, 'the supervision opinion is not necessarily more or less valuable than any other expert opinion which may sometimes be difficult for students to appreciate given the centrality of the student–supervisor relationship' (Carless et al., 2024, p. 540). However, supervisors will typically provide the bulk of the feedback that enables you to continue learning and progressing across your period of candidature, and it can be contended that 'the pivotal role for a supervisor is that of a guide, or feedback provider, while developing the thesis and shaping the candidate's identity as a researcher' (Stracke & Kumar, 2020, p. 266).

High-quality feedback can sustain you across your journey, and a lack of this feedback has been identified as a source of stress for doctoral students, perhaps leading them to question the direction of their research (Dai et al., 2025). While some supervisors may be naturally gifted in effectively providing feedback, generally this could be considered to be a *learnt skill*, and not all supervisors will necessarily have been exposed to someone who provides excellent feedback, enabling them to learn the skill; training may be needed. Furthermore, not all universities provide high-quality supervisor development support to deliver this training. As such, while your supervisor might want to do their very best for you, they might not have the best skill set, and in areas such as feedback, may be forced to draw upon how they were given feedback back when they were doctoral students as their model (which is fine only if they were exposed to an excellent model at that time). As a result, some supervisors' ways of delivering feedback may be a little outdated and poorly aligned with what is currently viewed as best practice.

As a supervisor I understand that there is subjectivity in how feedback will ideally be delivered and received. For example, when it comes to research, personally I don't need a lot of warmth or care in how feedback is delivered to me; ironically if feedback is delivered very carefully and nicely, it makes me paranoid and I overthink it. I would rather feedback deliverers be *very clear and straightforward* than spend any word count protecting my feelings, as long as the feedback is justified and delivered in an impartial and unemotional manner. That said, just because I like my feedback delivered robot-style doesn't mean I expect my students to have the same preference, which is why it is important for me to get to know their individual differences, which are also potentially going to change across candidature as students develop their confidence: 'Candidates with limited academic experience reported that they prefer to receive positive and encouraging feedback along with critical comments' (Stracke & Kumar, 2020, p. 269). It's also why my feedback delivery style is something on the table that students know they can have some input on: I don't view it as one size fits all and I'm happy to make reasonable accommodations that are realistic for me to manage within time constraints.

So how might they direct my feedback?

Students know that they can ask me to provide feedback on *specific sections of content only*, and *give me a specific role* in delivering that feedback. For example, when providing feedback on written material, such as the proposal, they might want me to focus purely on how the literature review aligns with the subsequent RQs, ignoring any theoretical concerns in this read, as that's something they are currently polishing. *They tell me what to read for*, also adding any smaller considerations in comments on the document they send to me. This means that my perfectionist students feel comfortable sharing work in progress, knowing that I am only going to provide feedback on the parts where it has been requested, enabling me to (temporarily) pry the work out of their hands so that we can start working together on tuning it up to where it needs to be for submission.

One way to get on the right track with feedback is to have early conversations about feedback expectations. This can be supported by the use of the Feedback Expectation Tool (FET), which has been described as 'an easy-to-use and flexible pedagogical tool to encourage dialogue on feedback between supervisors and candidates' (Stracke & Kumar, 2020, p. 265). The FET contains statements that have deliberate contradictions to open up this dialogue and allow both supervisors and candidates to explicitly explore and understand their own approach and preferences, those of the other party, and how to approach compromise and flexibility and optimise mutual respect and understanding (Stracke & Kumar, 2020).

Understanding supervisory workload

When tensions arise about supervisor responsiveness, sometimes this is because the supervisor is negligent, but sometimes it is because a student's expectations are not realistic, in part because they don't understand supervisor workload in relation to their PhD supervision allocation. Research from the UK found that the vast majority of university researcher supervisors enjoy being a supervisor (UK Council for Graduate Education, 2024), so there's a good chance that your supervisor loves this part of their job. Unfortunately, academic workload allocation for PhD supervision often falls very far short of what is needed, and supervisors may also be really struggling with the workload commitment, given how overloaded academic workloads are in many contexts: 'while 74% of respondents noted that their workplace or institution formally acknowledged supervisory responsibilities in workload allocation to some degree, many expressed a desire for a more concrete acknowledgement of the time dedicated to supervision' (p. 10). Supervision can also have a negative impact on supervisor wellbeing in some cases, given that 'around a third agreed that supervision made them anxious or that concerns around the role kept them up at night' (p. 7). While the supervisory workload issues briefly discussed here are no excuse for neglect or poor treatment from your supervisor, I believe that it is useful for TBP students to understand a little about how supervisor workload sits within the broader academic workload where it is recognised as such. For example, you may wish to meet with your supervisor several times a week for an hour or so each time, and this simply may not be practical among the supervisor's other work commitments. Similarly, if you provide them with a 10,000-word manuscript and you want detailed feedback within 48 hours so that you can meet a submission deadline, this may not be reasonably accommodated within the supervisor's workload, again highlighting why finding alignment between expectations and having clear communication are crucial so that expectations are realistic and shared.

If it doesn't work . . . maybe get rescued

Changing your supervisory team can sometimes be the best possible solution where the relationship with the supervisors has broken down to the point where your productivity and wellbeing are suffering. If this happens to you, it may be a comfort to know that you are not the first student who has experienced this, and it's actually pretty common and known as 'rescue supervision' (UK Council for Graduate Education, 2024, p. 9).

Supervisory changes occur for a wide range of reasons, including but not limited to the following:

> A dominant supervisory style, lack of communication and pedagogical skills and lack of belief in the students' abilities were examples mentioned by the participants for the supervisory changes. Some students also experienced a lack of structure and clarity concerning what was expected of them.
>
> (Schmidt & Hansson, 2021, p. 60)

If your supervisory team is no longer functional, once communicative solutions have been exhausted, I urge you to take prompt action to seek institutional support to make changes to your supervisory team, or if necessary, explore options at other institutions. The good news is that things can still end well for students: in some research related to changes in supervision, 'once the change was complete, they felt renewed, energized and capable of continuing with their studies' (p. 54). However, you do need to check that your expectations are realistic, as you are unlikely to find a supervisor who is able to meet unreasonable time and feedback demands.

Initial planning

Initial planning on a TBP has often been credited as a key element in TBP success. We can use it to develop *clear personal milestones* for what we want to achieve across candidature, in order to keep ourselves on track. If this is your first time being your own boss and setting your own milestones that are responsive to university expectations, this may feel both daunting and exciting. If you are working with an institutional policy that does not allow under-review manuscripts to be part of the thesis, early planning to optimise the chances of getting all of the SOs accepted by the time of thesis submission will be absolutely crucial.

As already briefly discussed, once you commit to doing a TBP there are specific implications for research project design that will need to be carefully considered in initial planning. For example, Cash (2023) described the pivotal role that this played in her own journey:

> When I was engaging in initial conversations about enrolling in a PhD programme, it was clear that both the institution and my academic supervisors preferred that I pursue a thesis by publication. Knowledge translation had been a key pull into research for me, so the idea of sharing my findings through publications seemed an obvious choice. My research proposal and my PhD were subsequently planned with this in mind, utilising a multiple methods project design so that I would have data to write up along the way. This commitment to the publication pathway from the outset really made a difference in the long run

for the PhD. Although there were changes and things that did not remain exactly the same as initially envisaged, planning for a series of publications that would create data and be publishable in chunks became a key to success using this method. Without this, I suspect that there would have been significantly more difficulty in completing the exegesis that ultimately pulled together the thesis into a cohesive document. (p. 148)

Many universities provide their doctoral students with a template for milestone planning, and this needs to be discussed and generated with your supervisors early in candidature, and adjusted along the journey as necessary. UNDA did not have one of these available when I began, so I developed a simple one for my students, with just three columns under the following headings:

- Month/year
- Key milestones
- Key activities.

While month/year is pretty self-explanatory, key milestones relate to what you specifically want to have achieved, and key activities will be what you need to do to get to those milestones. Here's an example:

- Month/year: June 2025
- Key milestones: Submit application to Human Research Ethics Committee (HREC)
- Key activities:
  - Rewatch HREC induction video online for guidance
  - Finalise research proposal, research tools, information letters and HREC ethics form for submission of all forms and required appendices to HREC
- Arrange for principal supervisor to review these before submission.

This is just one simple way of planning so that you know what you need to do, how you need to do it, and when it needs to be done by. Feel free to use something fancier or more detailed if that suits you better.

Be aware that in some cases, when a milestone document is provided by the University, it may be used to determine if a doctoral student is on track for completion, so perhaps resist the urge to be overly ambitious *on the document* if this is the case at your institution; best to give yourself some wriggle room while still setting far more ambitious personal milestones elsewhere if preferred. If you are working or have significant caring responsibilities during your PhD, you'll need to consider implications for milestones. For example, you might consider ramping up PhD activities during periods where those other commitments are less onerous, and being less ambitious about what can be achieved where those other commitments will demand more attention. For example, as my doctoral students are often full-time educators, we plan to get a lot done over school vacation periods, family commitments permitting.

Publication planning

Your publication planning sits within your overall project planning, and you need to have a very clear vision of how each publication works within the narrative of your thesis, contributing to the compelling 'story' of your research. As observed by Nygaard and Solli (2021),

> unfortunately, novice researchers are almost always tempted to put everything they know into every article they write. If you approach each paper as a mini monograph, where each one tries to represent your doctoral research in its entirety, you will struggle to figure out how to keep them separate from one another. Instead, you need to learn how to identify what the unique contribution of each article is, and how it contributes to the whole. This means deciding what should go where, and how much should possibly be repeated across articles. (p. 39)

In addition to avoiding repetition in your thesis where realistically possible, these kinds of considerations are also important to stay on the right side of the line in relation to publishing ethics. Initial publication planning is needed to avoid self-plagiarism, salami slicing and duplicate publication. How these practices are viewed varies widely in some cases across institutions, disciplines and countries, suggesting that just because something is okay at your university does not necessarily mean that it is broadly accepted within your field; you will need to speak to your supervisors if in doubt.

So for the uninitiated, what (generally) are these things?

Self-plagiarism

Self-plagiarism can come as a real shock if you are returning to learning having been out of academia for a while, but these days (at least in the Australian universities where I worked), we teach our students about avoiding self-plagiarism as part of our academic misconduct training from undergraduate level. Mature students who have had a gap, or who went to a university where this mandatory training was not available, can move through to the doctoral journey with no idea that self-plagiarism is even a thing, and while this is less likely to affect your life if you are doing a traditional PhD, it almost certainly will affect you if you are doing a TBP, which commonly involves publishing multiple SOs from the same research project.

Self-plagiarism can be defined as

> the presentation of your own previously published work as original; like plagiarism, self-plagiarism is unethical. Self-plagiarism deceives readers by making it appear that more information is available on a topic than really exists. It gives the impression that findings are more replicable than is the case or that particular conclusions are more strongly supported than is warranted by the evidence. It may lead to copyright violations if you publish the same work with multiple publishers (sometimes called *duplicate publication*).
>
> (American Psychological Association, 2022, para. 7)

So how can we avoid self-plagiarism? As a rule of thumb, you need to treat your previously published work with the same citation principles you would use for the work of others: cite it accurately and without fail. As per Chapter 1, you may be able to get around self-plagiarism rules when citing a prior published thesis written by you, but remember, some journals don't accept work from published dissertations, or they do so only if they are significantly developed beyond the thesis version (Klein & Müller, 2022), so I would avoid doing this as far as possible.

Journals expect to hold the *right of first publication* when you submit to them, which is one of the reasons why they ask you to declare that you haven't submitted elsewhere (often by checking an applicable box during the submission process) (Muñoz-Carpena et al., 2020). Plagiarism may be a surprisingly common reason for desk rejection. Similarity checking is often done at the very outset, acting as 'an initial filter' (Wu et al., 2024, p. 3). Klein and Müller (2022) note that 'we run all submissions through very thorough duplication detection software', and that even minor unattributed paraphrasing 'will not escape detection' (p. 543).

If you have been outside academia for a while, you need to know that depending on the software used, plagiarism detection software may often flag every suspect passage or clause, *including those that are correctly cited*. The reviewer then goes in and looks at the flagged passages to see which have been correctly cited, and which have not; this is why a document with 8% duplication can pass, while one with 6% can fail if the 6% includes unattributed quotes. However, *even where attribution is correct,* you can't just paste in large amounts of your previous work and cite it correctly and expect to have no issue; given the right of first publication, it might be deemed a duplicate work. You also can't be heavily reliant on another person's work—for example, if you submit an article that is 25% attributed quotes from a single work of another author, this may attract scrutiny.

So how much duplication from your own work, or the work of others, is too much? Again, it will vary between journals, and accurate citation will make a big difference to how this is interpreted, but here is an explanation from one editorial team, which used

> software that automatically provides the Editors with a Plagiarism and Duplication score (% of the text from other sources) identified from present and archived materials in the internet. During the screening process the Editors evaluate carefully the score and the duplicated parts of the text, considering also the impact of the overlapping with other journals on the new contributions identified in the manuscript. Typically, manuscripts with greater than 20% duplication, particularly from a small number of sources, are returned to the authors. When the duplicated text is plagiarized in large quantity from other sources this can be considered as a violation of scientific publishing ethics, and the Editors may report it to Elsevier for further action. The same applies if authors attempt to offer material for publication that is very similar to work that they have already published elsewhere.
>
> (Muñoz-Carpena et al., 2020, pp. 1–2)

At another journal, the acceptable rate of similarity was even lower; 'higher than 10% will certainly result in a desk rejection', with the authors of this article suggesting that where an acceptable similarity rate (SR) is not indicated, 'it is probably safe to keep SR below 15%' (Wu et al., 2024, p. 4). When you are publishing multiple SOs from the same project there will be some unavoidable repetition, but make sure you accurately self-cite aspects such as reproduced demographic tables. That way when they trigger the plagiarism detection, there is a clear explanation and citation. In some cases, plagiarism can see you banned from submission to a particular journal for a set period of time (Stolowy, 2017).

Don't use unattributed generative AI, and only use attributed generative AI if you are permitted to do so both by the journal and by your university, bearing in mind that your work will be included in your thesis. If either say no, that's a red flag for you. Academic publishers are constantly working to enhance their capacity to detect the use of AI-generated content in submissions (e.g. Springer Nature, 2024).

Also, doing a TBP does not give licence to ignore ethics norms in relation to salami slicing and duplicate publication, which I will briefly explain herein.

Salami slicing and duplicate publication

Salami slicing (also known as *redundant publication* and *salami publishing)* relates to 'the "slicing" of research that would form one meaningful paper into several different papers': 'as a general rule, as long as the "slices" of a broken up study share the same hypotheses, population, and methods, this is not acceptable practice' (Elsevier, 2017, p. 1). I avoided salami slicing in my TBP by *never publishing on the same RQ in relation to the same data across SOs*. If you follow this simple rule of thumb, it can help you to avoid allegations of salami slicing.

Duplicate publication is 'the practice of submitting the same study to two journals or publishing more or less the same study in two journals', and 'these submissions/publications can be nearly simultaneous or years later' (Springer Nature, 2023, para. 1). I've encountered this as a peer reviewer and questioned my own brain: the sense of déjà vu was overpowering. As the paper is basically the same, even though you've sent it to different journals, it will often go out to the same peer reviewers who can flag duplicate publication if this happens. Simply, don't write the same (or a materially similar) paper twice with slightly different wording and expect to get over the line at two different journals. Cite yourself if necessary and make sure you're not doubling up, as even if you get over the line, this can damage your reputation if/when discovered. These questionable practices won't be an issue as long as you understand them, and you've planned your TBP in advance to work as discrete units, clearly citing yourself where there's overlap. Editors *will* ask what's going on if they get a sense that you're intending duplicate publication, and journal article submission portals require your honest disclosure confirming that your work has not been submitted elsewhere.

When undertaking a TBP, it's useful to head off these editorial concerns at the pass by openly acknowledging where your paper sits within the whole project. Beyond my TBP, I've often been involved in research projects that yield multiple publications, and while sometimes I have received an editorial query, this has always been easily resolved through transparency. Since I started very explicitly flagging where multiple publications from the same project relate to different RQs across the whole project in both the manuscript and also the cover letter I don't even receive editorial queries anymore (touch wood!).

So how can we do this?

Here is an example of a direct quote from a journal article where we have flagged this for the editor:

> The 2024 International School Library Workforce Survey collected data from SLPs relating to a diverse array of research questions (RQs). The survey was sectioned into four separate and comprehensive blocks: reading engagement (this article), workforce (Merga and Mat Roni 2025), wellbeing (Merga in press), and digital information literacy (Merga and Mat Roni in press). This paper from the study focusses solely and comprehensively on the data from the survey block collecting SLPs' views on school libraries fostering student reading engagement. As such, at the outset, a brief review of the literature on the school library mediated elements of RfP that informed the survey items in this block is provided.
>
> (Merga & Mat Roni, 2025a, p. 2)

While the other papers from this project also reported on survey data, none of them reported on the same specific research and survey questions apart from the overlapping data reporting on the demographic components of the sample.

How to go about it

Hopefully, you are now convinced of the importance of using the initial planning stages to design a project that lends itself to discrete SOs that can stand alone without causing ethics issues, while also being cohesive to work together as building blocks in a single thesis. While doing this, you also need to ensure there's scope for achieving the minimum number of SOs needed as per your TBP policy if specified, while meeting the requirements of *all* PhDs, not just a TBP: as mentioned earlier, the design needs to deliver 'enough' to constitute a notable contribution to the body of knowledge in your research area. While this might seem like a pretty big ask, if you are working with supervisors who are used to designing and conducting these kinds of projects, you may get good quality guidance while learning how to do this.

As your PhD research is going to be conducted in the real world, there needs to be some wriggle room. Once you have your data, there may be some slight changes to how you work with it across the series of SOs; in some cases, successful TBP students have noted that the number and content of SOs was not planned at all at the outset, and was instead decided upon during the research process, and at the stage of analysis

(Pozniak et al., 2023). Where a doctoral journey involves multiple sub-projects where each project or phase corresponds to an article, rigid pre-planning is impossible as the PhD journey is completely responsive and evolving rather than set in stone at the outset, with even the RQs themselves expanding across the journey as more is progressively learned through the research process (Pozniak et al., 2023). While this sounds great, you can only do this if your policy allows you this kind of freedom and flexibility. Also, while you might start out expecting to write one SO at a time, in reality there is likely to be at least some overlap (Nygaard & Solli, 2021). For example, recently while I was collecting the data on a project, in my spare time I was also writing the literature reviews for the four separate papers planned from this project.

Even if your initial plan can't be specific, you can still plan not to have a plan if this can work with your policy. I'll break down four of the more common of these possibilities for your consideration.

1. Planned distinct findings

This is where, at the outset, you've planned publications to report on distinct findings. While not a PhD, my aforementioned project, the 2024 *International School Library Workforce Project* (ISLWP), also fits this approach, showing its transferability beyond the TBP. As can be seen in Table 4, the SOs often report on different RQs, and where they report on the same RQ(s), they do so using different data from the project.

These publications clearly and unambiguously can stand alone, as findings are responsive to different RQs, or groups of RQs, or different models, such as in the following case, where a student 'developed three research papers structured around her three related but independent logistics models that were designed to promote efficient and sustainable supply chain practices to deliver regional Australian products across the country and overseas' (Shrestha, 2023, p. 169). Others had an overarching RQ with sub-questions, each of which constituted an SO. For example, in his research in geography, Asante used 'one main question and five sub questions', and 'each of the five sub-questions was developed into an article', four of which were published before he submitted his thesis (Asante & Abubakari, 2021, p. 95).

Where you have multiple SOs reporting on the same RQ, ideally you will be using data from different research tools and/or questions on tools. For example, four of the SOs from my TBP report on RQ 3, which is: 'What is the influence of parents, English teachers, friends and peers on adolescents' attitudes toward recreational book reading?' However, findings are distinct because each SO reports on different data from the project as follows, bearing in mind that data collection on the project came from both surveys and interviews, and honestly, this was a very broad RQ, which also made this differentiation possible.

Table 3 *SO data sources from the TBP addressing RQ 3* (adapted from Merga, 2015)

SO title and citation	Data source for SO
Peer group and friend influences on the social acceptability of adolescent book reading. (Merga, 2014b)	Quantitative survey data specific to peer group and friend influences
Exploring the role of parents in supporting recreational book reading beyond primary school. (Merga, 2014c)	'The data that formed the basis of this article were gathered from the semi-structured interviews. The data were primarily derived from the answers and discussion that arose from two questions from the semi-structured interview, which focused on perceived parental valuing of the practice of recreational book reading, and comparison of parental encouragement received in primary and high school. Students also provided additional relevant information as part of discussion of other, indirectly related questions, and where this occurred the data have been included.' (p. 153)
What would make them read more? Insights from Western Australian adolescent readers. (Merga, 2016a)	Qualitative interview data on what would make students read more, as well as comments from an open field on the survey.
Should Silent Reading feature in a secondary school English programme? West Australian students' perspectives on Silent Reading. (Merga, 2013)	'The data that is the basis of this article was gathered from the semi-structured interviews, where students were asked about their current and past participation in Silent Reading programs.' (p. 234)

2. Built on findings

Other interesting approaches to SO writing, planning and delivery emerge from recent work in France, where Pozniak used an approach where subsequent articles addressed questions and issues raised by the previous one (Pozniak et al., 2023). Again, the RQs for the publications will be sufficiently different for there to be no potential issues arising relating to salami slicing or duplicative publication.

3. Findings with methods

It is also important to think broadly about the focus of the SOs beyond reporting on research findings to illuminating new knowledge on methods. For example, in one TBP which contained six articles, half of these focused on aspects relating to methodology, while the other half reported research findings (Pozniak et al., 2023).

4. Literature + findings

It may also be common for a TBP to include a published literature review as a first publication, as recommended by Mason (2018), which can be completed early, perhaps in a project lull, such as while waiting for ethics approvals for data collection. In this approach, a publishable literature review does more than present the literature; it justifies the research gap and thus the need for the doctoral project (Shrestha, 2023).

5. Planned distinct findings: TBP-friendly design and implications for RQs

You may be looking for a bit more advice on how to design a project with distinct components warranting separate publications. While hopefully Table 4 was useful, another example might help, so here's a more recent one. In 2024, with Saiyidi Mat Roni, we designed and conducted the aforementioned (approximately PhD-sized) ISLWP. The survey for this project collected data from 971 respondents across 63 countries.

The project design would have been appropriate for a TBP had it been undertaken as a PhD. This is because there was a strong unifying strand around needing to know more about issues impacting on the international school library workforce. However, there were also distinct elements within this goal that warranted close attention which could form the basis of individual publications. These were identified through a comprehensive understanding of the school library workforce through my networking with this group, my reading of the literature in this area, and my previous research that contributed to this field (e.g. Merga, 2020a; 2021b).

These were the project RQs guiding the whole project:

1 What are the most significant current international and context-specific issues influencing professional satisfaction in the school library workforce?
2 What are the most significant current issues influencing the capacity of the school library to foster student wellbeing, reading engagement and digital information literacy?
3 What are the most pressing predicted international and context-specific issues that will impact on school libraries in the future?

As briefly touched upon previously, the survey had four separate blocks, each with a unique and distinct focus and its own body of related research: workforce (Merga & Mat Roni, 2025b), reading engagement (Merga & Mat Roni, 2025a), digital information literacy (Merga & Mat Roni, 2025c) and wellbeing (Merga, 2025), and Table 4 shows how these four articles covered the project RQs with focused SO-specific sub-RQs.

Table 4 *Research Questions and scholarly outputs from the ISLWP*

Block	Article title	Citation	Project RQ	Focused sub-RQs
Workforce	School library professionals' perspectives on current and future workforce challenges	Merga & Mat Roni, 2025b	1 & 3	1 Do SLP*s feel valued? 2 Is collaboration between SLPs and classroom teachers supported? 3 What are the current and projected future SLP workforce challenges at school and country levels?
Reading engagement	'An uphill battle': School library professionals fostering student reading engagement	Merga & Mat Roni, 2025a.	2	1 Do students have access to the library to support RfP**? 2 Do students have support for choosing reading materials for RfP? 3 Are contemporary school libraries reading supportive environments? 4 What is the role of the school library in supporting teachers to model RfP? 5 What is the role of the school library in supporting parents to encourage RfP? 6 Are students exposed to reading aloud in the school library? 7 Is RfP and related reading engagement a priority across international contexts? 8 Does country income influence student reading engagement supportive factors?

Continued

Table 4 *Continued*

Block	Article title	Citation	Project RQ	Focused sub-RQs
Wellbeing	The library as a safe space in contemporary schools	Merga, 2025	2	1 Is developing students' wellbeing perceived to be a universal goal in schools? 2 Are school libraries seen as accessible safe spaces in contemporary schools? 3 Are school library environments conducive to promoting student wellbeing? 4 Do school libraries support student access to current wellbeing-supportive information? 5 What key insights are shared by respondents in relation to their school library as a space for fostering student wellbeing?
Digital information literacy	School library professionals' perceptions of student digital information literacy	Merga & Mat Roni, 2025c	2	1 To what extent do students have access to technological affordances to support DIL*** learning? 2 How is DIL learning positioned and valued in contemporary schools and contexts? 3 Are students perceived to have strong DIL in source credibility and expertise evaluation? 4 Is consistent DIL instruction related to perceived student DIL attainment? 5 Is a role for school libraries in DIL instruction related to perceived student DIL attainment?

*School library professional (SLP)
**Reading for pleasure (RfP)
***Digital information literacy (DIL)

As such, to be completely accurate, the project had three RQs, but also 21 focused sub-RQs as per Table 4, which were covered across four articles. You can see that these four articles are related to the overarching

RQs, and you can also see that they are sufficiently distinct at a focused sub-RQ level. For absolute clarity around how the SOs in your TBP deserve to be individual publications while also making an important contribution to the overall thesis, you might want to consider including a table like this early in your TBP to support the examiner in making these connections. Furthermore, creating this table at the initial planning stage could be a good idea as it may also be a notable asset to your proposal, demonstrating that you have done the necessary planning if you are taking a planned distinct findings approach.

Ethics and ethics approval

It is widely understood that academic research needs to be conducted in a verifiably ethical manner, with different contexts applying specific regulatory frameworks to this end. At your earliest meetings with your supervisory team, you need to get access to all applicable ethics policies and requirements of your institution to ensure that you are compliant from the very beginning of your journey. For example, I have had students wanting to collect data from colleagues prior to gaining institutional ethics approvals as an opportunity to meet with them had organically arisen. However, this would have been highly problematic had they proceeded. These policies will probably also refer you to national institutional frameworks and governance to ensure that your research is compliant beyond the university.

But is it enough to comply with institutional and national ethics norms?

On your PhD project, part of getting started and positioning for success involves building a comprehensive understanding of what it means to conduct ethical research. If what is permissible in your institutional and national context doesn't align with more rigorous expectations specific to your field, or scholarly outputs, you need to shape your work to be responsive to the higher standard. You may also find yourself working in a research space where the rules are still being written on what we should and shouldn't be doing in regards to data collection and analysis. As a novice researcher that can be an uncomfortable space, leaving you grappling with difficult questions that both you and your supervisory team may not find easy answers to.

For example, at present time, there are huge differences in ethical constraints on how researchers across nations use social media data in their research. With burgeoning social media content enabling 'exponential increase in access to naturalistic data' (Nicholas et al., 2020, p. 3), analysing social media posts may seem like a very attractive option. It can yield compelling insights into people's attitudes, values and activities without collecting data from them on purpose-designed tools or other interactions, and having the research activity shape the way respondents present themselves. Stewart et al. (2024) analysed comments on a YouTube video, noting that 'the advantages of using existing secondary data such as this posted freely in a public sphere without researcher prompting are that it is often considered to be more authentic and truthful than data collected for specific research purposes' (p. 90).

However, there has been growing attention on the ethical considerations that come into play when you analyse content that was not produced or collected for research purposes, and which therefore lacks the producers' knowledge and informed consent. What is ethically acceptable in this context has rapidly shifted in recent times, so social science researchers wanting to conduct content analysis of social media content will need to remain abreast of this evolving space in relation to human research ethics. While initially there was debate about whether social media data 'should be considered human subjects research or published data' (Sellers et al., 2020, p. 28), increasingly these data are seen as the former, rather than the latter.

It can be contended that 'the security, confidentiality, and appropriate use of personal digital data is a prominent issue in today's digitally engaged society' (Nicholas et al., 2020, p. 3), and this needs to be reflected in research norms. The currency of this issue can be seen in

> legislative changes including the introduction of the General Data Protection Regulation (GDPR) in the European Union. In addition, the US congressional hearings over Cambridge Analytica accessing over 75 million Facebook user profiles without knowledge or consent from the majority of those users, have brought the power and value of personal data, and issues around data privacy, further into the public consciousness . . .
>
> (Nicholas et al., 2020, p. 3)

Of course, recent changes in US politics may see another shift in this space. The limited extant research suggests that social media users may not be comfortable having their content analysed without their consent (Ford et al., 2019), and there have been very high-profile retractions in this space. For example, a retracted article that analysed social media posts (Hardouin et al., 2020) achieved significant media coverage and a social media backlash:

A medical journal is retracting an article that called some social media posts 'potentially unprofessional' after outraged health professionals flooded Twitter with photos of themselves posing in bikinis and holding alcoholic drinks.

The hashtag #Medbikini quickly trended Friday after the Journal of Vascular Surgery posted the article titled 'Prevalence of unprofessional social media content among young vascular surgeons.'

The article specifically mentioned photos that included 'provocative posing in bikinis/swimwear' and 'holding/consuming alcohol.'

(Johnson & Ebrahimiji, 2020, paras. 1–3)

As such, the consequences of research missteps in this space can also be amplified and ironically become social media content in their own right.

While ethical guidelines for social media research may be patchy or entirely absent in some contexts, as our understanding advances in this space, research regulatory bodies and policies are beginning to reframe expectations for researchers' practice. For example, in Australia, where I am based, all university researchers need to comply with the *National Statement on Ethical Conduct in Human Research* of the National Health and Medical Research Council (NHMRC) (2023). This includes stipulations around 'secondary use of data or information' relevant for research that involves 'access to and use of data or information that was originally generated or collected for previous research or for non-research purposes, including routinely collected data or information', noting that 'the main ethical issue arising from this use is the scope of consent provided or, alternatively, the impracticability of obtaining consent' (NHMRC, 2023, p. 36):

... using data or information without consent may undermine public trust in the confidentiality of their information. Privacy concerns arise when the proposed access to or use of the data or information does not match the expectations of the individuals from whom this data or information was obtained or to whom it relates. These issues are especially complex in the context of the access to or use of information relating to individuals that is available on the internet, including social media posts ... The guiding principle for researchers is that, although data or information may be publicly available, this does not automatically mean that the individuals with whom this data or information is associated have necessarily granted permission for its use in research. Therefore, use of such information will need to be considered in the context of the need for consent or the waiver of the requirement for consent by a reviewing body and the risks associated with the use of this information.

(NHMRC, 2023, p. 36)

As such, while this research can still be undertaken, researchers (at least in Australia) will require ethics approval to undertake it, demonstrating that they have considered the issues of consent, and minimised risks to the humans whose content they intend to use.

So if you are living in a country and/or working at an institution where there are limited regulations around the ethical use of social media content, how might the much stricter rules elsewhere impact the success of your TBP?

Research is absolutely lagging in this area, given that it is a very current and emerging issue. However, it is foreseeable that if your research is sent to peer reviewers from countries with stricter standards, this will be reflected in the responses that you receive concerning your methodology. You may find yourself being held to a higher level of ethical accountability than what is necessarily expected in your context. As such, while you need to understand the expectations in your institution, you also need to keep across evolving broader ethical expectations as far as possible to avoid finding yourself in a position where you have conducted research but cannot publish it because it does not meet new ethical norms.

As a bottom line here, if you are asked to collect or analyse data in a way that feels ethically or morally questionable, even though it's sanctioned in your working context, take a pause, read more, and get some advice from outside of your supervisory team if necessary. Research ethics are not just about what's already fixed in stone, they are evolving alongside growing possibilities for data sources and methods.

Ongoing targeted training

Ongoing learning in research will be a lifelong pursuit for those who enter into a research career; even the most senior academics will continue to build their research knowledge and skills (Arrieta et al., 2024). There is no point where a researcher knows everything, and to be honest, for me personally the constant learning and upskilling is part of what I really love about the job, as it never gets boring. Theories and methods do not remain static, and the knowledge area is constantly evolving, with constant contributions being made to its scope and depth. One of the things I love about being a researcher is constantly having my ideas reshaped, and it is very stimulating to engage with this, and to make material contributions to this process. For example, in my recent work I have expanded understandings of legal and ethics implications for autoethnography (Merga, 2024c), and made novel suggestions for quality controls in systematic reviews (Merga, 2024d). This noted, the learning curve for research training may be particularly steep during doctoral degree completion while the foundation knowledge is being acquired and consolidated. This may feel overwhelming at times, but just bear in mind that almost everyone who got a PhD had to go through a similar process.

TBP students will need much of the same research training as those pursuing a traditional thesis. However, they will also need exposure to specific training in how to manage aspects relating to the publication journey, particularly where this cannot be covered in their supervisor-directed learning opportunities. For example, TBP students might need training on how to make strategic choices when targeting journals 'to increase the chance of their work being accepted, and how to set legitimate timelines for various stages of publishing such as manuscript writing, submission, review, revision and resubmission' (Oboirien, 2024, p. 165), though guidance in all of these areas is also covered in this book. Depending on their academic English competence, they may also need a great deal of training and support in this area if this is required (Hidayat et al., 2024).

At the time of writing this book, my university (UNDA) did not have a functioning Graduate Research School or equivalent facility, which meant that the responsibility for providing ongoing training for TBP students arguably primarily rests with the supervisors in the area where I worked. Since starting at UNDA I tried to contribute to this provision through running the Method of the Month (MOM) training programme. MOM was designed to provide clear guidance on how to adopt a new research method or strategy, even if there was limited prior knowledge of this method. The emphasis was on the basics, and how the method might be creatively used, so these sessions were suitable for both fledgling research students and experienced academic staff looking to add to their methods toolkits; indeed, those who attended came from a variety of Schools and had greatly varying levels of seniority. TBP students need to stay on the front foot in regard to research training as they don't have the luxury of time to get their heads around new methods and concepts, so they need timely support, and I hoped that MOM could, to some extent, meet this need, both for my students and for any others across UNDA.

In addition to attending any relevant training taking place at your institution, you should also look out for guest lectures at other universities (online or in person), as well as making the most of free learning affordances available through social media, when produced by reliable and reputable creators. Joining networks and professional associations can also open up additional opportunities for training.

Peer support and spaces to engage

Doing a PhD can be an incredibly isolating experience and much has been written about this. Pretty quickly you can get to a point with your family and friends where their eyes will justifiably glaze over at the mere mention of something related to your PhD. Sadly, there aren't many people outside academia (or let's face it, even in academia) who actually want to hear about your theoretical framework. The deeper you go into your PhD, the less interesting you may be at parties, though if you have any friends who suffer from insomnia, you may find them calling you more often around bedtime, and asking you probing questions about your literature review.

While you may have vastly different desired levels of PhD-related social interaction depending on your own preferences and the stage of your PhD (Kitano & Lane, 2024), there may be times when being able to interact with like-minded peers is of huge benefit. It's great if you can get a group of other TBP students to hang out with either in real life or online, and/or an experienced academic mentor who can devote some time to supporting you by fostering a sense of belonging and helping you to network within your academic community.

However, don't despair if that doesn't work out for you: many novice researchers have really struggled to find someone to fill these roles. Our research in this space found that 'mentor and peer support are not universal, and some respondents did not have a mentor or significant peer influence supporting their production of academic or translational research outputs' (Merga & Mason, 2021b, p. 5). Here's how it felt to be one of them:

> I've never had a real proper mentoring relationship like a patron or anything like that. It was very much blindly groping until I figured out the way forward. A lot of trial and error. And I was fortunate enough that I didn't have any really major setbacks in that while I was doing that. I think if I'd gotten sick or I'd had some kind of family responsibility or something that came up . . . I did get divorced but, apart from that, I think I've been quite fortunate in having a kind of space to figure it out and I think a lot of people don't.
>
> I've seen a lot of people kind of go underwater in that kind of phase where they're trying to figure out how do I actually do this and not really having the person there to go, 'All right, this is what you need to do, this is what you don't need to do, here's some funding that I've got for you, here's a project that I want you to work on to train you up on this particular skill set that will help you off down the line.' I never really had that. Most of my colleagues that I went through the process with didn't have that either. (Vince)
>
> (Merga & Mason, 2021b, p. 5)

As such, while it's great to have mentors and peers invested in your PhD journey, they are not essential to your success.

In my own experience, as I briefly mentioned earlier, I was fortunate enough to work in a paid academic mentoring role from the second year of my PhD candidature. If a similar opportunity comes your way, I strongly urge you to take it. As a SOAR Ambassador and Mentor I facilitated dyadic meetings with doctoral students

> to assist with problems specific to a candidate's research, along with group SOAR seminar sessions on a variety of topics related to the research journey. While performing the role is centrally concerned with knowledge and skill support, in practice SOAR Ambassadors also provide a large degree of social support for clientele.
>
> (Booth et al., 2016, p. 386)

Focusing on other people's research was a really welcome break, and I really loved learning about knowledge areas widely removed from my own, such as factors impacting on seagrass oxygenation and preventing infant mortality across cultures. This role made me really aware of the transferable skill set I was learning; for example, I found myself providing advice and seminars on negotiating academic journal article publication *as I was learning it myself* with my very junior status widely known. To deliver quality learning, I needed to be a deeply reflective educator in the space, able to tap into the practical and emotional dimensions of the challenges faced by novice researchers while living them myself. Even the students seeing me for the most technical reasons also sought wellbeing and social support as part of that exchange. Recent research found that for distance doctoral students who were also carers, 'peer connections with other doctoral students were emphasised as critical sites of care that enabled wellbeing and success' (McChesney et al., 2024, p. 106). As a doctoral supervisor many years later, I have still been very much shaped by those early experiences in the SOAR role, considering knowledge and methodological needs, but also social and emotional needs.

Publication options for early stages

Where you are working with an institutional policy that requires a minimum number of SOs and/or they all need to be accepted by the point of TBP submission, you may be particularly interested in designing a project that allows for publication options for early stages. At my former institution (UNDA), most literature reviews and autoethnographies did not require an extensive ethics approval process, so students could easily get permission to undertake *narrative or systematic literature reviews*, or reflective *autoethnographies*. If this is also the case where you are, these SOs can be particularly good early options.

It is often logical to include these two kinds of publications in a TBP project design. For example, even a traditional thesis would usually include a literature review, and autoethnographies are relevant when the TBP student wants to situate themselves in relation to their research by connecting their own story to their broader project:

> Being situated means being mindful or aware of the relationship between oneself and one's context. We argue that, since research is intersubjective, and since it is the researcher who initiates and takes charge of the research process in order to produce as reliable data as possible, the more the researcher knows about why they have chosen to attempt data production about phenomenon X rather than Y, how they go about producing that data and how they produce their stories about X, the better the data, and the better the texts.
>
> (Neumann & Neumann, 2015, p. 799)

If you would like to attempt one or both of these kinds of publications early in your candidature, you will need to read extensively about the methods informing them. I'll provide you with a very brief overview here to get you started.

Narrative and systematic literature reviews

Literature reviews investigate the extant research to better understand what is currently available, identify gaps in the research, make an argument for the merit of the proposed research and, increasingly, deliver implications for real-world purposes (Merga & Oddone, 2025).

While the publishable literature review may be the most organic and logical of choices for a publication early in the doctoral journey, given that you need to do this work anyway, I know of many instances where TBP students have created a literature review only to have it remain unpublished. While there can be many reasons why a literature review does not get accepted for publication, I feel that sometimes there is a fundamental misunderstanding about the point of a *publishable* literature review. I would argue that in most cases, even when the literature review is a chapter within a traditional thesis, it should ideally do more than just summarise the available research and weigh in on research gaps, and if you want your literature review to be publishable, it probably needs to take the next step of contributing new knowledge through the way this existing literature is analysed, interpreted and critically interrogated.

First, I'll briefly cover the difference between the narrative and systematic literature review. They are not the only kinds of review, but in my experience, they are the most common for social science TBP students to undertake, so I focus on them here. The systematic review will follow an explicitly articulated process for selecting the research that informs it with a view to that process being *replicable*, whereas the traditional narrative review will be unconstrained by systematic process and instead be a 'creative process through which a researcher identifies and examines prior research and develops increasing understanding of a phenomenon under examination and in the process constructs the relevant body of knowledge' (Boell & Cecez-Kecmanovic, 2015, p. 164). For example, in my 2024 systematic review on TikTok and digital health literacy, I clearly describe the systematic process that I adopted in the methods, also providing a supporting diagram (Figure 2) which is hopefully pretty simple.

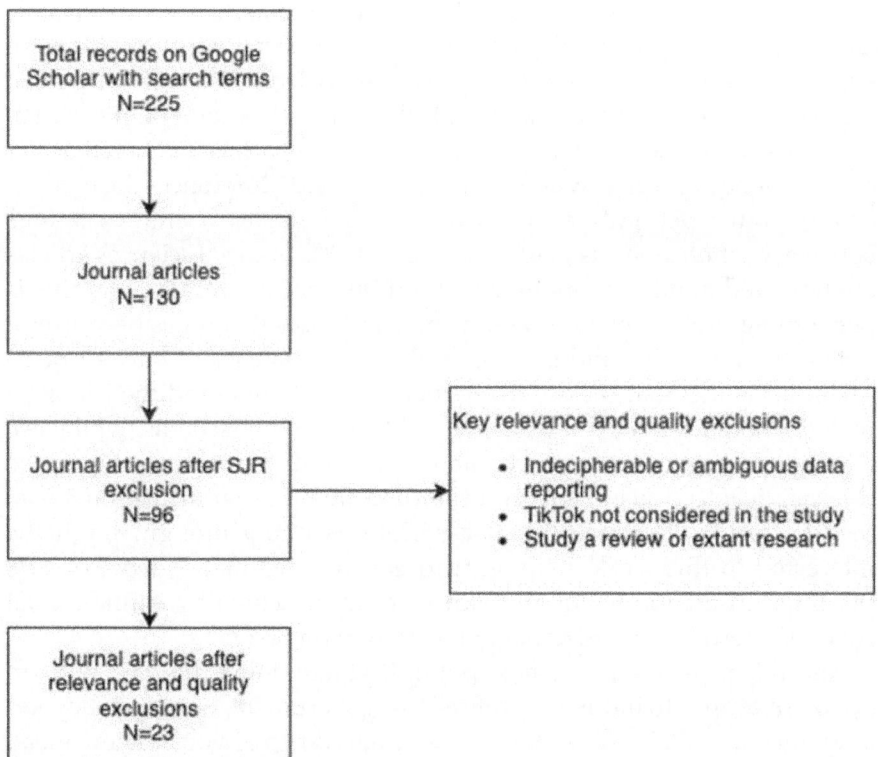

Figure 2 *Systematic review process* (Source: Merga, 2024d, p. 3)

In contrast to the narrative review, 'the explicit and systematic approach' is what 'distinguishes systematic reviews from traditional reviews and commentaries' (Khan et al., 2003, p. 118). While the systematic review has this kind of prescribed approach, there can still be flexibility in how you approach it, and the best way to prepare to write a systematic or narrative review is to read many current examples from within or beyond your discipline and see which style and method resonates with you.

While narrative literature reviews are often denigrated as being the least rigorous of review types, particularly when compared with systematic reviews and meta-analyses, they can add value within and beyond research fields when created with a clear audience in mind, and where the findings and application of the literature meet a significant immediate need, they may perform very well in some of the readership metrics I unpack in the chapter on KMb later in this book. Indeed, some of my narrative reviews have outperformed my empirical research in terms of reads, downloads, and/or citations, and I believe that this is because these narrative reviews have been carefully constructed to meet a very specific end-user need. For example, a 2020 narrative review that I undertook to support a grant application (which was successful!) is one of my most viewed papers of all time (Merga, 2020b), currently sitting on more than 29,000 views on the journal page, and 60 citations, which isn't too bad for social sciences norms; while there are marked differences in median citation rates per publication within social sciences, and variations between citation analysis platforms, around 68% of social sciences articles are not cited at all (Tomaselli, 2019). I think that the reason why this is performing pretty well with views and citations is that it has been useful for professionals beyond academia; there is a paucity of current peer-reviewed works that seek to bring together the different dimensions by which school libraries can promote wellbeing within schools, while also clearly articulating a research plan to expand research in this space (Merga, 2020b). I also actively promoted this journal article on social media, tagging in professional associations that I thought might be interested in this work, helping it to get to an Altmetric score of 114, placing it in the top 5% of all research outputs scored by Altmetric. I'll cover Altmetrics in more detail in the section on KMb.

And this takes me to my next point. If you're doing this TBP with an eye on relevance to industry, professions, government, or society beyond academia, definitely think about what the findings of your review mean for these audiences. Our recent review of KMb contributions of narrative reviews in higher education found that most of these reviews 'included a novel KMb contribution that had been extracted and developed during the review process, demonstrating a common willingness to engage with the review findings to derive practical implications' (Merga & Oddone, 2025, p. 698).

Having both written and peer-reviewed a number of literature reviews across disciplines in the social sciences, here is a brief summary of what makes a literature review publishable in my experience:

1 The synthesis needs to be seamless and it needs to flow. By that, I mean that if your review reads something like 'Ho and Smith (2023) said this. Blogs and Singh (2021) said this. Bilge (2020) said this', what you have reads more like a shopping list than a literature review; you need to find the commonalities and the differences in what you are reading, and position the research in your review accordingly.
2 If you are going with the systematic review, the logic behind your methodology needs to be really clearly articulated and justified, with limitations acknowledged. You will probably want to use a diagram to represent the steps that you took, as is commonly employed in this method. Figure 2 is a really simple example.
3 Ideally, you need to find something in the literature *that others have not already uncovered,* perhaps something that others would miss/have overlooked. This is part of what can give your literature review its novelty and value within and/or beyond academia. What is your point of difference with similar reviews (if applicable)?
4 It helps to have some real-world expertise, where you can show genuine utility in the findings of your review for a group of end-users, and it might be easier for you to locate this in the literature if you know what you are looking for from a practical standpoint. Don't be afraid to take it to the next step, finding the implications for future research and current practice where applicable, while acknowledging the limitations of the extant research and what can be claimed in analysis of it.
5 Take the time at the very outset to firm up how you are framing key concepts. Consider what you need to define in terms of concepts to even know what you're looking for, and what sources you can legitimately draw on to justify your concept framing. You don't need to include every relevant study ever done in the history of humankind; what you do need to do, particularly if conducting a systematic review, is consider and justify what filters and limitations are reasonable to place on your study. For example, in my systematic review on TikTok I wanted to only engage with current literature as

this is a rapidly evolving platform, so I made the related decision to only include literature published in 2020 onwards (Merga, 2024d).

Autoethnographies

As mentioned earlier, many doctoral students, particularly those using qualitative methodologies, may seek to situate themselves within their research at the outset by including an autoethnographic component. As a thesis examiner, it's something I particularly like to see *where relevant*; rather than pretending that we bring a blank slate to our research, we can use autoethnography to describe, acknowledge and even celebrate how our previous experiences can (inevitably) inform how we conduct and understand our research project.

As with literature reviews, there are many ways to approach an autoethnography, so if you decide to include an autoethnography in your TBP, you will need to read many examples to decide how you wish to go about this, though I will provide a very basic overview here:

> Rooted in the principles of narrative inquiry, autoethnography is a qualitative method that involves the intentional connection of personal experiences to social and cultural phenomena, often to illuminate or challenge extant norms (Trahar, 2009). It involves an iterative process of 'focusing outward on social and cultural aspects' of personal experience, then looking 'inward, exposing a vulnerable self that is moved by and may move through, refract, and resist cultural interpretations' (Ellis & Bochner, 2000, p. 739) . . . While autoethnography may be subject to criticism on many grounds, not limited to a perceived lack of scientific value, as contended by Wall (2006), postmodernism allows for the possibility that there are diverse ways of 'knowing and inquiring' that hold legitimacy, allowing for the potential of the 'sharing of unique, subjective, and evocative stories of experience that contribute to our understanding of the social world and allow us to reflect on what could be different because of what we have learned'
> (pp. 147–148)
>
> (Merga, 2024c, pp. 1–2)

In autoethnography *you* are the data source; we engage in dedicated reflexive introspection within the limits of our subjective possibilities and conditionings. For this reason, at the time of writing this, in some contexts you may not need to get institutional ethics approvals in order to conduct autoethnography; a waiver may be granted, but you need to confirm this.

However, this ready access to human data from yourself does not mean that autoethnography is without significant issues and challenges. It is certainly not the case that an autoethnography is an 'easy option', and peer review of this methodology may be particularly agonising when reviewers want greater disclosure about your personal experience than you are willing or able to provide, as I have experienced first-hand. The process of making the personal public can be personally risky; as you read examples of autoethnography from your discipline, you may be somewhat surprised by just how revealing these pieces can be (and how easy it is to identify unnamed antagonists in autoethnographic depictions based on the descriptive detail about them). One of the four conditions of autoethnography outlined by Sparkes (2018) is 'embracing vulnerability with a purpose', but as a novice researcher, will you always know where to safely draw the line to protect yourself and others? There are also other ethical, professional and legal risks involved in the contemporary research space that should be carefully considered (Merga, 2024c).

As such, while reviews and autoethnographies are often viable publication options for the early stages of TBP, there is much to learn about how to conduct these methods with rigour and care, engaging in this kind of text production in a manner that mitigates risk and will enable these texts to sit within your TBP, adding value.

## CHAPTER 3

Navigating Journal Article Publication

If you have some familiarity with academia, navigating journal article publication might be the thing that you are most apprehensive about with regards to completing a TBP. As someone who likes to plan and be in control of my work, I personally find detaching somewhat at the point of submission and accepting that my SO is now out of my hands an ongoing challenge.

Navigating journal article publication is a complex skill set to develop, and institutions do not provide equal support for your acquisition of these skills as novice researchers. Moving from being an ECR into mid-career, with peers I have reflected on how career progression has influenced my understanding of the role of the institution in supporting this:

> ... there can be great variation in quality and affordances of research training across institutions . . . As we have persisted in academia, we have also become increasingly aware that research supportive training, facilities and related cultures are not static variables within an institution, and they are sensitive to internal changes in quality of delivery, even where outwardly resourcing... (may) appear the same or comparable.
>
> (Merga et al., 2025, p. 10)

The ease with which you acquire this capacity is not all on you, and you should draw on institutional support as well as supervisory support where possible.

If you are planning on moving into academia after your PhD, acquiring this skill set now will be hugely advantageous. It's likely that many readers of this book have decided to undertake a TBP at least in part to further develop their skills in navigating journal article publication:

> Scholarly publishing, a central feature of the TBP, was an important motivator for many participants in this study, 'in order to be competitive in the job market

after completing my PhD' (Jenny). There was a keen understanding of the important role that publications play for those pursuing an academic career . . .

(Mason et al., 2020a, p. 863)

Research has found that in the HASS TBPs, 'the majority of the publications were journal articles, with almost 99% of all candidates including at least one journal article' (Mason & Merga, 2018a, p. 146).

Assuming at least some of your SOs are journal articles, how do we write one that can survive peer review?

It helps to build an understanding of what the editors are looking for. As we've covered previously, a lot of this more practical knowledge can be tacit (Merga et al., 2018), and it is often learned through discussions with your supervisors, reading the somewhat limited extant research, via 'mentors, peers, or the vast number of materials on the Internet' (Wu et al., 2024, p. 1), as well as more brutally through your own trial and error. Not every student has an experienced and knowledgeable supervisory team who have published recently and extensively in their specific field, or exposure to high-quality training within their institution. Even if you are fortunate enough to be this well-resourced, it's still useful to have a strong understanding of what editors are actually looking for to avoid stumbling at the multiple hurdles to peer-reviewed publication.

Journal selection

I'm kicking off this section with a comment on journal selection as it's really key to navigating the journal article publication journey smoothly. Fun fact about journal selection: while I have provided professional development on how to do this in the social sciences at several universities, as well as offsite, for external research teams looking to partner with an academic mentor on an academic journal publication, I used to be *spectacularly terrible* at this as a TBP student. As I was the sole author on all of my SOs, my journey was unusually solitary, and all of the (many) mistakes I made were uniquely my own. At that time, I didn't understand that many journal expectations were tacit. For example, just because a journal does not say that it is *only open to quantitative work* in its author guidelines does not mean that it will welcome articles reporting on qualitative work.

So how can you maximise the chance that your journal article will be accepted, and how can you ensure that it will be published in a well-regarded journal? Here are some tips for absolute novices.

Impact and outputs

Before you select the journal, you need to understand any impact expectations as they may have a significant influence over your (permissible) choices. I have already briefly touched on journal impact in Chapter 1, so if you are reading this book out of order, I suggest familiarising yourself with that content before jumping here unless you are already aware of how journal impact is evaluated. The extent to which your publication choices will be dictated by metrics is context- and discipline-specific (Merga et al., 2025), and may also be dictated by your supervisory team.

One place to learn about expectations is institutional policy. Perhaps in response to research excellence agendas and their association with impact factors and related metrics (Kamler, 2008; Osterloh & Frey, 2015), TBP policies can be quite specific around SO quality expectations. In recent research, a third of TBP policies used 'adjectives to describe characteristics of publications, publishers, and/or outlets' (Mason et al., 2024b, p. 8):

> Around one-fifth of policies (n = 34, 18%) make mention of citation-based metrics, such as quartile rankings and/or Impact Factors. This includes five policies that require journal metrics to be reported with their submission, and 15 cases where doctoral researchers are required or strongly recommended to publish at least one article (if not all) in journals in the top quarter (n = 1), top half (n = 11), top three quarters (n = 1), or top four quarters (n = 2) of journals in terms of citation ranking. (p. 8)

As such, there may be a significant narrowing of options when it comes to selecting where you can send your manuscripts. Whether the directive on permissible journals comes from your university, supervisory team, or another source, you will need to get clarity about where to go in order to get a list or database of permitted journals. In some cases, this may be compiled by your academic librarian, but in others, students are expected to enter journals into an online platform to learn of their current impact status in relation to these expectations.

While you can't ignore metrics and impact factors in journal selection unless not relevant in your context, if you are new to academic publishing, you might not be aware of how your journal selection and citation practices serve to reinforce existing inequities in higher education. In our 2021 blog article we explain that

> the 'top' journals in any discipline are those that command the most prestige, and that position is largely determined by the number of citations their

published articles garner. Despite being highly problematic, citation-based metrics remain ubiquitous, influencing researchers' review, promotion and tenure outcomes. Bibliometric studies in various fields have shown that the 'top' journals are heavily dominated by research produced in and about a small number of 'core' countries, mostly the USA and the UK, and thus reproduce existing global power imbalances within and beyond academia.

(Mason & Merga, 2021, para. 2)

When you go with a lower-impact journal if permitted by your policy, you run the risk of not ideally positioning yourself for favourable academic outcomes, but on the bright side, you are probably providing your free content in support of a journal that is more inclusive:

. . . Q4 journals are statistically more likely to include research and researchers from outside of the core anglophone countries. In doing so, Q4 journals make an important contribution to scholarship through the inclusion of research from and about regions that are otherwise under-represented. Further, it was only in Q4 journals in which articles written in languages other than English were considered. (para. 4)

The other thing that no one really talks about is the fact that every researcher plays a role in shaping these impact outcomes, because of whom we choose to cite: 'citation is an area in which researchers can exercise agency, and an opportunity to reflect on our own sometimes constrained practice' (para. 5). Furthermore, if you only ever cite the giants in your field and never the junior scholars who are also innovating in your space, you are contributing to further bloating the advantage of established scholars over new entrants into the scholarly space.

What to look for

Once you know where you are permitted to publish if such limitations apply, when choosing the right journal for your work, you'll need to closely consider what the journal is both explicitly and tacitly looking for, as well as what your work offers various fields and stakeholders. Personally, as a more experienced researcher now, I prefer to write for a specific journal rather than choose a journal once I am done with my draft, as this enables me to tailor every aspect of the manuscript to that journal's unique needs. To this end, I've made a table for you with some things to consider, in no particular order (Table 5).

Table 5 *My tips for choosing a journal*

Focus	A few reasons why it matters	Some related questions	How to find out
Relevance	Journals will sometimes explicitly state that they're looking for manuscripts that join an existing conversation taking place in their journals. In simple terms, this means that you need to cite those existing works from that specific journal.	*Which journal have I cited the most in my literature review (or completed manuscript if you are at that stage)?*	Check your reference list. Familiarise yourself with what is currently being published in your target journals, particularly in relation to hot topics.
Audience	As I also explore further in Chapter 7, there are many different kinds of research journals, some of which may be reaching professional as well as academic audiences. If you are particularly keen for your work to reach stakeholders beyond academia, give some consideration to publishing in research journals that have already forged these connections. However, if you are required to publish in journals with strong journal metrics, you will need to find journals that are both sufficient in metrics *and* connection with your desired audience beyond academia.	*Who do I most want to read this article?* *Which journals with sufficient metrics (if required) are already connected with these audiences?*	Read the author guidelines. Connect with relevant professional associations or industry groups and try to find out which (if any) research journals they are connected with or source information from.
Context	There may be some journals that will reject because they feel that research done in your context is not relevant for their journal. While this can be mitigated to some extent by actively writing your manuscript for an international audience, for international resonance, sometimes even that is not enough. If you are writing outside a privileged context, prepare to be disappointed in some instances at the unfair practices that still prevail in some dominant journals.	*Does this journal regularly publish articles from my context?* *If not, are they demonstrably open to publishing work from marginalised contexts and voices?*	Read the author guidelines. Scan recent journal articles, taking into account the origins of both the data and the researchers.

Continued

Table 5 *Continued*

Focus	A few reasons why it matters	Some related questions	How to find out
Methods	If you submit an article to a journal that does not usually publish the kinds of methods that you have used, they may not be interested in it. There are many reasons for this including but not limited to a lack of a qualified peer-viewer pool, and methodological preferences of the editorial board. Sometimes you'll be using a method that is really new, so if you follow this rule to the letter you literally will not be able to publish anywhere. Luckily there are some journals that are open to innovation and flexible in relation to methods, but you cannot assume that this is the case without some diligent investigation.	*Has this journal regularly and recently published the kinds of methods that I have used?* *If no, are they demonstrably open to innovation and flexibility in research methods?*	Read the author guidelines. Familiarise yourself with the kinds of methods that your journal has published in recent times; this is important because changes in the composition of an editorial board sometimes lead to shifts in what is given preference in terms of methods.
Accessibility	If you or your university can afford to pay open-access fees, you can opt for journals that allow for open-access publication to ensure that your work can reach the widest possible readership. If you can't afford open access, there are other ways to share your work in some cases, and I cover these in Chapter 7 in the section on open access and paywall workarounds.	*Will other academics be able to read this article in diverse contexts?* *Can my stakeholders beyond academia access this article?*	Speak with your supervisor team and/or your academic librarian to find out what agreements are in place with regards to open access, or where open access funding may be accessed. If you cannot afford open access, choose journals that allow you to freely store and share the pre-print of your article (more about this in Chapter 7).
Journal metrics	As mentioned above, you may be required to submit only to journals meeting certain impact requirements as defined by approved metrics. Metrics do not necessarily remain stable over time, so you will want to choose a journal that is trending upwards rather than	*What is the impact of this journal in relation to the metrics approved at my institution and within my field?* *Have these metrics been typically stable over time? If no, are they trending in a*	If constrained by this factor, use the current metrics and related list/platform recommended by your supervisory team, and remember to revisit and recheck the page before

Continued

Table 5 *Continued*

Focus	A few reasons why it matters	Some related questions	How to find out
Journal metrics (*continued*)	downwards where possible. This is because a Q1 journal can become a Q3 journal, and if you want to report on your general metrics in job applications at the end of your PhD, you'll typically be reporting on where the metrics are *at that time*, rather than where they were when your journal article was originally published. Yes, it's a gamble!	*positive or negative direction?*	submitting again in the future, given that these metrics change.
Journey length	As you are doing a TBP it's not a great idea to submit to a journal where the time from submission to decision is very lengthy, *particularly* if your TBP policy requires that your article be accepted in order for inclusion in the thesis.	*How long does it typically take for an article to be given a decision at this journal from the point of submission?* *Given my current stage of candidature, university TBP policy and future plans, is this a realistic wait time?*	Read the author guidelines. If the typical journey length is not published in these guidelines, ask staff at your university who have published in this journal recently, bearing in mind that your circumstances may be very different to theirs.
Acceptance rate	If you send an article to a journal with a very low acceptance rate, obviously you're more likely to be rejected. I would tend to send my more competitive research to the low-acceptance journal; this will be the article that covers my most compelling RQs if appropriate in relation to the other areas of focus.	*What is the acceptance rate of this journal?* *Given my current stage of candidature, university TBP policy and future plans, is this a viable acceptance rate, or am I probably wasting my time?*	Read the author guidelines. If the acceptance rate is not published in these guidelines, ask staff at your university who have published in this journal recently.
Format	There's no point in trying to write a journal article requiring a	*What is the word count for this journal?*	Read the author guidelines.

Continued

Table 5 *Continued*

Focus	A few reasons why it matters	Some related questions	How to find out
Format (*continued*)	substantial word count for a journal with a very firm and limited word count.	*What is the style for this journal?*	
Quality of review and editorial oversight	While this partly relates to publishing and journals where the 'giants' in your field are on the editorial team, there are wide differences in the quality of peer review and editorial oversight experienced across journals within a field, and I discuss this further in Chapter 7.	*Have other authors (e.g. your supervisors) reported a reasonable peer review process at this journal?* *Do editors intervene in instances of major contradiction between reviewers?*	Ask staff at your university who have published in this journal recently about the quality of the peer-review process.

Within and across disciplines

This section is most relevant for those undertaking research that may have cross-disciplinary implications. If this is not you, feel free to skip along to the next section.

While I work across a range of areas (see Appendix), a lot of my work is relevant for *both* audiences in education and library and information sciences (LIS), so when it comes to choosing journals, I think about which discipline the findings will most resonate with, and therefore where it will be easiest to get the findings over the line.

For example, in the recent ISLWP, all four outputs could have been published in education or LIS journals due to the clear cross-over relevance. In this instance, one of the four papers was published in an education journal (Merga & Mat Roni, 2025a), with the other three appearing in LIS journals (Merga, 2025; Merga & Mat Roni, 2025b; 2025c). The key factors that determined the journal selection in this instance were journal quality, positive past experience, relevance and speed. In our view, the findings had urgent implications for policy, given our data captured a school library workforce that is dwindling in many contexts, and/or facing significant threats: in my experience, it takes a lot longer (in general) for manuscripts to pass through review in education journals compared with LIS journals. Also, personally, when my work has relevance across disciplines, I always try to publish *at least once per discipline* without duplicate publication or salami slicing, to reach the broadest relevant audience possible.

Choosing and hiding your identity

Once you have selected your journal and prepared your manuscript, you have further decisions to make before you can submit, and some of these relate to your own naming and related identifiers needed at the submission process, which might not be as straightforward as you expect.

Choose your name and get your number

Once you start publishing under a certain name, remaining consistent to that name where possible can help minimise metrics confusion (see Merga, Mat Roni & Mason, 2020 for more on this). Names do not necessarily remain static, so this can be a challenge for people who choose to take the name of their partner after marriage, or change their name after divorce or other life circumstances.

I also want to note that there are all kinds of challenges faced by people with compound last names. For example, my regular co-author Saiyidi Mat Roni has the first name Saiyidi and the last name Mat Roni; he is often incorrectly listed on our papers (as Roni, S. M. instead of Mat Roni, S.) despite my efforts to fix this where detected at copyedit stage.

Understandably, Saiyidi doesn't want to have to change his name so that he can be correctly attributed by academic publishers. So if you have a compound name:

- Pay attention at copyedit stage both to how the name is presented on the article in the main text and in any related headers or footers;
- If the article is published with incorrect naming, contact the publisher to ensure a correction is made;
- Where possible, enter metadata yourself. For example, when I publish with Saiyidi I make sure that I manually enter the publication information into Google Scholar so that his name is added correctly.

You will also need to do due diligence when deciding on your name to see who is already out there in your field with the same name, potentially leading to confusion. If there is already someone publishing under your name, you can consider adding your middle name as an additional distinguisher, or the reverse. For example, when I recently discussed co-authoring a chapter with one of my TBP students, we checked her name on Google Scholar to see if there were any matches. Somewhat incredibly, the only match had the exact same middle initial, and used it consistently, so instead of listing her author name with her middle initial, we opted not to in order to minimise the likelihood of metrics confusion.

Once you have selected your name, and you have begun to undertake research (even as a student), it is a good idea to sign up to a numeric persistent identifier:

> A persistent identifier (PID) is a long-lasting, unique reference to an entity or resource, such as an organization, researcher, or research output. PIDs unambiguously identify resources and contribute to research outputs being findable, accessible, interoperable, and reusable (FAIR). As recognized by the UNESCO in its 2021 Recommendation on Open Science, PIDs are a critical component of Open Science infrastructure.
>
> (Douglas Research Centre, n.d., para. 1)

Some journals will not even allow you to submit a manuscript without including your Open Researcher and Contributor ID (ORCID). ORCID is a persistent identifier commonly used by researchers. Signing up will provide you with a unique 16-digit numeric code that is your individual identifier for free, that you can use across your academic career to distinguish your work from others, even where they have exactly the same name, and work in exactly the same field. Your ORCID can also act as an externally visible CV that will show your publications, affiliation, grant wins, and other related data of interest to the academic community.

When you want to be nameless

Writing this in 2025, there is an additional consideration that I need to raise here. There is no universal protected freedom of speech for researchers (Merga, 2024c), and you may find yourself doing a PhD in a higher education context with known or new risks, not limited to traditionally authoritarian regimes (Scholars at Risk, 2024). Given rapidly evolving limitations on research in some contexts (e.g. Palmer, 2025), you may find yourself in a situation where you want to do a TBP but *you don't want your name on the SOs*.

For example, a student might do a TBP that includes SOs on their own sensitive personal experiences. In this instance, you may be confident that the examiners of your TBP will be able to preserve your anonymity, and that you can embargo your thesis, but the SOs pose another issue. However, the major academic publishing groups are trying to be responsive to scholars at risk. The following is from the editorial policies of Taylor and Francis (2025):

Where there is a credible risk of serious harm or threat to their life or liberty, as a result of their research or findings, researchers should contact the journal Editor or editorial office to discuss what options for publication may be available to minimise risk to the researcher.

Please note that the purpose of naming authors on scholarly publications is to ensure that the appropriate individuals receive recognition, and are accountable, for the published work. Therefore, anonymous publication may only be considered in exceptional circumstances. Requests will be evaluated on their own merit by the journal Editor and Publisher, and an editorial note or footnote to accompany the publication may be warranted. The Editor and Publisher have full and sole discretion as to whether a request to publish anonymously will be granted and do not provide any guarantee that requests will be granted.

If the Editor and Publisher grants a request to publish anonymously, they cannot and do not make any guarantees with respect to the author's total anonymity and the author acknowledges that they proceed with publication of the article at their own risk. The Publisher will also require the author to enter into any requisite publishing agreements and copyright documentation under the author's legal name. (paras. 1–3)

While I also explore implications of high-risk projects for KMb later in this book, knowing that there can be editorial policies with flexibility to at least endeavour to protect your anonymity on SOs can provide some security for students, bearing in mind that there is no guarantee that anonymity will be successfully preserved, or necessarily permitted. Where you do not want your name on SOs due to potential legal risks related to your disclosures, also seek legal advice; supervisors are not always across what you can and cannot say in a publication unless they are research active in this area of law in the relevant context.

Anonymising the manuscript for peer review

As seen in Table 1 earlier, double-anonymised peer review (also known as double-blind peer review) is the most common kind of peer review undertaken in the social sciences. Now that you have decided on your name, you will need to make sure that it is completely removed from the anonymised manuscript that you would typically submit to a journal for double-anonymised peer review.

At journal submission stage, you will be asked to submit your manuscript typically in one of three approaches:

1 Anonymised manuscript with all identifying information removed;
2 Anonymous manuscript for review, *and* final manuscript not anonymised, not for review (as two separate files, under two separate designations in the submission portal);
3 Final manuscript not anonymised (editorial team will undertake the anonymisation for you).

This third option is the least common in my experience; that noted, one journal where I often publish requires my submission in this form.

Where anonymisation is required by a journal, this is taken very seriously. If they ask for an anonymised manuscript and you do not completely anonymise it, it may be unsubmitted and returned to you. If you upload your anonymised manuscript under the wrong designation, it may also be unsubmitted and returned to you.

But what is expected when we anonymise a manuscript? In my experience, expectations vary.

As the bare minimum across the board, we remove our name, contact information and affiliation from the manuscript. We will also be expected to remove any acknowledgements, conflict of interest statements, and identifying features relating to our project funding source.

Depending on the publisher, you may be required to substitute any self-citations with (Author) in text, keeping the year. The references at the end also need to be swapped out, and here is one way you might do this (see Table 6 opposite). This is just my personal preference and I've never been told to do it differently, so I'm sharing it with you; read author guidelines and listen to your supervisors and follow their preferences over what I recommend.

However, you should note that some publishers *do not want self-citations to be anonymised* (e.g. Sage, 2025), which is actually pretty logical, given that anonymous self-citations are often totally identifying, particularly if you directly quote yourself. A few seconds on Google will reveal your identity once the quote text is pasted in as long as the source has been published.

Also, where self-citations are anonymised, it is not uncommon for peer reviewers to question why you haven't cited yourself, when they don't know that you are in fact the researcher that they want you to cite! This puts you in a very difficult position trying to respond to this peer reviewer query without identifying who you are.

There are instances where you will want to waive the right to double-blind peer review because it is completely impractical, only submitting an identifiable manuscript. For example, if you write an autoethnography,

Table 6 *Anonymising references if required*

End-text anonymised example	What it means
Author (2019)	This is an article published in 2019; I am the sole author.
Author & Other (2025)	This is an article published in 2025; there is one additional author.
Author et al. (2021)	This is an article published in 2021 with two or more additional authors.
Author & Other (in press-a) Author & Other (in press-b)	In this instance, there are two in-press papers by the same team of myself and another author, so I have them listed as in press-a and in press-b. I can list them as in press as they have been formally accepted for publication and I have evidence of this (i.e. a formal email of acceptance from the journal).
Author & Other (under review)	This is a reference to an under-review paper, not yet formally accepted. You will typically be discouraged from including a lot of under-review work, but most journals in my experience accept some under-review citations if they are needed. Check author guidelines as some will specifically ask you not to include reference to under-review content.

hiding your identity can be virtually impossible if you choose to reveal details about yourself and your story that make you identifiable – one of the reasons that this approach has some pretty unique ethical considerations that must be taken into account (Merga, 2024c). Not all academic publishers have systems that accommodate this easily, and you will need to speak with the editorial team if this applies to you, to get permission to submit an identifiable manuscript, and direction on how to best do this without triggering unsubmission.

Getting off the desk

Once you submit through the journal portal, before your articles even go out for peer review, they need to pass through an initial evaluation process at a managing editor's (or related) desk; if they are rejected at that stage, we refer to this as a 'desk rejection'.

Getting off the desk is a growing challenge; given the scarcity of peer reviewers, editors prefer to only attempt to find reviewers for papers deemed viable (Forsyth, 2022), saving everyone time (which I'm sure you have noticed, is in very poor supply in academia). Desk rejection is incredibly common. At some journals, the vast majority of rejected papers will never have seen peer review (Wu et al., 2024). The percentage of manuscripts rejected at desk stage can widely vary, and the rejection rate can be 70% or higher (Wu et al., 2024), so it's quite strange that in academia, we talk about rejection *after* peer review more often than we talk about desk rejection, given that so much scholarly work is being rejected at this stage. It is not only the academic authors who feel the pain; being the person in charge of desk rejection can be a very frustrating role: one editor noted that given their primary concern 'is to find papers to publish', 'the fact that half of our submissions so miss the mark that they cannot even be sent out for review means that a huge pool of talent is misdirecting its efforts' (Billsberry, 2014, p. 3).

As the first stop for the manuscript after submission, the desk is the stage where submissions are reviewed by the managing editor (or similar) for initial quality control, journal alignment and author guidelines compliance, including meeting any specified formatting requirements and submission directions. Papers that don't meet the guidelines are unsubmitted, so adhering to any specified guidelines when you submit your work will save everybody time and prevent wasted effort (Klein & Müller, 2022). Given that the managing editor is often working for no remuneration, showing respect for their time is really important, so pay close attention to detail before submission and make sure there is strong alignment with the author guidelines. Where you have submitted a manuscript to a journal where it is perceived to be out of scope, editors also see this as giving you a chance to find a journal that is a better fit, saving both their time and yours (Stolowy, 2017). In some cases, they may even suggest a journal that you can target (Evans et al., 2021).

A desk rejection is often final, though in some instances it may be accompanied by permission to resubmit once specified changes have been made, but this depends on the reason for rejection (Forsyth, 2022). It is also worth noting that in some cases, the article must get approval at more than one desk before going out for peer review (e.g. Klein & Müller, 2022), highlighting the possible high level of scrutiny and quality control at desk stage.

Beyond the guidelines, there are other aspects of a journal article that can see it rejected at this early stage. A recent article explored the criteria that were used to determine if journal articles progressed from the desk. The focus was on the fields of linguistics, language and education (Saragih et al., 2024):

> Journal editors assess six key factors when determining whether to accept manuscripts during the desk evaluation process, including originality, significance, and novelty. . .
>
> According to data from 42 editors, the primary reasons for manuscript acceptance were: relevance of the topic (95.02%), alignment with the journal's

scope (92.85%), novelty of the research (90.47%), significance of the research (88.09%), appropriateness of the topic (85.71%), and originality of the research (80.93%). (p. 4)

How do you practically demonstrate these things in addition to carefully adhering to the author guidelines?

Know the target

Be a regular reader of your target journal's content; 'the easiest and quickest way to get your manuscript instantly rejected is to write about something that the journal does not publish' (Billsberry, 2014, p. 4), and submitting a manuscript outside of this tacit or explicit scope is felt to be the most common reason for desk rejection (Wu et al., 2024).

While author guidelines and journal scope will often provide an overview, reading them is no substitute for keeping across the recently published content. While you're at it, check that recent issues' content even aligns with what is in the guidelines—sometimes a journal claims to publish a breadth of methods, or is silent on methodological preferences, but when you actually read recent issues, there's very clear emphasis on certain methodological choices (Merga et al., 2018). It has been noted that 'some papers submitted give the impression that the authors have actually never seen or read' an article from the target journal (Stolowy, 2017, p. 415); your paper needs to look and feel like it belongs.

Unfortunately, it is also important to note that a journal may claim to be international in scope, but when you look more closely at where authors are based, clear patterns of privilege can be identified (Mason, Merga et al., 2021), and it may be harder to get work accepted, as we discussed in relation to our experience as ECRs:

> Both Shannon and Margaret had experiences that they perceived as parochialism when submitted to or reviewing for US journals.
>
> *Shannon: I have had papers rejected from so-called 'international' journals because they did not have enough data from the US.*
>
> *Margaret: In one instance as a reviewer, I was privy to all of the reviews submitted for a paper, and I noticed that one of the other reviewers had pointed out the lack of relevance of the research based on the fact that it took place outside the US. I wonder how seriously editors take these kinds of reservations. I recommended acceptance in this instance, as I*

strongly believed that the paper had cross-contextual relevance, but the other two
reviewers suggested rejection, so it didn't get over the line.

(Merga et al., 2018, p. 385)

If there are no authors from your context recently represented in a journal, I would love for you to submit anyway and run the chance of being the first, but I also don't want you to have to deal with the kind of ridiculous prejudice that persists in some journals and their reviewers.

Know your readership and show this in your focus. For example, writing an article with no implications for your profession, and sending it to a research journal with a strong focus on KMb for a profession or group of stakeholders is not going to be a good fit. For example, I've published a few articles in the *Journal of Adolescent & Adult Literacy*, including work from my PhD (e.g. Merga, 2014b). This journal has a strong professional readership and is formatted to be highly accessible to this readership:

An official journal of the International Literacy Association, *Journal of Adolescent & Adult Literacy* (JAAL) is the only literacy-focused journal for teachers of older learners, providing high-quality, classroom-tested ideas as well as reflections on literacy trends, issues, and research. Exploring innovative teaching methods, literacy assessment tools, and strategies for improving reading and writing skills in diverse populations JAAL features research articles, reviews, and practical insights related to literacy instruction, reading strategies, and language development.

(Wiley, 2025b, para.1)

The practical and professional focus of this research journal has implications for the kind of details you may need to add. This meant that in the peer reviews for one article, I was asked to explain in-text what correlation is, so that the work could be more reader-friendly (Merga, 2014b). Being a common term in scholarly journals, I had not previously been required to explain this term in an academic journal article, but I was happy to make this reasonable accommodation to enhance the accessibility of my work to the specific audience.

In this vein, knowing your journal is about knowing which kind of voice to use to meet the needs of the audience. There is a plurality of academic voices, and choosing the right voice is important. Yes, this will mess with your cohesive narrative in your TBP (see Chapter 5) as a thesis with distinct voices will be a departure from the traditional monograph style, so you may wish to include comment on this in your introductory content so that the switches between voices are not as jarring, and they are recognised by the examiner as part of attempting to engage broad and diverse audiences.

During my own TBP journey, journals I selected were located across diverse contexts, and some were designed to resonate primarily with researchers, with others looking to speak to professionals (while still making a research contribution). After writing for a journal with a strong professional focus, I then attempted to submit to a research journal with a solely researcher audience, but *I failed to switch the voice back*, a pretty major rookie error. This resulted in a rejection at peer-review stage, with some of the harshest criticism of my writing that I have ever received.

Cite the journal. While many editors may be reluctant to admit this, citing a journal matters, showing you are joining an existing conversation in the journal (and let's face it, the impact benefits for journals that are able to rack up a few additional citations in this manner can be sweet for them). Billsberry (2014) observes that when there are no, or very few citations of his journal in the reference list of manuscripts on his desk, he reviews the manuscript with extra scrutiny to ensure that it is relevant to journal readers, and that it adopts 'our conventions and approach' (p. 7). Appropriate current citations can also 'help editors and associate editors to identify appropriate reviewers who may be willing to perform the review' (Dwivedi et al., 2022, p. 4). Ethically, if you cite a reviewer, it is not supposed to increase the likelihood of your paper being accepted, but given that its publication will enhance the citation count of that reviewer, there is certainly a conflict of interest.

Align the cover letter, and attract the target. I have a tendency to treat my cover letter like marketing material. I want my manuscript to get off the desk as fast as possible, and in order to do that I try to capture the editor's attention and interest, and argue for impact either within or beyond academia:

> Authors should not hesitate to use the cover letter to convey some important messages, such as the existence of related papers or explaining the real and main contribution of the paper. Simply copying the abstract in the cover letter is not necessary. They should make sure that the cover letter is addressed to (journal name) and not to another journal (real case I had some time ago).
>
> (Stolowy, 2017, p. 417)

By illustrating the value of the article in my cover letter, I seek to demonstrate likelihood of citations, accesses and downloads, all performance indicators collected by journals, and some of which are associated with KMb-related journal impact measures, as I explore later in this book.

Know the literature, fill the gap

Don't submit your manuscript until you're sufficiently across the literature, and seek confirmation of this from your supervisory team or external mentor. This work needs to be done, and done comprehensively: 'if you do not show your awareness of previous writing on a subject and how your paper builds on it, the outcome will be inevitable and swift' (Billsberry, 2014, p. 4).

Show that your research fills a research gap, and where applicable, also show that your research has broader value (Merga & Oddone, 2025). There are advantages and risks in publishing in popular spaces as opposed to emerging or less favoured spaces. On one hand, your peer-review journey can be smoother if there are multiple experts in your field who can review your paper, but conversely, it can be harder to find an innovative and novel research gap in a field that is already saturated with active researchers. Furthermore, it is possible that research in heavily saturated spaces may be subject to more intense scrutiny; 'in cases where editors receive an overwhelming number of submissions on a particular topic, they may become more selective, even if the submissions are relevant to the journal's scope' (Wu et al., 2024, p. 6), leading to unexpected desk rejection.

The conundrum around originality has an odd kind of irony; PhD research should ideally be novel and groundbreaking. It has been noted that 'while originality appears to be the basic requirement, other expectations such as creativity and innovation, and associated criteria of usefulness and economic advancement have recently appeared on the agenda' (Baptista et al., 2015, p. 63). However, it can be really challenging to get truly new and innovative ideas and methods over the line, perhaps the biggest barrier being the resultant lack of experts who are qualified to assess the quality of this kind of research. Right at the beginning, at the design stage, you need to check with your supervisors that potential examiners for your thesis and peer reviewers for your SOs exist. They can be a little tangential to your area of focus, but one of the risks of novelty is creating something so new that no one can confidently assess it beyond your research team.

For example, this was a risk we took back in 2018 when Saiyidi led a paper that used artificial neural network as an adjunct analysis tool in education (Mat Roni & Merga, 2019). It took a little while to get that one published and we expected that to be the case, given that this wasn't really a known approach at that time, and the *Australian Journal of Education* turned out to be an excellent fit as their editorial team were supportive of, rather than resistant to, innovation.

I'm not saying that you shouldn't do anything novel or new; far from it. However, if you are working in a very methodologically conservative space and try to innovate, you might find notable barriers to timely publication, and issues when it comes to examination. I would love to see more research on this.

Balance, correct and cook

Avoid section overkill, and try to get a good balance in your coverage of different sections. It's really obvious when a student has really mastered the literature, but doesn't fully understand the implications and limitations of the method they used. You also need to give yourself enough word count to really critically engage with your findings. Klein and Müller (2022) contend that 'submissions that overemphasize the analytical details often overshadow and limit the positioning and phrasing of their findings in the discussion and conclusions sections' (p. 545).

Edit it, probably more closely than you've ever edited anything in your entire life. Like many other academics, I like to use the 'read aloud' function in Word to capture errors that I can hear but no longer see because I have read my article so many times. I also use the 'dictate' function in Word in order to write, reducing strain on my wrists, which really take a beating given the word count I try to reach each day, but unfortunately this involves the introduction of errors that I wouldn't personally make if typing, particularly in relation to apostrophes and homophones. If you're someone who will pick things up better in the paper form, print off your final copy and read over it closely before submission; I only do this at the final stage to minimise environmental impact, and then recycle these pages as shopping lists and scrap paper for planning.

Give yourself time between reads; returning to an article after a weekend off, you might see otherwise evasive errors with fresh eyes. Writing quality is a common reason for desk rejection (Saragih et al., 2024), and inattention to detail reduces confidence in the quality of your work (Dwivedi et al., 2022).

Fully cook it. While you don't have forever to work on each journal article, restrain the urge to send out something half-baked because you are in a rush to meet milestones, and again, take advice on this while you are a novice researcher, whether this advice is from your supervisory team or an external mentor:

> If you really want a quick rejection, just send in an abstract or a few pages containing some notes. Or write it as if it were a book chapter or a section from a textbook. Or write with one-sentence paragraphs, unexplained diagrams, missing tables, endless bullet point lists, poor grammar, spelling mistakes, and so on and so forth. The sad reality is that the review process is designed to hone manuscripts that are close to publication into publishable papers. Papers need to look and feel like finished papers when they come in.
>
> (Billsberry, 2014, p. 5)

One of the points of having supervisors is to have this guidance while you're developing your ability to ascertain readiness; it's not realistic to expect you to magically learn this overnight, but this is where again a close editorial eye is crucial. If you complete a TBP, you should experience massive growth in your skills in this area as they will be constantly needed. However, anyone who tells you that undercooked writing can be refined through the peer-review process (Stolowy, 2017), is giving you really bad advice, and setting you up for high likelihood of desk rejection. Similarly, in a recent article, a TBP student sees themselves as a 'paper factory', 'for me, the goal of a PhD student is to build the capability to produce many papers in a short space of time, regardless of their quality' (Sammon et al., 2024, p. 7). I would contend that this kind of orientation raises the risk of rejection.

Ghosted

Given that doctoral students are typically expected to complete the degree within a set institutionally defined time period, and some institutional policies require manuscript acceptance for inclusion as explored earlier, you may be watching the clock from the point of submission, psychologically willing your manuscript over the line, with very little control over the journey from that point. One of the most common questions asked by novice researchers is, 'When should I follow up?'

We don't want to enter into stalker territory, putting the journal off us by being too intense (so that's a no to hiding in the hedge at the front of the editor's house with a pair of binoculars), but at the same time, we are desperate for news on the progress of our fledgling manuscript. Sadly, it can't send us postcards or text message updates from where it is on its journey, but many academic publishers have made good advancements on the presentation and clarity of their online Author Centres, Dashboards or similarly named in recent times, enabling you to log in and see what stage your article is at.

So what does this look like? Here's an example of the journey an article I published with Sage went on as it moved through the stages of peer review, as available at any time on my Dashboard (Figure 3). Please note that this one moved unusually smoothly and quickly, perhaps due to the currency of the topic. I wanted to show a more dramatic and bumpy journey, but I could not find an example from my submissions with other publishers that had the correct dates in the dashboard (for some reason there is a tendency for them to be consistently out of chronological order in Taylor & Francis), or had the journey presented in a format that was easy to capture for this purpose (Wiley's dashboard is detailed and useful, but does not show the trajectory in an easily captured format).

Manuscripts with Decisions

ACTION	STATUS	ID	TITLE	SUBMITTED	DECISIONED
Forms Completion submitted (03-Dec-2024) - view	☑ Contact Journal ADM: Goulding, Anne • Accept (03-Dec-2024) view decision letter	LIS-24-0473.R1	School library professionals' perspectives on current and future workforce challenges View Submission	02-Dec-2024	03-Dec-2024
a revision has been submitted (LIS-24-0473.R1)	☑ Contact Journal ADM: Goulding, Anne • Minor Revision (25-Nov-2024) • a revision has been submitted view decision letter	LIS-24-0473	School library professionals' perspectives on current and future workforce challenges View Submission	13-Oct-2024	25-Nov-2024

Figure 3 *The journey of one article*

So can you just sit back and relax and trust that your article will move smoothly through this process?

In my experience maybe not; as recently as last year I pulled a paper from a journal review process because the peer-review process was extremely lengthy, and communication unusually reticent. This was really disappointing as I had previously had a wonderful experience publishing with that particular journal, but editorial boards and teams change, and all kinds of untoward activities can occur behind the scenes that might impact on the progression of an article.

To further illustrate this point, one of my co-authors once found out the hard way that failure to follow up can result in an unexpected surprise:

> Julia: I submitted an article to a high ranked journal in my field, as the journal aims and scope stated that they were interested in mixed methods research. I knew that it would take some time to get through review, so didn't think too much about it until 12 months later. I logged into my author dashboard and noticed that the article had been rejected a week after I submitted it, with an editorial comment that it was outside of the scope of the journal. However, I didn't receive any notification of this rejection. I emailed the editor asking for more feedback. A month later when I hadn't heard anything, I went back to the journal's homepage, and found that the aims and scope of the journal had been changed to a wholly-qualitative focus. My article was now out of scope! I really wish they'd told me and I could've resubmitted my article sooner. It is now in review with another journal, and I'm being more careful with my follow up!
>
> (Merga et al., 2018, p. 384)

So when should you follow up, and how often?

Some journals will provide an estimated expected timeline of progression in their submission guidelines, which will include anticipated length of peer review. Where that is the case, I recommend following up as soon as that length of peer review has been exceeded. For example, if it is stated that peer review is expected to take 8 to 10 weeks, I would touch base in the 11th week.

Where that information is not available, at present I recommend following up at the three month mark, and then at least every month following this. Once an article has been under review for more than six months in a research area where a decision might be *reasonably expected* far sooner (and in my experience, what can be reasonably expected can vary a lot between research areas and journals), and where there has been very little communication from the editorial team with no decisions made such as requests for revisions, I will seriously consider withdrawing the article and placing it elsewhere. It is a very difficult call to make, but there are unfortunately instances where articles seem to fall into some kind of virtual gap in the peer-review process, never to be seen again.

If you find yourself in this position, don't take it personally and remember it may be happening due to issues unanticipated by the journal. While this is very frustrating from an author's perspective, bear in mind that it must also be frustrating for the editorial team who have to find and then chase up peer reviewers.

I always appreciate it when editors give me a brief update about what is going on when a significant lag comes into play, and it makes me far less likely to remove a paper under submission. For example, the review process took a little longer than usual on one of my recently accepted papers because of issues finding reviewers, and when the editor let me know about this problem, I offered to propose some possible reviewers who had expertise in the research area to support their efforts. You will find that some journals specifically ask you to list possible reviewers at the point of submission as standard; and some journals also include an opportunity for you to list any academics that you do *not* want to review your paper, which is kind of interesting, indicative of some of the gatekeeping that can sadly happen in this space.

Realistic expectations of success: don't get discouraged

My first son Gabe was a nightmare sleeper. He didn't sleep through the night for many months, despite my getting all kinds of professional help and reading every available resource on the matter. He did not like being alone, not even for a single second, which made self-care (e.g. showering) a fun challenge, punctuated by outraged screaming. I was so severely sleep-deprived that I nearly burnt the house down at one point, putting something on the stove and forgetting about it until the smoke alarm went off. I'm obviously somewhat biased, but I think that he's a great adult, so no one would know to look at him what a villainous baby he used to be.

Then my second son Sam came along and was the complete opposite. He'd just look at me with dreamy eyes and check out, sleeping through almost from the beginning, and he could sleep anywhere.

So why am I telling you this random parental story about my now adult children? Not *just* to be an embarrassing mother. I want to flag that there is no 'typical' journal article publication journey; even if your first experiences are brutal and discouraging, this does not mean that your work is objectively poor, or that all of your experiences will be like that. Yes, now that I am a more experienced author my work does pass more smoothly through peer review *in general*. However that doesn't mean I never get rejected; rejection in some form, whether related to journal article publication or grant submission, is a delightful constant in the lives of most academics whether they be junior or senior, and I am certainly no exception.

It can also be frustrating if early success is then followed by more challenging experiences, as initial confidence can be rattled. Cash (2023) describes a very laborious peer-review process on their third paper, giving you some insight into the intensive level of labour and emotional challenge that peer review can involve:

> I was 18 months into my candidature, and halfway through my scholarship, before I had completed my first study and had sufficient data to develop a paper for publication. Fortunately, I had an early win and this paper was accepted on the first submission with very minor revisions. Although this was a thrilling confidence boost, it gave me a somewhat rose-coloured view of the pathway ahead. The second paper required a more time-consuming process of review, although one I felt was ultimately fair and useful to the overall paper, my thinking and the thesis. It was at the third paper stage that the challenges inherent in publication processes became more problematic. The first journal to which I submitted took nine months to review it, before rejecting it with minimal feedback . . . Two more re-writes and rejections followed with other journals on this third paper . . . The paper was eventually published in an excellent journal, though one with half the word limit of the original manuscript. Although the paper was published, the significant cutting and rewriting markedly changed the scope of what was ultimately published from that stage of the project . . . the process did create a lot of anxiety about the risks of relying on publications to complete a thesis and the potential need to adapt sections of the thesis to a more traditional format if publication plans are unsuccessful. The final paper planned for my thesis was written as a methods paper . . . I wrote the paper and submitted it, only for it to bounce back with significant changes requested. Four rounds of major review later (no, I am not kidding . . .), the paper looked nothing at all like I had intended. (p. 150)

This account highlights the challenges and lack of control TBP students can experience, which can impact on TBP students' wellbeing, and also be incredibly high pressure given that in some cases, revisions are accompanied by requests for a tight turnaround, and they can be very time-intensive, particularly where editorial direction is minimal, and reviewer comments are unclear or untenable. It also shows how the peer-review process can transform a manuscript so that it no longer sits effortlessly within the broader thesis, involving further labour around facilitating cohesion.

However, whichever way it turns out for you, there's much that can be done to prepare you for the challenges you may encounter, even though your control is limited.

At the outset of navigating the journal publication journey, you need to familiarise yourself with its norms. For example, you usually cannot submit to more than one journal at a time. If your manuscript is rejected and resubmission is not explicitly permitted, you cannot resubmit the same or amended manuscript to the journal that rejected it (Dwivedi et al., 2022).

It is also important that TBP students have realistic expectations of the extent to which a senior supervisor's involvement and co-authorship can insulate them against the likelihood of revisions being required, or even rejection occurring. Even 'big names' in the field are rejected during the double-blind peer-review process. Jalongo (2024) illustrated how this scenario can play out where expectations are unrealistic, and how an expert supervisor can model a productive response in the instance of a recently graduated doctoral student and her advisor, who co-authored an article:

> When the reviewers' comments came in, she was stunned. Her advisor was widely published, and she expected prompt and uncritical acceptance. Instead, the reviewers raised numerous questions and the editor's decision was 'revise and resubmit.' When the student met with her mentor to discuss the project, she was surprised by his response. Instead of being offended, angry, or defensive, the senior professor immediately got to work categorizing the comments and noting ways to address each one. They revised the manuscript accordingly, agreed that the modifications had improved the work, resubmitted their paper, and it was accepted for publication in a prestigious journal. (p. 4)

As such, an experienced and level-headed supervisor can play an important role in helping you to tailor your expectations and respond effectively to feedback, regulating emotional response, but it is worth noting that they don't have a secret free pass to get you through peer review entirely unscathed. On the bright side, having to meet stringent peer-reviewer demands on a TBP publication is a valuable training opportunity for you, enabling you to develop revision skills which I cover in further detail later in this book.

## CHAPTER 4

Negotiating Authorship

Supervisory authorship during the PhD has been happening for a really long time, though before the TBP there was less scrutiny on it.

I've never really understood it when people argue that a TBP is inferior to a traditional thesis as it includes SOs where supervisors have made an authorial contribution. Supervisors have been contributing varying amounts of their intellectual property to their students' traditional monographs as a norm, perhaps in greater quantities with students who enter into the programme with lower ability, experience, and/or familiarity with academic culture norms in context (Bøgelund, 2015), or where the PhD student is essentially a funded research assistant on a project devised by the doctoral supervisor. It can be argued that rather than being the less ethical option, the TBP model may be superior in this regard, as when done correctly (as will be outlined in this chapter), the authorial contributions of supervisors and others if applicable are actually recognised explicitly, with attribution given in the authorship of SOs.

While for some students their supervisors will dictate author order, I don't agree with that approach. I think that the TBP student should be the Chief Investigator on their own PhD project (or component of a larger supervisor project as applicable) and the TBP student should be first author on related SOs where at all possible, with a key role in negotiating author order.

It's perfectly reasonable to feel daunted by the prospects of negotiating authorship on your TBP SOs. Some may prefer dealing with a zombie apocalypse than having to engage in such a potentially contentious act. Even more seasoned academics can struggle with this, and 'determining co-authorship is one of the most difficult negotiation processes that academics encounter' (Schneider & Gur-Arie, 2017, p. 71).

I believe one of the reasons that many academics continue to work with the same people with some consistency is because they can trust them to be able to be open and reasonable in this regard; it's certainly a factor that

I consider when forming teams. While it is not realistic to expect TBP students to be experts in negotiating authorship without training and/or access to supportive resources, explicit training in this area may not be available for PhD students at all universities.

This chapter seeks to give you an overview of some of the research relating to the ethics of authorship, ideas about how to source further resources, and also insights into the practicalities of negotiating author order, which may be of particular concern where your supervisors are not already openly communicating with you about this.

Ethics of authorship and author guidelines

You may gain a lot through the co-authoring experience, with research linking it to developing understanding of academic research culture, supporting the development of academic voice and identity, and giving students real-world experience of how their choices can shape their publication outcomes (Guerin, 2016; Merga, 2015).

However, there is also a lot to learn that is specific to the (often unfamiliar and/or ambiguous) ethics and expectations in this space. Researchers have called for 'more research on pedagogical practices and ethics surrounding co-authorship' relating to TBP (Solli & Nygaard, 2023, p. 996). We also need further research on *what authorship actually is*, with Pruschak (2021) noting that while 'social scientific literature has especially discussed author orders and the distribution of publication and citation credits among co-authors in depth', 'only a small fraction of the authorship literature has also addressed the actual underlying question of what actually constitutes authorship' (p. 1). While these gaps exist, I've primarily drawn upon the broad body of literature on authorship and author guidelines to inform this chapter.

I can't assume that you've been given any training on authorship and author order. Ethics in TBPs are a messy minefield that may be typically neglected in doctoral education; 'ethical discussions in current doctoral training programmes tend to be focused on the conduct and process of field research and collection of data' (Robinson-Pant & Singal, 2020, p. 860), leaving the ethical implications related to authoring relatively untouched. This is problematic as students can't be expected to magically know how to do this, leaving them open to potential exploitation and errors in author attribution. As I will explore in further detail herein, the consequences can be serious, and even career damaging.

While I also can't assume that *every* university has a current functioning author guidelines policy, it is common for universities' TBP policies to include explicit guidelines and expectations in relation to author order in TBP publications (Kubota et al., 2021), often also linking to institutional authorship policies. Relevant to the previous discussion around qualifications frameworks and the autonomy, knowledge and skill requirements that must be demonstrated by a doctoral graduate, author guidelines and TBP publications may stipulate that students be the lead author on their TBP publications, and or have contributed at least 50% to the publication in order to meet the requisite contribution levels for SO inclusion in the thesis (Kubota et al., 2021).

Where your university has a current author guidelines policy, it may or may not be particularly practical and useful. In some contexts, such guidelines are so ambiguous in their expression that they are of limited utility. Perhaps this is because, at a broader level, there is no common universally agreed-upon set of author guidelines that can be applied across all research areas for universities to draw on; *what constitutes authorship in one space does not necessarily constitute authorship in another*.

For example, one of the dominant guidelines often used in social sciences (e.g. Pruschak, 2021), despite coming from the medical field rather than the social sciences, is known as the *Vancouver Convention*, the Vancouver Recommendations, the Vancouver Guidelines, and the Vancouver Criteria. It was created by the International Committee of Medical Journal Editors (ICMJE). According to the most recent version of the Vancouver Convention, to be an author, individuals need to be able to demonstrate the following:

1. Substantial contributions to the conception or design of the work; or the acquisition, analysis, or interpretation of data for the work; AND
2. Drafting the work or reviewing it critically for important intellectual content; AND
3. Final approval of the version to be published; AND
4. Agreement to be accountable for all aspects of the work in ensuring that questions related to the accuracy or integrity of any part of the work are appropriately investigated and resolved.

(ICMJE, 2024, p. 2)

However, other guidelines allow for *far less to be done* in order to 'count' as an author.

For example, the Australian NHMRC (2019) notes that an author is someone who 'has made a significant intellectual or scholarly contribution to research and its output', and who 'agrees to be listed as an author' (p. 1). The NHMRC are a significant funder of research in Australia: during

2021–2, they provided research funds to a value of 971,135,895 Australian dollars (Australian Government, n.d., para. 4). While again, they are primarily peripheral to social sciences with a STEM focus, I selected their model for comparison because, like the Vancouver Convention, it includes an explicit medical focus. Delving into the specifics around what a significant intellectual contribution actually is, this is framed as follows as a 'minimum threshold':

> While authorship conventions vary across disciplines, a significant intellectual or scholarly contribution must include one and should include a combination of two or more of the following:
> - conception and design of the project or output
> - acquisition of research data where the acquisition has required significant intellectual judgement, planning, design, or input
> - contribution of knowledge, where justified, including Indigenous knowledge
> - analysis or interpretation of research data
> - drafting significant parts of the research output or critically revising it so as to contribute to its interpretation.
>
> (NHMRC, 2019, p. 1)

Compared with the Vancouver Convention's specifics stated previously, the threshold for minimum compliance for the NHMRC *is far lower*. Someone can theoretically contribute to the design and knowledge of a project at its early stages, leave your team, and then claim authorship on an article that they have never even read under the NHMRC minimum threshold, which is not possible under the Vancouver Convention.

As I have illustrated, author guidelines can wildly vary, so you must pin down exactly what your university and faculty are working with, and use this as a basis for your discussions and decision-making in this space. However, if you're working with supervisors or other potential co-authors across institutions, you need to be aware that their author guidelines may be *very different* to the ones that you are operating with, as you can see from the two compared examples, and you need to supply these guidelines to these external team members early, and talk about authorship expectations clearly, so that everyone is on the same page.

For whatever reason, many researchers in social sciences 'apply very broad authorship criteria that do not accord with the criteria laid out by the ICMJE' (Pruschak & Hopp, 2022, p. 14). If you want to see how badly things can end where there is a foreseeable misalignment in authorship expectations and/or order, consider this case:

> All authors cannot agree on a revised author order, and at least one author
> continues to dispute the original order. In this case, the original article is being
> retracted on the grounds that the journal does not have permission to publish.
>
> (Retraction Watch, 2017, para. 4)

Such extreme outcomes are rare but they do happen, highlighting the importance of having a clear and shared understanding of author guidelines to avoid adverse consequences such as retraction.

It's also not uncommon to hear of a sleeper supervisor or related person appearing on a paper despite not even remotely satisfying any related authorship criteria. I conceptualise a *sleeper supervisor* as a supervisor who has made no material intellectual contribution (covered in the next section) to their students' doctoral journey. Just because a supervisor is listed next to your name, and they exist and are alive, does not make them an automatic co-author of your work, no matter what anyone tells you. Many established scholars have doctoral and early career horror stories where senior academics have been added as authors on SOs where they had not made any contribution to the informing research or the paper, which they may not have even read. I know of one instance where a co-author was unaware of the existence of an article until after it was published, and they received congratulations for their work on it. In this day and age, let's not do this anymore if we can possibly resist it (and I understand that in some cases, that won't be possible for you given the power imbalance in play).

So what are the major issues we often see in their space?

Ghost and gift authorship

While there's a whole interesting taxonomy of author-related ethics issues, academic misconduct in this space often occurs around the following.

First, authorship denied to, or resisted by contributors who did enough to count as an author as per the agreed guidelines (*ghost authorship*).

Second, granting authorship to individuals who didn't make the required level of contribution to the work as per the agreed guidelines (*gift, honorary or guest authorship*) (Pruschak & Hopp, 2022).

In cases of ghost authorship, Pruschak and Hopp (2022) identify three main reasons for the missing author:

1 'Pressure from co-authors, can lead to researchers declining or being declined authorship' (p. 3).

2 The ghost author doesn't want to be associated with the work 'because they perceive the findings in the research as controversial, dubious, or weak' (p. 3), and it may be a bad career move.
3 The ghost author and/or team wants to hide their association with the work due to 'potential conflicts of interest', such as where this helps to hide commercial funding.

Gift authorship is equally sketchy, though the strategic advantages of gift authorship may be one of the reasons behind its relatively high prevalence (e.g. it's felt to be at around 41% in Cochrane reviews!) (Gülen et al., 2020):

1 Supervisors may demand authorship from their TBP students 'in return for supervising them' (Pruschak & Hopp, 2022, p. 4), even though they have not done enough to warrant inclusion as per author guidelines.
2 You may actually *want* to add the gift author, perhaps to attach the paper to a big name in the field, but that doesn't make it ethically okay (Pruschak & Hopp, 2022).
3 There can be a quid pro quo scenario: you add the name of a colleague 'on the understanding that s/he will do the same for you, regardless of your contribution to his/her research, but simply to swell your publication lists' (Albert & Wager, 2003, p. 34).

In many instances, gift authorships constitute a kind of 'free-riding', 'a phenomenon where certain researchers contribute minimal effort, resources, or expertise to a research project but still receive recognition, publications, or other rewards from the collaborative work, despite not fulfilling their fair share of responsibilities' (Khodakarami et al., 2025, p. 2).

So will you be pressured to grant gift authorship and enable a free-rider?

Research suggests that around 30% of PhD students from across disciplines actually did this, and half of these 'indicated that they had done so because they had been told to do so by the person in power' (Goddiksen et al., 2023, p. 1). Moreover, while further work with larger samples and across contexts is needed, recent research suggests that students may identify this as a bigger problem than faculty members (Khodakarami et al., 2025). While I'm giving you the basics around the ethics in this space, I understand that in reality, you may feel that your options are limited in relation to both ghost and gift authorship where these pressures are being exerted on you, a student, and I would like to see institutions do a better job of protecting and supporting students who find themselves facing undue pressure in this space.

Academic norms vs ethics

We need more research on why some academics think that ghost and gift authorship are par-for-the-course, normal and acceptable. Research often looks at why this is done in terms of reward and risk, without considering the possible role of enculturation in perpetuating these issues going forward.

I'd like to draw attention to the power of 'upbringing' in academia. As I've addressed briefly previously (Merga, 2015), during my TBP journey I was able to access excellent ongoing research training that was very valuable to me (I attended a lot of high-quality and relevant training run by Natasha Teakle, who has since shifted her remarkable research and project management skill set to industry consulting). However, I was also introduced to norms on ethics and authorship that were explicitly taught to me through my participation in research training. I was brought up in academia to believe that ethics in research are incredibly important; that norms in this space are evolving rather than static, requiring agility and policy, planning and training; that as a student I had rights and responsibilities; and that there were systems and processes that would support this available to me. Not everyone is lucky enough to be brought up in this kind of academic environment.

It's not just about the power imbalance; if you are told that these unethical authorship practices are norms or unwritten rules, you are likely to accept them. One of the roles of the supervisor is to inculcate the student in the norms of academia; we are expected to trust and believe that the information they provide us is correct. Furthermore, sometimes the supervisor who asks you to do sketchy things may *also* have been 'brought up' in academia to accept these now very much outdated norms without question, and breaking with that mindset can be very challenging. This doesn't make it okay; institutions should provide ongoing training for their senior academic staff to ensure that these kinds of unethical dispositions are adjusted to align with author guidelines. In reality, students still find themselves in the (involuntary) position of challenging norms in their supervisory teams, but also perhaps in their departments and universities, depending on the extent to which these practices are normalised and uncontested.

I believe that some of the issues that we see on identification and quantification of an intellectual property contribution come from differing notions of what constitutes an intellectual property contribution, caused by different guidelines (as outlined previously), research upbringings, and many other factors. I also think that in addition to subjective misunderstandings about the weight of contribution, people genuinely forget what others have done unless there's documentation.

Often contention in this space is complex and like most issues in relationships, due to unaligned expectations and understandings. Here are some examples that I've actually seen in the wild in other people's supervisory groups, and that I disagree with:

- Supervisor A thinks they have done more than Supervisor B, because even though they made an identical intellectual contribution, it took Supervisor A a lot longer to do it due to a comparative lack of skill;
- Student A had a very supportive Supervisor B who did a lot of intellectual work on that project and the article (in my opinion, probably too much), but Student A wants to leave Supervisor B out of the author line-up because they were 'just doing their job';
- Supervisor A won the grant that funded the PhD and therefore devised the project, but did not contribute to the article; Student A wrote the entire article, and did all of the data collection and analysis. Supervisor A contends that because the article was focused on their grant-winning ideas, they should be the first author.

As you can see from the above, issues in aligned expectations and understandings can extend beyond what is covered in most author guidelines. We'll learn more about author order now.

The practicalities of author order

While students may be made aware of institutional or disciplinary author guidelines to support them in determining what constitutes authorship and how to allocate author order among other concerns, they may get less exposure to the practicalities of how to negotiate fair author order despite the power imbalances at play in student–supervisory relationships.

While you can use this chapter in consultation with your applicable author guidelines to decide with (some) certainty whether someone even counts as an author, ordering authors fairly and correctly is an additional challenge. You're in a position where you need to provide clear communication in a power imbalance; all of your actions and decisions as a researcher build or undermine your reputation and trustworthiness (Schneider & Gur-Arie, 2017), and you may face pressures to make decisions that don't align with guidelines and ethics norms in the worst-case scenario.

Where co-authorship is indicated, the more reasonable, supportive and cohesive your supervisory team is, the easier this is going to be for you. For example, supervisors can disagree about author order, both wanting the higher position; 'obviously, supervisors should not put their learners into awkward positions and should work out their issues collegially, including those related to authorship order', but that doesn't stop them from falling out dramatically over this if you are unlucky (Kuper et al., 2023, p. 1368).

If you are coming from outside academia, you might find the controversy in this space mystifying. When I've had to explain this to new students in the past, I usually draw on the fact that in academia, our currency is our intellectual property; when authors find themselves in what they perceive to be (realistically or not) the wrong position in the author order, they may feel like their contribution was devalued.

I've been pretty lucky with author order so far, and I attribute that to being fortunate enough to mostly work with very ethical and reasonable people who were *comfortable speaking openly* about these matters in an early and ongoing manner during our publication process. I reiterate that knowing who is doing what, and what that means for author order before you even start an SO has been vital for this. For example, if I (Author A) am contributing 80%, Author B is bringing 15% and Author C 5% according to our agreed-upon tasks, Author C will easily resist the urge to overwork beyond their scope given that in terms of author order, they are only getting credit for 5%. It also means that if Author B gets sick and needs to offload work to Author A or C, we can adjust the author order if applicable with high transparency.

However, I understand that PhD students may often have the least say over whom they find themselves working with, so you might need some more detailed guidelines that you can follow on author order. There are publicly available and free rubrics, schemas, frameworks and scorecards that you can use to calculate the weight of contributions (some of these are listed in Martins et al., 2023, along with their own). If none of these quite work for you, you can create your own (as long as it aligns with your applicable author guidelines) and then get the whole team's agreement on using it, again *before* writing commences, and ideally before tasks are allocated.

Equal contributors

Let's say I'm the first author, but the other two authors did the same amount of work. How will I decide on author order?

There's been an increase in equal contributor (EC) statements on articles, but readers may still instinctively credit the earlier listed EC author as a greater contributor due to established protocols in author order (Mattoon et al., 2024). So even where you have explicitly designated two authors as ECs, you still won't escape the need to decide on an author order.

Some will suggest going with alphabetical order, but ask those with last names starting with Z how they feel about being bumped down author order based on the first initial of their last name, particularly if equal contribution is something that happens quite often to them, or if they are at a career stage where they are still demonstrating seniority and need to show a good position in author order to support their claims of research contribution.

There are better, fairer ways. Use a 'list randomiser' or 'random name selector' from the range of free tools online. Alternatively, for maximum accountability and transparency, you can use the American Economic Association's (2024) free online Author Randomization Tool. After entering the names in the fields along with the associated title, it will confirm that you want to proceed given that the results will be archived and publicly available. This is great, because it prevents an unscrupulous operator from just constantly generating the author order randomly until they get the result they want. Results include the random author order, a unique confirmation code, and the date/time the randomisation was run (see Figure 4).

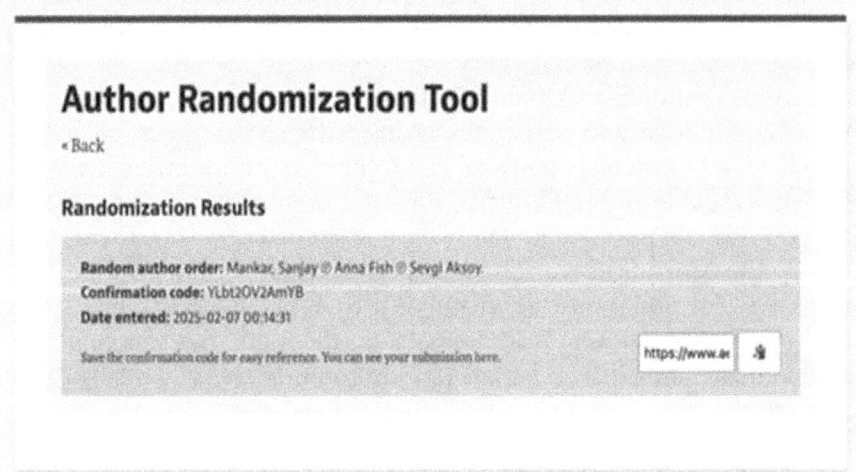

Figure 4 *Output of American Economic Association's (2024) Author Randomization Tool*

If it goes wrong

Where viable and available, I urge you to seek institutional support to protect yourself if authorship becomes a sticking point for you, or if you foresee that it may become one.

The Committee on Publication Ethics (COPE) has published a guide for new researchers with advice on managing authorship disputes (Albert & Wager, 2003). You may:

- Make sure your faculty/department library includes current material on publication ethics.
- Get your university author guidelines, or spur their creation if they don't exist.
- Have early conversations about author order with your research team, and record information on agreed decisions and contributions; have the author order of each SO decided before you start to write it, to be revised based on what people actually contribute.

(Albert & Wager, 2003)

However, to be honest, a lot of the COPE suggestions won't be feasible if you find yourself working in a space with an extreme power imbalance and very low HDR student support. I understand that university cultures vary widely both across universities and within them, and it's not realistic to expect that you will have a lot of agency in shaping these cultures.

If it goes wrong and your supervisor is the cause, you may find yourself in a pretty difficult position, and you need to get institutional support, but I know that there is an added layer of difficulty when you are in a precarious position, such as where you are an international student on a scholarship and your supervisor is a highly respected name in your field.

While institutions and contexts will hopefully have specific policies and guidelines in place for these kinds of issues, you might be wondering whether it is even an institutional responsibility if the manuscript has been submitted before issues arise. Does this mean that the journal should be the arbitrator around this? It's useful to note that COPE (2017) forums situate these issues as institutional responsibilities rather than for external arbitration particularly where authors are situated in the same institution. For example, in considering a case study on 'a lengthy disagreement between the four authors regarding the order of authorship' (para. 1), the forum made the following observations:

The Forum advised referring this to the institution, and asking the institution to verify who should be authors on the paper and what the authorship order should be. It is not up to the editor or journal to investigate this issue. As three of the authors are based at one institution, it would be reasonable to ask the institution to mediate in this situation.

There may be copyright issues, if the dissenting author no longer agrees with the content of the article, as all authors have joint copyright. Again, the institution needs to resolve this—this cannot be decided by the editor. (paras. 8–9)

Again, it is pretty wildly unreasonable to expect TBP students to be in a position to negotiate these kinds of challenges without a great deal of support. I wish that I didn't have to include this section at all, but I have heard of far too many cases where supervisors have acted in an untoward manner when it comes to author order and author attribution. Please do not despair if you find yourself in an impossible position concerning authorship, and engage the support services available to you as early as possible.

Finally, recent events have drawn attention to the possibility that misconduct in relation to authorship might not always be about students and their co-authors; there is a very slight chance that your work can be appropriated by others during the peer-review process. For example, in March 2025, we learned of the following case:

A chemist at a university in Pakistan found a surprise when he opened an alert from ResearchGate on a newly published paper on a topic related to his own work.

When Muhammad Kashif, a chemist at Abdul Wali Khan University Mardan, looked at the paper, he noticed 'substantial overlap' with an unpublished review article he had submitted to other journals. On closer inspection, he found it was indeed his paper – published by other authors.

(Retraction Watch, 2025b, paras. 1–2)

The manuscript was submitted for publication by Sujit Kumar, one of Kashif's peer reviewers from a journal where Kashif's work was withdrawn after the first round of review. According to Retraction Watch, Kumar claimed that he had accidentally submitted the wrong paper. While this kind of incident is unusual, it is useful to set up alerts in your knowledge area to help you stay across the literature, and also detect such incidents.

## CHAPTER 5

Structure and Cohesion

While the traditional PhD monograph is often the sole expected output on the PhD journey, on a TBP you are producing SOs as well as the thesis. As a result, the cohesion of the thesis as a whole can be neglected, given the urgency often attached to meeting SO-related goals, as covered previously in this book. Supervisors have raised concerns about the quality of theses where SOs are given the bulk of TBP student time and labour to the detriment of the thesis. In one high-profile falling out between an international student at a European university and his supervisory team, while I can't weigh in on the legitimacy of any of the claims made, the misalignment between the student's investment in the SOs and the supervisors' concern that the thesis was being neglected seems to be one of the contributing factors that can be discerned from the private conversations the student published online (Zhao, 2025). At institutions where there is ambiguity around norms in TBP production at policy level, and if gaps are not adequately addressed at Department level, there can be a fundamental misalignment in expectations of where priorities need to lie. Yes, attention on quality SOs is crucial to the TBP, but a TBP is not just a pile of SOs.

Excessive focus on SOs to the perceived detriment of the whole thesis has been linked to 'managerial dispositions' felt to 'undermine professional quality', with a supervisor making the following comment:

> This foolishness, that a PhD should be granted for writing three articles – that is setting the bar too low . . . It is important, that you learn how to combine theoretical and methodological considerations . . . At this faculty . . . many say. . . that now PhD students should take part in making 'deliverables', and later we call them theses . . . the basics are neglected. (Supervisor 3, A)
>
> (Bøgelund, 2015, p. 49)

A grouping of three 'deliverables' or SOs does not constitute a thesis in many contexts. While much of this book focuses on getting SOs over the line, it is also extremely important that students pay close and careful attention to the writing of their thesis, and to understand the unique textual requirements specific to a TBP in their context.

So what do we need to focus on when seeking to produce a high-quality TBP?

Many books have been written on how to write a thesis, and rather than competing with these works, I'll focus on the two areas that I feel may receive inadequate attention that are specific concerns on a TBP: *structure* and *cohesion*.

First, as a TBP is not structured like a traditional monograph, you need to know what your choices are in this space. Second, the majority of TBP policies include a requirement that your TBP is *cohesive* (Mason et al., 2024b). However, there could be quite a lot of ambiguity around what that means: how to write a cohesive thesis and objectively assess if this has been achieved may be pretty subjective. Criticisms around 'lack of cohesion' in a TBP are not always adequately supported by a description of how to actually attain this cohesion, so I'll try to provide some insight here based on what is currently available, and how I personally have sought to address this issue.

How can a TBP be structured to promote cohesion?

So how can you structure your TBP?

While there may be some differences in preferred structure related to discipline, there are many online resources that provide guidance on how to structure the traditional thesis by monograph. In many cases, this will include the following sections:

- Abstract
- Introduction and literature review
- Methods
- Results or findings
- Discussion
- Conclusion.

(University of Queensland, n.d.)

However, while the TBP can be expected to sufficiently cover these aspects somewhere within it, it can be argued that the TBP does not have a one-size-fits-most approach; there are many possible structural models that your thesis can adopt, some of which are covered extensively in our 2018 article (Mason & Merga, 2018b). We found that 'the most common TBP structure . . . uses an introduction chapter and a conclusion chapter to encase papers which are positioned within the centre of the thesis', often positioning 'each paper in its own chapter' (p. 1459).

To find the right structure for you, you'll be looking for an approach that enables you to tell your research story in the most accessible and logical manner, minimising repetition as far as possible and inviting the reader to appreciate the depth and breadth of your exploration. I strongly encourage you (where permissible) to draw on extant models *just for examples*, and to understand how varying choices can work in telling the story of your research journey. Feel free to adopt any sound approach that works for your TBP structure in consultation with your supervisory team (as long as this is permitted by your institutional policies).

As you will note from the following content, there is a notable role for the use of features such as binding text, used to link content for cohesion. It can be contended that in binding text, 'you are doing more than talking about what is self-evident from looking at the articles themselves but are also directing the reader's attention to the significance of what you have done' (Nygaard & Solli, 2021, p. 55). The role of every component of the thesis other than the SOs themselves, appendices and references is to make the text work as a whole. For example, the introduction in a TBP can be an opportunity to focus on the 'content of the thesis itself instead of the content of the articles, so that the reader can clearly understand the final document as a whole, whether he/she is the board examiner, or a future researcher interested in the work' (Kubota et al., 2021, p. 4).

If this all seems pretty opaque, don't worry, I'll give you some clear examples in this section.

An anatomy of my own TBP: how was it structured?

While I will outline the structure I used for my own TBP here, this is *just one approach* to give you ideas, so it is certainly not meant to be prescriptive: instead, I want to give you the confidence to take your own logical path that works with your research design and SOs. I also want to add that some features, such as the abstract length, are likely to be regulated at university level, so make sure you follow any required dictates on structure that are set by your university.

Before deciding on my own TBP structure, I consulted available TBP theses online and explored how other people had approached this decision-making stage. I then shoved all of that to the back of my brain and took a good look at the pieces I needed to strategically assemble in my own work.

While some people's TBPs can be chained in a logical progression, my TBP dealt with some pretty different RQs around a broad area of inquiry, and I wanted to draw the 10 SOs in my TBP together where relevant, with the idea that this could make it easier to negotiate for the reader, as well as more logical and cohesive, drawing attention to where my research investigated dimensionality in relation to a common branch of inquiry. I weighed up the pros and cons of different kinds of SO grouping and text-binding approaches before deciding on the following.

Before we get into detail on my decision-making here, I'll orient you by providing the abstract so that you know what my thesis was even about:

Recreational reading has a significant impact on school performance and life outcomes. The West Australian Study in Adolescent Book Reading (WASABR) aimed to discover current attitudes toward and levels of engagement in recreational book reading among Western Australian adolescents. It also examined the role of social agents in influencing the recreational book reading (RBR) in this cohort, examining the influences of parents, English teachers, the peer group and friends on adolescents' RBR, in order to understand how adolescents' engagement in RBR is affected by social factors. These understandings were sought with a view to ultimately enhancing participation in RBR.

This mixed method study utilized an explanatory design, whereby qualitative research provided additional depth to quantitative findings. However, student-generated qualitative findings were also central, rather than an adjunct, to several of the routes of inquiry, and the student responses provided the framework for subsequent coding of data. Key insights were developed into ten journal articles, which were submitted for publication to peer-reviewed journals in the areas of education and literacy. These articles form the basis of this TWP.

The articles explored a range of areas within the broad scope of the study. Firstly, the current attitudes toward and frequency of engagement in RBR by adolescent readers were gauged. Findings showed that the majority of respondents were not regularly engaging in RBR. Within the sampled group, boys read less, and had a less positive attitude toward the practice, than girls. Reasons for infrequency of engagement in RBR were examined, with personal preference taking primacy over other potential factors.

Despite high levels of access to devices with eReading capability, this cohort still predominantly chose paper books for RBR. Frequent readers were also found to be comparatively infrequent users of social networking in general, though some keen avid readers were frequently engaged in reading and producing fiction on social networking sites, and others were dependent on social networking sites with peer ratings to select new books. The use of movie adaptations to increase motivation to read the source books and also address comprehension issues was also explored.

RBR was seen as a relatively socially acceptable recreational activity. Students who deemed book reading as socially unacceptable were less likely to engage in and enjoy the practice than students with a more favourable perception. The study also found that students were generally receiving little encouragement to read for recreation from their friends, with boys receiving less encouragement than girls. While friends were influential, the influence of the peer group as a whole was found to have no significant impact on this cohort.

Parental influence on RBR was explored. Favourable characteristics for maintaining parental support of RBR into the high school years were identified and analysed.

Finally, the influence of teachers and schools on RBR was examined. The value of continuing a Silent Reading program into the secondary years was supported by the findings of this study. Students identified specific in-class practices that supported RBR, with these forming the foundation of a provisional framework for best practice. Student responses to the question 'What would make you read more?' highlighted how a multi-faceted approach to this heterogeneous group would be required to support an increase in RBR.

(Merga, 2014a, pp. 2–3)

Introduction to the thesis: rationale and structure

My approach here was pretty standard; the biggest departure from the introduction found in a traditional monograph was that I included a specific section on the structure of my TBP.

Here are the subsections in this introductory component:

- Abstract
- Acknowledgements
- Contents
- Definition of key terms
- Structure of the TWP
- Rationale
- Thesis structure.

I'll go into a bit more detail on my coverage of the structure of the TWP. As I've explained, TBP was pretty new both in my field and at ECU when I undertook it starting in 2012, so I wanted to include a rationale, knowing that it was highly unlikely that my examiners would have experience assessing the merits of this kind of thesis. If TBP is common in your field and context and your examiners can be expected to be familiar with this mode, including this kind of content may be redundant. However, given that TBPs can take quite different forms structurally, and we may be responsive to different motives in adopting a TBP approach, you may find it useful to include this kind of rationale early in your thesis to guide the reader.

Here's what I included in my Rationale for TBP, which I termed TWP as aforementioned:

> Thesis with publication is an unconventional format for dissertations in the field of Education. Some explanation is therefore needed to orient the reader.
>
> The decision to undertake PhD by Publication, instead of the traditional thesis route, was driven by a number of factors. Thesis with publication offers advantages of timely dissemination of findings and lengthy feedback from the peer review of each paper constituting a thesis chapter, both of which are highly beneficial particularly for an early career researcher. In the changing academic culture, publication is increasingly an imperative for securing ongoing academic employment (Lee & Kamler, 2008). In the current academic environment, even entry-level academic positions require a publishing history in addition to a doctoral-level qualification (Brien, 2008).
>
> The broad design of the study, which was given the working title of the *West Australian Study in Adolescent Book Reading* (WASABR), lent itself readily to the thesis with publication approach. Dowling et al. contend that PhD by publication is 'particularly suited to doctoral research that addresses a number of related but potentially stand-alone empirical or conceptual issues' (2012, p. 295). This kind of research readily separates into discrete papers, which are subsequently brought together as a whole in the form of the thesis.

I chose to describe my thesis structure so that my examiners wouldn't be triggered by any perceived gaps, given that TBP can require different organisation of the required components of a thesis, orienting the examiners to negotiate the thesis. Here is most of the guidance I provided in my introduction about my thesis structure:

> The structure of the thesis by publication differs from the traditional model. An introduction provides an outline of the research and brief overview of some of the general supporting literature, theoretical and conceptual frameworks, and methodology employed. The aims of the research and the research questions are explained, and a current audit of the publication status of all of the articles is included. Finally, a brief outline of the research papers that function as the chapters of the thesis is provided.

The body of the thesis consists of publications that are published, in press, or under review that act as chapters. These chapters are grouped into sections. Each section of the thesis begins with a descriptive introduction, and each of the papers includes a summative abstract at the outset. As the publication chapters contain a clear explanation of methodology and a review of the relevant literature, additional detailed sections dedicated to these components have not been included.

A detailed discussion examining key findings and critically reflecting on the study concludes the thesis.

In this vein, a more recent thesis (Dryden, 2024) also combines a rationale with a description of structure. Here is an abridged excerpt from their section on thesis structure to give you a sense of the logic informing decisions around mode and structure:

This thesis is centred around multiple themes intrinsic to translingual discrimination that acknowledge how this form of discrimination shapes linguistic integration in Australian society. The thesis presents these findings through six peer reviewed publications, presenting as a thesis by publication . . .

The choice to compile a thesis by peer-reviewed publication meant that subsections of theory and data were focused on within each article, meaning that the articles combined to explore multiple themes within the broader thesis topics of 'linguistic integration' and 'emotional wellbeing,' through the conceptual framework of 'translingual discrimination.' Doing a thesis by publication had two benefits: the dissemination of the participants' voices, ensuring that their time and effort in participating reached a larger audience; and the external peer review of each article by experts in the field meant that the feedback they provided was unencumbered with subjective assumptions of the body of work, which assisted in improving its quality (Merga, 2015). Having individual publications meant that each article and chapter stands as a study on its own, with the publications containing sections that provide theoretical context, such as the introduction and literature review, a methodological outline, data analysis and discussion, as well as concluding sections that contain implications that will be expanded upon in the thesis' concluding chapter. Compiling a thesis in this manner allowed for the ethnographic exploration of various sociolinguistic realities that occur within Australia. These realities were then combined to form a larger picture of how linguistic integration in Australia may or may not occur, and the emotional outcomes of this, providing critiques on how sociolinguistic interactions and translingual discrimination shape both these major themes in the thesis.

(Dryden, 2024, pp. 7–8)

You will note that the last sentence in the above speaks to the combined value of the individual publications 'to form a larger picture' of an issue or phenomenon.

Introduction to the research

After introducing my structure, the next section covered an introduction to the research that included many of the components covered in the traditional thesis as previously outlined. However, to avoid repetition, the coverage could have been relatively lean where detail was rich within publications. What seems like a generous word count at the start of your thesis journey may begin to feel meagre by the end, so you need to prioritise content that adds value and builds cohesion, avoiding duplication where possible. For example, having a large methods component where this is also fulsomely covered in a dedicated SO is a waste of words.

So how deep do you need to go in this introduction? You also need to be thinking about whether the journal articles deliver enough to meet examiner needs. As noted by Nygaard and Solli (2021), 'what might be considered a sufficient degree of detail about methodology for a reviewer of a journal article might be considered inadequate for an examiner of a doctoral dissertation' (p. 31). If it's not enough in this instance, it's easy to add a chapter, an appendix or binding text that expands on methods as required; as long as your TBP policy allows it, you'll have the flexibility to adopt what works best for you. If I had written a separate SO as a literature review or methods paper, there would have been an SO in my introductory section in place of that content, but all of my SOs were reporting on research findings.

I included the following headings in the introduction:

- Background to the project
- Theoretical framework
- Conceptual framework
- Exploring the field
- Examining social influences
- Limitations
- Methodological approach
- Research aims
- Research questions
- Method overview
- Instruments

- Participants
- Interview respondents
- Undertaking the research
- Publications
- Organisation of research papers.

You will note that the last two points are the most significant departure from structural possibilities related to the traditional monograph. In the component on publications, I provided an up-to-date table on the publications that were included in the TBP audited against RQ coverage, very similar to Table 4. I also stated that 'all papers were sole authored by the primary researcher' (Merga, 2014a, p. 31), given my unusual circumstance as sole author of all of my SOs.

The component on organisation of research papers is once again concerned with examiner reader experience, guiding them through the logic that informed my decisions across four sections with SO chapters:

> The papers have been broken into four related sections, though a number of the papers could legitimately appear in other sections.
>
> The first section provides insights into the current adolescent attitudes towards and engagement in recreational book reading. The chapter 'Are Western Australian adolescents keen book readers?' reports on the frequency and volume of recreational book reading in the cohort, in addition to current attitudes toward recreational book reading. Data is then split by gender, which suggest that boys may read less than girls, and have a less positive attitude toward recreational book reading. The social acceptability of reading, for this cohort, is explored in the chapter 'Peer Group and Friend Influences on the Social Acceptability of Adolescent Book Reading,' with the influence of friends and the peer group, and how this varies by gender, also examined. In the paper 'Western Australian Adolescents' reasons for infrequent engagement in recreational book reading,' the factors leading to infrequency of engagement in recreational book reading are quantified . . .
>
> (Merga, 2014a, pp. 33–34)

Each of the four sections is introduced in this manner, providing the examiner with an early overview of what to expect. The four sections have the following headings, with the SO distribution of the 10 SOs noted:

1 Current adolescent attitudes towards and engagement in recreational book reading (3 SOs)

2 Technology, popular media and adolescent recreational book reading (3 SOs)
3 Parental influences on recreational book reading (1 SO)
4 English teacher influence on recreational book reading (3 SOs)

Body (sections and their chapters)

The binding work that began in the introduction continues throughout the thesis. The aforementioned four sections include preamble content followed by the article(s). Again, you absolutely do not need to have both sections and chapters, but as previously articulated, I felt that this worked best for my approach to link my SOs meaningfully and relate them back to the research inquiry. I used the preamble content to introduce the SO chapters, but also to point out how they were related to each other. The final paragraph of the preamble could include a statement about the research contribution of that section. For example, the first part of the final paragraph of the preamble for section one notes that 'from the first section of the thesis, current trends in attitude and frequency are presented, and an understanding of the complicated impact that social influences can potentially exert on adolescents begins to be outlined' (Merga, 2014a, p. 37).

Preamble text was also used to relate sections to each other. For example, here is the first paragraph of the fourth section:

> This section focuses on identifying variables within the scope of potential teacher mediation that could encourage a greater frequency of recreational book reading, in addition to increasing the social capital of engaging in the practice. The papers in this section also revisit areas of research identified in previous sections, such as reasons for not reading, in greater depth, and with additional supporting data, connecting findings to teacher practice in more detail.
>
> (Merga, 2014a, p. 229)

Again, this is a reminder of the interrelatedness of the sections that I have separated, reinforcing the cohesion of the thesis.

End narrative

Your end narrative on a TBP will do the work of drawing together research results previously described in the SOs, further emphasising cohesion and interrelationships, highlighting conclusions and considering limitations and implications for future research (Remenyi, 2015).

One of the best things about the end narrative is that unless you saved all of your SOs to the very end of your journey (which would perhaps be undesirable given the time constraints on a TBP), you were writing SOs along the journey, always dealing with an incomplete picture.

Your end narrative is a chance to take a breath, look back at what has been achieved, and critically consider the contribution that has been made, and how your research informs future directions for additional research and real-world purposes, while at the same time being transparent about key limitations that need to be taken into account when considering your findings as a whole. You started out conceiving a whole but segmented project, then started primarily working with it in these SO-aligned segments, and now you are reverting back to the whole again, switching lenses to zoom out.

I have very clear memories of writing the end narrative of my TBP. For me, it felt like a kind of arrival—I could see that I had some solid SOs and findings, and the intense labour of data collection and SO writing and revisions on the TBP project was (mostly) behind me. The end narrative of the thesis had a different job to do, but it also felt like saying goodbye, the wrapping on a present, all kinds of nostalgic images with one toe still in it. At the same time, having achieved some peer-review success across the process suggesting that my research was basically sound, I felt emboldened to take a really critical look at how my project could have been better (with a particular focus on what could have been achieved with more time and resourcing). One of my favourite sections to write was my limitations section.

Here are the headings from my end narrative. This part involved overview and critical coverage of what was presented in the thesis:

- The impact of parents, English teachers, friends and peers on adolescents' attitudes toward recreational book reading
- Parents
- Friends and the peer group
- English teachers
- Implications for method and design
- Peer group and friends
- Frequency as an attitudinal indicator
- Mixed-method design.

This part dealt with limitations and areas for research in far more detail than what was included in the SOs:

- Additional limitations & areas for future research
- Self-report
- Issues with saturation achievement
- Generalizations from the qualitative data
- Issues with consent
- Uniqueness of Western Australia
- Emerging issues for further study
- Broadening the cohort
- Longitudinal perspective
- Final comment.

(Merga, 2014a)

Across the journey, as you are writing your SOs and editing sometimes brutally in order to be compliant with rigid word-count limits set by SO publishers as well as reviewer requirements, you may find yourself cutting or severely limiting content on important related tangents and considerations. I suggest that you keep a separate file where you put all of these additional components to revisit at the time of writing the end narrative, where you will have a chance to breathe new life into warranted additional considerations, perhaps with more word-count freedom.

References: introduction & discussion

When writing a TBP, deciding how the references will be presented is a relevant consideration. Including references throughout may feel interruptive, but just including all of the references at the end as is often done in the traditional monograph probably won't be an option where you have chapters that are SOs, therefore containing the references cited in those SOs. So if you are providing references throughout your TBP anyway, do you then start including a reference list at the end of each component?

I made what I thought was a logical choice in the case of my TBP to move the introduction- and discussion-related references to the end of the thesis. Reference lists in the body of the thesis only related to the SOs.

Interestingly, this means that in my TBP there is no list that includes every single reference cited in the thesis due to these multiple lists throughout. I think that an argument could potentially be made to include a reference list that encompasses *all* of the references cited throughout the entire thesis, including the individual SOs. Of course, you can only make this decision if you are within the (often university-stipulated) acceptable word constraints.

Appendices

Finally, as is the case with the traditional monograph, my TBP included appendices specifically relating to the devised research tools and ethics requirements. I also made my survey data available in this section for the interest of the examiners. Here is what I included:

- Survey tool
- Semi-structured interview guide
- Survey results
- Student consent letter
- Parent consent letter
- Department of Education site manager consent
- Department of Education ethics approval.

Academic writing for TBP level: a few tips and observations

There are many ways that you can improve your academic writing to get it to the standard needed for success in the SO publication journey *and* the thesis and, as mentioned earlier, there are numerous books written to inform improvement in academic writing, so I won't be duplicating these works here. Others have made an entire career out of being amazing at teaching this, and if this is an area of concern for you, you will need to access a far more fulsome coverage of how to improve academic writing for the production of SOs and your TBP. You may also access writing consultant support if available at your institution, and if you do so, make sure you remember to tell the consultant that you are writing a TBP so that they know that they need to help you upskill to arguably the highest level of academic writing, and perhaps master discipline-specific textual features for SOs if applicable. For example, the first time I presented findings of (non-parametric) quantitative data analysis was in a manuscript for a journal, and learning the norms around how to present the data was important self-directed learning that I undertook at that time. Instead of encroaching on a space already well-covered by others, I will provide a few tips and observations that are TBP-specific.

As briefly touched upon earlier in this book, writing for SO audiences will be subject to more scrutiny than you have probably ever encountered previously. As a former teacher of English and literature, I came into my TBP with a lot of confidence in my writing ability, having taught others how to write effectively. However, I had a lot to learn about writing for specific academic audiences.

It has been contended that 'writing is assumed to be a universal skill students learn prior to doctoral studies' (Doyle & Caissie, 2024, p. 4). However, if you do not have experience writing for academic peer-reviewed journal articles, you might find this writing to be on a whole new level. As such, the intense scrutiny on your writing quality, and perhaps a scathing critique of its perceived limitations from peer reviewers as you develop, may initially be quite overwhelming.

Read

This may sound incredibly obvious, but one of the most useful things that you can do to prepare yourself for this jump is to read a lot of SOs relevant to your knowledge areas, methods and theories, and you'll be doing this anyway in order to cover the literature review component of your thesis. It's almost impossible to have a *realistic understanding* of the writing level needed without being an avid reader of academic journal articles from your target journals. In addition for reading to understand the field, methods and key current findings, you also need to read with attention to how the research story is being told; for example, how is the contribution of a journal article presented in its abstract? When you read an article that you find compelling and innovative, or choose to read one SO before another based on the title, take a close look at the role the writing played in engaging you as a reader.

Get feedback

Novice authors have indicated that group meetings with supervisors and students can also play an important role in enhancing writing skills and combatting emerging challenges encountered in this space (Xu et al., 2024). Explicit, logical supervisory feedback focused on writing can do much to support academic writing skill development; in my own experience, this is most effective when accompanied by a model so that students can see what you mean beyond your explanation. For example, in the past, some of my really excellent students initially struggled to determine when to write with an advocacy voice, and when to write with a researcher voice, and the difference between these two positions. As a supervisor, providing early and clear feedback on this, and what kinds of language are used in both contexts, helped the students to quickly adapt to find their researcher voice for the proposal presentation they needed to pass in order to achieve confirmation of candidature.

Review

Another excellent way to improve your writing is to act as a peer reviewer for journals or conferences. Evidence of reviewing will also be handy if you are looking to move into academia post PhD, as you can add this to your CV around service.

It's amazing how the same limitations in our own writing that we readily overlook will absolutely grate when you encounter them in someone else's work. For example, there is nothing like reading someone else's circular writing that never actually gets to a point to motivate you to have far greater clarity in your own written expression. You may not see the point of topic sentences until you attempt to read a manuscript that does not have them. Experience as a peer reviewer has made me more forgiving of the writing issues of others as long as they are still clearly communicating ideas, while at the same time, it has made me far more rigorous in my editing of my own work (though I am still not perfect!).

However as a note of caution, do not let reviewing work become all-consuming; once you put your hand up to review, given the paucity of reviewers, you may receive a never-ending procession of offers to review landing in your inbox until the end of time.

Consider readability

One of my personal opinions is that academic writing that is so advanced in sophistication as to be virtually impenetrable by anyone outside of a very small circle of scholars is not necessarily a flex.

I'm of the view that *where possible*, when writing SOs we should endeavour to be as accessible as reasonably viable while being responsive to the required nuances necessary to accurately convey our research, and in a sufficiently academic tone. I'm not saying we must 'dumb it down': we can write in an academic voice while still at a level where advanced EAL readers can access our complex ideas, and so that an exhausted peer reviewer doesn't have to activate psychic powers to understand us. The lower the level of English reading comprehension required to understand our research, the broader the scholarly community it can resonate with. While I understand that highly accessible writing may not always be possible, given that we must convey very complex ideas and findings, and voice and tone must meet disciplinary and journal norms, it should be our goal as far as possible as it is aligned with a broader global scholarly inclusivity agenda. I'm not going to go so far as to insist that you run all your work through a readability tool, but if you are writing for audiences beyond academia, that can be a good idea in some instances, potentially yielding benefits for citation count (covered further in Chapter 7).

You won't be 'on' every day

Given the serious time constraints that you'll be operating under if producing a TBP, you need to get really good at managing your time, energy and attention levels.

You may have health issues, be raising a family, caring for family members, experiencing periods of economic instability, working a side gig, or any number of other life obstacles. Life doesn't stop during a PhD and you may find yourself facing challenges that have nothing to do with your research project but compound stress related to it by denying you downtime and peace of mind. During your PhD you may learn more about how to get the most out of yourself in terms of academic productivity while endeavouring to protect your wellbeing, and part of that is being responsive to what can realistically be done at any given time without causing yourself harm.

In this vein, on research, I do the low cognitive demand stuff (e.g. tidying references) when my brain is not as 'on', and the higher demand stuff (e.g. thematic coding) when I am fresh, rested and functional. It all needs to get done anyway, so manage yourself reasonably and responsively while maintaining momentum: you are your own human resource. Finally, while I was able to pass through my PhD without having to suspend my candidature at any point, not everyone is this fortunate, and you need to know when to put things on pause if possible so that you have a chance to recover and regroup.

CHAPTER 6

Revising and Resubmitting without Losing the Plot

Revisions can make your SO manuscript a lot better. Insights from field experts, often from beyond your professional reach, can enable you to strengthen your argument and increase its relevance to cross-contextual circumstances (Merga et al., 2018). For example, in our recent article I noted that

> I recently had a paper published in a UK based journal . . . and while I tried to make it resonate with a UK audience, being outside the UK, there's only so much I can do to try to fill the gaps without current lived knowledge of what it means to be a UK-based educator. The minor revisions on this paper were all very helpful, and mostly tweaks I could make to create that alignment. I like that the paper will now appeal to a broader audience thanks to peer-reviewer intervention.
>
> (Merga et al., 2025, p. 4)

However, even if you're at the earliest possible stages of your PhD journey, you have almost certainly heard about the personal and professional challenges involved in the peer-review process, many of which revolve around dealing with suggested revisions, and the reality is that you will almost certainly do some kind of revisions on your SOs.

For the uninitiated, your journal article will probably be given one of the following designations (or a variation of these) as a decision after peer review. Most of the options require you to be responsive to peer reviewer feedback, ranging from very minor tweaks to substantial reimagining:

1 **Accepted, no changes (acceptance).** This is pretty rare, and has only happened a handful of times in my career; it certainly has happened more often later in my career than in the early stages when I was still learning the ropes and submitting manuscripts out of scope among

other infractions. When you land an accepted, no changes decision, just like the wording implies, there's nothing more to do until you get the copyedit sent through (covered later in this section) apart from ordering a cake and then eating it with your research team.

2 **Accepted, minor changes (acceptance).** It's pretty much accepted; you just need to make a few minor changes to prepare it for publication, such as clarifying concepts, adding additional references, or reframing a section to make it more appropriate to an international audience. Pay close attention to what you've been asked for and respond in a timely and clear manner, and you'll get over the line.

3 **Accept with major changes (conditional acceptance).** The journal wants your paper, but you need to make some notable changes first. These are big enough to hold off on giving you the green flag.

4 **Revise and resubmit (conditional rejection).** While this may initially feel disheartening, it is actually a good outcome; it is after all way better than being rejected. Revise and resubmit means that the editors and/or peer reviewers see genuine merit in your work, but substantial changes will be needed in order for it to be given further consideration. When you agree to go down the revise and resubmit path, you may face multiple rounds of revisions to get the article to the level where it needs to be to warrant publication.

5 **Rejection (outright rejection).** This may be a desk rejection, or it may be a rejection after peer review. Either way, as I explore further in this section, you should pay close attention to the reasons for the rejection as this will usually offer crucial clues to support you in getting your manuscript into publication at another journal.

(partly adapted from Wiley, 2024a)

We all have different life journeys in the lead-up to a PhD, and I have seen students who are quite dumbfounded when they first encounter relatively minor revisions having never been subjected to that level of scrutiny before. It can be deflating. While as I argue above, getting an opportunity to revise your paper rather than having it rejected outright is a good outcome, it can still be emotionally tough to find out that you are still some way from the finish line, particularly given the exertions you've already put in:

> If there was labour in constructing the article, there is certainly labour in dealing with its return and the accompanying reviewers' comments. Our goal was to produce and submit a quality article and we got there. But – not really. The horrible realisation that there is still so much to do dawns on us. We're not really

there yet. And this realisation is always emotionally draining because we now have to accept the need to unstitch and unpick the careful argument we crafted and thought was complete.

(Thomson & Kamler, 2012, p. 127)

I really like how these authors normalised the fact that it is natural to experience a range of emotions on learning that a revision will be necessary, and frustrations can be compounded by the kind of revisions requested, as explored further herein.

The peer review experience can be a very supportive process that enables you to grow your skills and knowledge, particularly around communicating your research. It can also be deeply demoralising. For example, in her opinion piece, Hu (2023) describes encountering 'bias, interests and jealousy of reviewers':

I believe that the fairness of academic publication includes not only whether reviewers can maintain objective neutrality and review each manuscript fairly in the face of researchers of different countries, races and languages, but also whether reviewers can objectively and fairly evaluate the value of each research result without delaying or even failing to publish the papers of other researchers due to personal interests or jealousy. (p. 1)

As such, it is possible to encounter a really mixed bag in the peer-review process: having a piece accepted with no changes by one reviewer with the other requesting a revise and resubmit is certainly not unheard of, and while the reasons for this disparity can be sound, in some instances they may not be (see previous on parochialism), and it can potentially be difficult to navigate these distinctions with the disadvantage of inexperience. While there is a great deal of literature that looks at the challenges, inequities and issues associated with peer review, in this chapter I will primarily focus on those with a specific TBP application, though I encourage you to do further reading to better understand this contentious space.

In my experience, the more controversial or unfashionable the ideas in a journal article, the harder to get the work published, which should not come as a big surprise to you. Reflecting on my TBP, I noted that

while arguably all theses should contain potentially insubordinate ideas, the reception of these ideas is not dependent only on the manner in which they are communicated; the culture that receives them can also significantly determine whether or not they will ever be heard.

(Merga, 2015, pp. 295–296)

Just because this is a barrier to publication doesn't mean that it should stop you from challenging the status quo. Since doing my PhD I have always found it extra satisfying when I manage to get risky, unfashionable or contentious ideas over the line (e.g. Merga, 2024c): it feels more useful.

Also, if you're planning to share your research outside academia, you need to learn how to respond to having your ideas challenged, responding with agility and credibility, and the peer-review process can help you refine these skills. For example, a live radio interview I did in 2025 raised a controversial issue in one of my research spaces with no prior warning, and while this sent my blood pressure through the roof having to address this on live radio, luckily, thanks to my experiences in peer review, I knew exactly what to say to deal with the situation, control damage and placate all parties without compromising my values, or misrepresenting the research or reality.

When I talk about revising and resubmitting without losing the plot, I'm being both literal and figurative. While doing reviewer-dictated revisions may be stressful, there are also risks for your thesis cohesion that you'll have to think carefully about as you weigh up literally every suggested or demanded change. Undergoing the revision process on journal articles that form part of a TBP is risky, particularly on those not-uncommon occasions where reviewers want you to adopt a stance that is *tangential to your original RQs* (yet often mysteriously aligned with the peer reviewer's niche area of research, making them identifiable through feedback in the double-blind process, particularly when they ask you to heavily cite their work).

Where this is warranted, it must be done. Where it is deemed not warranted after close discussion with your supervisory team, and ideally some input from external mentors and advisors, it should be avoided *if possible*, particularly where changes would make your thesis less cohesive. Once you have the pressure of time constraints of peer review and candidature milestones, it can be hard to resist changes that could get an article over the line, even where they could disrupt the 'plot' of your thesis, while not enhancing your SO. While each SO needs to be responsive to individual journals or other requirements, it also needs to fit within the thesis; it may start out very well aligned, but reviewing processes can shift it substantially. Trying to figure all of this out, so that you don't lose the plot emotionally, or lose the plot of the thesis, can be really hard without sustained and substantial input from an experienced and knowledgeable supervisor or supervisory team.

Also, it is important to add that revision is another new academic textual form for you to understand. When you are asked to provide any kind of revision, it is common for journals to be explicit about the form in which they want to receive this revision. For example, they might ask you to attach a *table of changes*, and/or a *tracked changes version*, alongside a final manuscript.

It is really important that you closely follow the requests of the journal; if your revisions are difficult to locate within your submitted materials, it's only going to take longer for your work to move through peer review. Do everything in your power to make this an easy experience for the editors and reviewers. If there is any difficulty in this regard, expect to have your manuscript returned to you: 'Lack of experience in revising reviewed manuscripts led to our manuscript being returned to be rerevised by us using track changes as suggested by chief editors/reviewers' (Indrayadi, 2024, p. 1340).

Substantial revision/redirection

So you have received a request for revisions, and you've never done revisions on a journal article before in your entire life. Where to begin?

Frame of mind

You need to get yourself in the right frame of mind before you even attempt to do this. In many cases, people should not immediately jump in and tackle revisions after reading them for the first time, unless they are particularly minor and innocuous.

When revisions land in your inbox on a rough day when you're already feeling pretty overwhelmed, it's important to not allow them to be the straw that breaks this camel's back. Look at them, get the general gist of them, and then close them and walk away. Come back to these revisions in a timely manner, but also at a time when you are better equipped to deal with them. Don't try to squash your frustration – draw on any *healthy* stress-reducing mechanisms that you find work for you (bearing in mind that if you become reliant on unhealthy mechanisms, particularly those that kill off brain cells, that's not going to help you in the long run). Go for a run, shout in a forest, have a whinge or a cry with a tolerant friend or play with your dog. Then get on it when you are ready and *treat it like it's someone else's work*.

Table of changes

Once you return to your revisions, read through them again carefully.

Hopefully, you'll find it less painful this time around. After you've roughly decided what needs to be done on each point, get your supervisor's input (unless they are unable to provide you with feedback in a timely manner).

Make a simple table of changes (see template in Table 7). Paste the reviewer comments into the 'requested revisions' column, and track changes on a separate Word document as well; respond to each of the comments respectfully and thoroughly where a change is genuinely needed.

Unless otherwise directed by the journal, you will need to submit:

- the revised final manuscript (with tracked changes as per Figure 5; the underlined text is the inserted text);
- the revised final manuscript (with changes accepted);
- the table of changes that clearly explains how each requested revision has been responded to (see Table 7), with some direction to the reviewer about where they can find it in the tracked changes version of the manuscript. This can be a page number or a clearly specified location, as seen in Table 8 opposite.

Be as clear as possible. The easier your changes are to locate, and the more respectful you are, the faster you get out of the purgatory of revisions and lock in an acceptance.

So how clear do you need to be?

Do not forget that *this is unpaid labour* that the peer reviewer is doing, falling into the category of *organisational citizenship behaviours* like many other unremunerated aspects of the academic workload. Imagine your peer reviewer is recovering from illness and battling post-viral fatigue while raising kids and working a full-time job. Have mercy upon them. How can you communicate your changes so that they can understand what you've done without having to do your job for you? It is your job to make it very easy for the reviewer; don't make them do the labour of interpretation when you can enhance your own clarity to help them out. If you are not sure if you have been clear enough, share your files with a

Table 7 *Table of changes (blank)*

Requested Revisions	Action
Reviewer 1	
Reviewer 2	

peer and get them to evaluate your clarity and while you are at it, ask them if they find your justifications and changes persuasive and sufficient.

Table 8 *Table of changes (example from a recent minor revision)*

Requested Revisions	Action
Reviewer 1	
This is an interesting article and provides a clearer international picture of the value (or otherwise) placed on school libraries and the SLPs in them, and some insights into how that relates to the value placed on RfP (reading for pleasure). My only real suggestion is to make the links to RfP more explicit in the conclusions – if part of the argument this article is making is that RfP is important to achievement then it would be good to see that emphasised more. I look forward to seeing more of the outcomes from this survey.	Thank you for your useful feedback. We have added the following to the introductory paragraph of the conclusion. Schools need to foster their students' reading engagement to build and maintain literacy skills, particularly given the benefits regular RfP can offer for enhancing vocabulary and reading comprehension (Allington & McGill-Franzen, 2021; Pfost & Heyne, 2023; Sullivan & Brown, 2015; Torppa et al., 2020). RfP needs to be understood, valued and communicated as an educative practice, particularly as children who recognise the ongoing importance of RfP read more often (Merga & Mat Roni, 2018). Fostering awareness of the importance of RfP within schools, and the role of SLPs in promoting and supporting it may be challenging in many contexts. A number of key issues with high relevance for SLPs' capacity to foster student reading engagement were identified in this research, warranting researcher, SLP, leadership and/or policymaker attention.

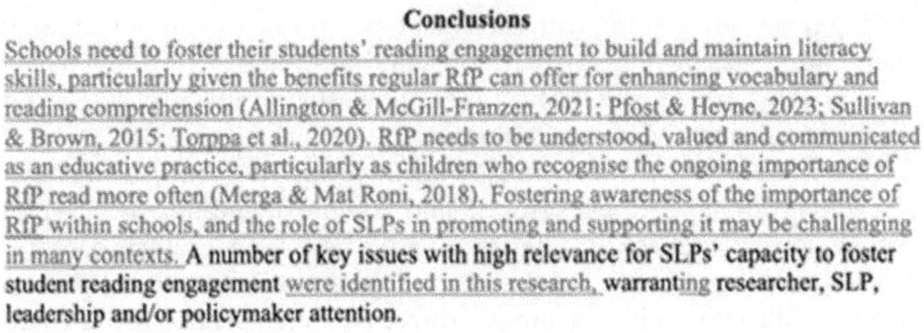

Conclusions

Schools need to foster their students' reading engagement to build and maintain literacy skills, particularly given the benefits regular RfP can offer for enhancing vocabulary and reading comprehension (Allington & McGill-Franzen, 2021; Pfost & Heyne, 2023; Sullivan & Brown, 2015; Torppa et al., 2020). RfP needs to be understood, valued and communicated as an educative practice, particularly as children who recognise the ongoing importance of RfP read more often (Merga & Mat Roni, 2018). Fostering awareness of the importance of RfP within schools, and the role of SLPs in promoting and supporting it may be challenging in many contexts. A number of key issues with high relevance for SLPs' capacity to foster student reading engagement were identified in this research, warranting researcher, SLP, leadership and/or policymaker attention.

Figure 5 *Screenshot from the tracked changes version*

While you are learning the ropes, you will need to liaise closely with your supervisor to get the balance right. However, perhaps one of the most disorienting moments that you may encounter is when the peer reviewer's issue is with the *supervisor's contribution* rather than your own.

If you already distrust your supervisory team, this may lead you to conclude perhaps correctly that aspects of their input are harming rather than helping your work. However, it is usually more likely that your supervisor has contributed a component that they knew to be controversial rather than making that your responsibility. Basically, it's important not to jump to conclusions purely based on a single peer viewer's feedback, just as it is crucial to be working with a supervisory team that you can genuinely trust, and whose expertise you can rely on.

A journal editor plays a really important role in adjudicating when it comes to deciding which proposed revisions are warranted, and when they do not enact this role it can lead to an impasse between reviewers. For example, while I was still relatively early in my research career, I withdrew a paper from the peer-review process at a journal for the following reasons:

> The reviewers started to actively contradict each other and the editor did not weigh in. For example, Reviewer 2 stated: 'The title for me is ambiguous. For example, I can see the authors have responded to a previous reviewer's comments about the age of participants, but I am not sure adding 'in primary school' works unless the authors are talking about children reading in primary school'. There were other issues too, including name-calling. After withdrawing the paper, it was quickly accepted elsewhere and with almost no changes. We knew it was a good paper, so we persisted, but if this had happened earlier in my career, I probably would have buried it.
>
> (Merga et al., 2018, p. 385)

Having reviewers arguing with each other over revisions without editorial intervention was incredibly frustrating, and despite easily finding a new home for this article, significant time was wasted in this process, and it was demoralising and disappointing.

I also wanted to add that there are some unique issues that can emerge if you come from an EAL background and you are attempting to interpret peer-reviewer feedback in English. Even where your English comprehension skills are very strong, issues emerge as reviewers do not always communicate clearly. For example, a directive from a peer reviewer could be worded as follows: 'I would suggest that the first two paragraphs be substantially revised with far more recent research added to this introductory content, given that the references that these paragraphs currently rely upon are extremely dated, and there is a significant volume of newer work in this space.' Despite the use of the word suggest, this is not actually a *suggestion*: you are expected to make this change.

Requested revisions: what exactly do they look like?

To write this section, I went back to look at some of the revisions I've made over the last 10 years or so.

Here's an overview of 10 different kinds of revisions I've been asked to make during that time across a range of different articles, and how I responded to them, just to give you a sense of the sorts of changes that you might be asked to make to enhance your manuscript, and how you could respond to them (Table 9). Of course, you may experience completely different issues. I include revisions from both sole and co-authored works, sometimes lightly edited so that they make sense outside their original table.

Table 9 *Ten examples of requested revisions*

#	Requested Revisions	Action
1	It would be useful to see the ORDER of the duties, and the # of words used for each duty. You could do a % in terms of words/duty to get an overall balance of jobs (pie chart or series of histographs).	Thanks, but I don't feel that this is appropriate for these data. Doing this kind of analysis with qualitative data interpretation can be misleading and messy, as a qualitative statement often incorporates duties that have been coded more than once, making it impossible to allocate a ranking order. For example, in the methods I've already noted: 'Overlap was common; for example, some of the 'Events and displays' were also closely related to 'Literacy and reading supportive activities and dispositions', such as participation in World Book Day. Such instances were subject to dual or even multiple coding as required'. (p. 3) As I've mentioned in the method, in some cases documents were merged where there was a job description and separate person specification form. To rank order, I'd have to weight one over the other, but this would be arbitrary. In addition, I'm not confident that order of duties listed necessarily indicates order of valuing/privileging by the schools, and until I see research that links order with privileging I hesitate to make this assertion.
2	The author was effective in focusing on the 'role' rather than the 'actions' of the school librarian. However, there were at least a couple times in the article where the author mentioned 'what school librarians actually do' (page1line48). It's important to keep these separate because there's a difference between the job description expectations and on-the-job librarian performance.	Good point; such blurring is inappropriate and I made minor changes to the abstract and on page 1 (see tracked changes version).

Continued

Table 9 *Continued*

#	Requested Revisions	Action
3	My first point is about our scope and readership: since our readership are publishers there needs to be a stronger message for them in the conclusions. How do your findings affect publishing and publishers? What information are you presenting which is of use to them when considering their business and their publications? I feel that this article is right on the edge of our scope and needs to be tied more closely to it to make it a suitable article for us. Related to this I felt that your abstract and introduction rather 'squeezed' this point in – you say that publishers are concerned with translation beyond academia – I am not 100% sure this is really the case, but they may have reasons for wishing greater visibility of the research they publish which could be brought out perhaps?	Thanks for this useful feedback. We added the following to the conclusion to better align the paper with the readership: Scholarly publishers should encourage institutions to support and reward research outputs for both academic and translation audiences. Scholarly publishers should also remain abreast of the trends and possibilities explored in this article as they have implications for the quality and quantity of research that informs their publication. Scholarly publishers can harness trends toward broader research dissemination beyond academia to expand the potential audience for consuming the research disseminated by scholarly journals, potentially greatly increasing the breadth and diversity of this audience and increasing the circulation of these research works. In addition, much of the work published in scholarly journals is funded by external (non-university) sources. When research is shared with end-users beyond academia such as industry and governance, these entities may increasingly value the work done by these scholars as they see the transferability and relevance of the work. In turn, it can be contended that these entities may be more inclined to fund future works, enabling the research that will populate scholarly journals with articles into the future. As such, a narrow vision of research audience that confines itself to academia falls to account for the shrinking pool of research funding which is increasingly dependent on government and industry; scholarly publishers cannot afford to ignore the importance of broadening their audience for increasing circulation and facilitating future scholarly material to publish. We added the following to the abstract: Scholarly publishers can benefit from the sharing of research beyond academia where it can exert societal impact, as this can increase the breadth of their readership and encourage funders in industry and governance to fund the research that informs scholarly publications. We added the following to the introduction (and the related reference): Scholarly publishers can benefit from the sharing of research beyond academia where it can exert

Continued

Table 9 *Continued*

#	Requested Revisions	Action
3		societal impact, as this can increase the breadth of their readership and encourage funders in industry and governance to fund the research that informs scholarly publications. Government-provided funding of research supports the diffusion of academic research (Tseng et al., 2020), and across the OECD, university research is increasingly funded by industry and 'the share of basic funding for universities is decreasing' (Gulbrandsen & Smeby, 2005, p. 932). When scholarly publishers support the connection between research, industry and policy, they are potentially bolstering the quality and quantity of the research informing future scholarly publications, and supporting the security of government and industry-supported research funding for scholarly work. As industry funding is 'strongly correlated with high publication productivities, even when adjusting for types of publication and co-authorships' (Gulbrandsen & Smeby, 2005, p. 947), the contribution of industry funding to the scholarly publishing community is noteworthy. We've also re-written the key points to highlight the significance for the community: • Scholarly publishers should support research translation beyond academia to expand their readership • Research translation can also encourage industry and governance to fund the research that informs scholarly publications • Early career researchers (ECRs) need more support from their universities to share their research. • Support for research translation may be particularly poorly supported. • Japanese universities may show greater valuing of translational outputs than Australian universities. Support for both academic and translational outputs changes in response to nations' changing research priorities.
4	A minor point but I was very alarmed to hear that an academic was terminated for not publishing! (I assume – and hope! – it was their contract that was terminated!)	Thanks; we've attended to this error; thanks. The Terminator was not involved as far as we know! ☺

Continued

Table 9 *Continued*

#	Requested Revisions	Action
5	I find the title cumbersome and confusing; nor welcoming.	We've changed the title to: **University support for sharing research with academia and beyond**
6	The abstract fails to explain the aims and objectives of the study clearly and it is also expressed poorly.	We have extensively re-written the abstract as follows: Abstract: There is increasing expectation that research be communicated broadly to share knowledge with industry, professional, governmental and public spheres. Scholarly publishers can benefit from the sharing of research beyond academia where it can exert societal impact, as this can increase the breadth of their readership and encourage funders in industry and governance to fund the research that informs scholarly publications. This paper draws on qualitative in-depth interview data from Australia and Japan-based early career researchers (ECRs) with the aim of identifying how higher education institutions may support the development of the diverse communication skills that ECRs need to effectively share their research both in academia and beyond. We found that sharing research in academia and beyond is often valued but not always supported. Output valuing was communicated in performance management, and there were compelling differences in output valuing between the two nations.
7	2) Methods I would like to know more about the details of language orientation of the participants. Would it be possible to add the column of 'English as an additional language' in Table 2 as well? This request is made because I wish to know to what extent Australian and Japanese samples had ECRs with English as an additional language. If the ratios were too high/low compared with the larger society population of each nation (I know this research is a qualitative and small sample study, so that can coincidentally happen), it should be noted somewhere.	Thanks. We haven't added this information in that table as we believe it could enable deductive disclosure of respondents when combined with the other information we provide. But we have addressed your interest in 'to what extent Australian and Japanese samples had ECRs with English as an additional language' by adding the following: Most (84.6%) of the Japan-based respondents were classified as using English as an additional language (EAL), but there was also a relatively high number of Australian ECRs classified as EAL, considering that the language used in Australia for official purposes is standard Australian English (47.1%).

Continued

Table 9 *Continued*

#	Requested Revisions	Action
8	Measures determining the quality of the model are missing in the text (recall, precision, specificity, F1-Score, area under the ROC curve). I'm concerned about the very low accuracy classifying those cases that do not belong to the target group (it is also important the precision result indicating that the algorithms of the network classified correctly substantially more cases relevant to each category than irrelevant ones).	We include ROC as Figure 2, and also a paragraph explaining the AUC of the ROC. We also include relative effect size of AUC on the basis of Cohen's (1988) d. The newly added Table 9 includes the percentage of correct and incorrect classifications together with recall, precision, specificity, accuracy, and F1-score.
9	There is a lack of definitional clarity regarding reading engagement. It is unclear if engagement comprises attitudes, frequency, and skills or only attitudes and frequency. This needs to be clarified.	We added a diagram to the first paragraph to further clarify our definition of reading engagement.
10	The piece is quite enjoyable to read, with an engaging narrative flow and clear structure. However, I would suggest fusing the section entitled 'Limitations' with the one describing the methodology. As it is now, this short section on the limitations breaks the flow shifting from the results to the analysis. The merging of these sections is also an opportunity to make the article shorter.	We have moved the limitations discussion to the end of the methodology section (p. 6).

Some things that really stand out in Table 9 are that I have a tendency to typically (but not always) 'match the energy' of my reviewers; critical feedback can be delivered in a wide range of voices, and reviewer input can be incredibly useful.

How to say no

Some people are better at saying no than others, and as a doctoral student you are indoctrinated to be responsive to feedback. Deciding not to enact it in some instances can be very hard to adjust to, and even impossible in some instances, given the power imbalances at play in the doctoral journey. However, even if you are the biggest people-pleaser in the world, you should not make changes that will make your article significantly worse, and what will you do when you get two reviewers suggesting opposite actions? You'll have to say no to someone. Alternatively, your first natural instinct may be to always say no to every single requested revision, but that will probably be to the detriment of your paper, and make the likelihood of publication low unless you can mount a very strong argument in favour of total resistance.

In my experience, there are three kinds of revisions. The first kind will make your paper better. The second kind won't lead to any material improvement, but it also won't make your paper any worse; that said, they may be time-consuming and therefore a poor investment. The third kind will introduce errors and issues into your paper. I used to only push back against doing the third kind, but now that I'm a more experienced researcher and even more time-poor than ever before, I often push back against any instances of the second kind that will take up too much of my time, given that they cannot be justified for notable benefit.

A 'no' needs to be expressed in a manner that is justified, professional, respectful and will preserve your relationship with the editorial team if realistically possible. Table 9 provides some illustrative real examples where I felt that my research would suffer if a change was made, or ethical concerns would come into play, requiring me to somewhat diplomatically say no.

So how does a novice researcher learn where to draw the line?

You need to accept that you won't always know at this stage of your career; it is not unusual for doctoral students to waste energy defending a position because they don't fully understand a method or a field. As mentioned earlier, you are urged to seek an informed second (or even third or fourth) opinion on the validity of your response, and this person can be referred to as a 'broker':

> Complex and difficult decisions need to be made about how to address reviewer comments in terms of the disciplinary knowledge, debates, structural framing and the discourses of the target journal. Publication brokering can be done by a variety of people – supervisors, colleagues, writing mates, writing groups and other academic professionals.
>
> (Thomson & Kamler, 2012, p. 134)

Be sure that resisting is the right choice, and not just a knee-jerk reaction to criticism. Once you know that you are not overreacting or underreacting and that your decision-making in this space is reasonable and informed by the current research, you can get down to the business of carefully and respectfully arguing your point in your table of changes, using substantiating references/evidence as applicable.

In addition to Table 9, here's some sample wording on how you can say no in three different scenarios, and when to use them.

1 When the reviewer wishes that your paper was about their own personal interest that is genuinely irrelevant or tangentially relevant to your work, and you couldn't make the changes anyway without a time-machine.
   We appreciate that the peer reviewer sees merit in refocusing the paper onto apples. While investigating apples would make a useful contribution to the literature, and it's certainly something in our sights for future research, for the purposes of this paper we are focusing on stingrays as we feel that the research gap in this space warrants more urgent inquiry. Furthermore, the research has already been conducted, and thus it would be impossible to accommodate this request without substantial additional resourcing.

2 When a requested change is outside the scope of the paper and it's not reasonable to introduce it.
   While Reviewer 1 introduces a unique and creative perspective that we feel warrants deeper consideration in future, more tailored works, it is outside the scope of this paper as defined in scope by our RQs.

3 When the reviewer asks you to make a change that is literally contradicted by the research.
   While Reviewer 3 introduces a novel point, we feel that it is contradicted by the more recent, larger scale work of Rodent and Broccoli (2023) (which we have now referenced in the paper on page 3, see tracked changes version). We have now also explicitly addressed this tension in our paper (also see page 3 in tracked changes version).

Sometimes when you say no, that will be the end of your journey with this journal (at least in relation to this manuscript). In our recent article (Merga et al., 2025), a journal associated with 'a prior negative experience' was given 'the benefit of the doubt' by my tenacious co-author Mason, but the experience was not better the next time around:

> The paper was accepted quite quickly, the reviews were fair, and I responded to them all. The paper was accepted and we were told to get ready for proofs. Then ... an email came saying we didn't address one of the comments. We had, but we responded in depth detailing why we couldn't accede, and the argument was

strong. There is no way I thought they would turn around and say, literally, change it or we don't publish. So, I pulled the paper. It was such a waste of our time, the reviewers' time, the editor's time. That one associate editor could hold a paper to ransom for a flawed argument, seemed like just a power play. (Mason)

(Merga et al., 2025, p. 4)

As such, while you may say no and provide what you believe to be a fulsome explanation and justification, there is no guarantee that this will be accepted, and rejection on what you perceived to be an invalid point can really rankle. When you plan on saying no, ensure you put enough time into your justification so that you have no regrets if this kind of worst-case scenario plays out.

Rejection

I have already written a bit about rejection in this book in relation to desk rejection. Your manuscript doesn't have to be scrapped, it just needs reworking and rehoning. Do not throw it in the bin or relegate it to the dusty drawer of doom that holds relics of all your past failings (am I the only person with a drawer like this?).

But before you can get your rejected paper accepted, you must understand and be honest about why it got rejected. And if you don't know, find out from your mentors, supervisors and other supports. It may feel a bit like ripping off a Band-Aid/plaster in slow motion to show them the negative feedback accompanying your rejection, but it's a very valuable learning opportunity and you may find solace as well.

The problem could be 100% in your control, 100% on your co-authors, 100% on the peer reviewers or lack of editorial oversight, or any combination. The main thing is, don't blow up or burn bridges if the people you go to for advice kindly and reasonably tell you that the main reasons for rejection were under your control. You are not supposed to be a master at this; again, a PhD is a research apprenticeship, and even when the supervisors have done their job well in terms of providing you with good mentoring and feedback, you still might get rejected because *it happens to the best in the field*. Problems that are 'you' problems are the best, as they are potentially easiest to change with training, reading, experience and good advice. Rejection is a chance to update, tighten, clarify, enhance focus and resonate more effectively with a clear audience in mind. See the previous section on desk rejection for more insights on how to do this.

The copyedit

The copyediting process should ideally be a smooth and speedy experience where your manuscript is given a final and close check by both you and a copyediting team. You will receive a marked-up manuscript with author queries to respond to, and have a final chance to read through, pick up any minor typographical errors, update any references, and if you have not already done so, reverse any anonymisation. Sometimes you will do this on a PDF, but in my experience it is more typical to do it on an online platform unique to the academic publisher; some of these have improved a lot in recent times and have become much easier to navigate, though one major academic publisher is still using a terrible platform that I can never use, forcing me to the Plan B of submitting an annotated PDF every time.

However, I must emphatically stress that *you cannot just relax at copyedit stage*. You can't safely assume that errors will not be introduced to your manuscript during this stage, and you should not assume that the copyeditor knows enough about the subject area you are covering to make corrections that are actually appropriate. You may also find yourself grappling with very unfriendly editing systems, being locked out after arbitrary password resets, and experiencing lengthy delays in communicating with the copyediting team over any issues that arise.

The pressure is on: copyedits are accompanied by a pretty tight turnaround in terms of timing (usually between 48 hours and six days). As I write this section, on the weekend I was sent an email from one of the big academic publishers letting me know that it was time to copyedit an upcoming paper. They sent me a new username to use the copyediting system but no password. While they included a link for me to reset my password 'if you do not know your password' (and how could I know my password if it has never been given to me?), this system doesn't appear to be automated, so it takes many hours to actually receive the password enabling me to do the copyedits. While their email stresses how time-sensitive this is, I'm not the one holding up the process. This is a constant issue with this academic publisher, and one that I have raised with them multiple times. Fun times are had when the password is finally reset and issued, but for the *wrong username* (each time I publish with them they issue me with a new one, as apparently the old one can't be reused). This has also happened multiple times, holding up the process and causing the requested turnaround time to be exceeded. Be aware that the inefficiencies of some copyediting systems and poor and lagged communications pose a challenge to getting this work done within the complex workload on your plate.

If you are fortunate enough to have open access funding covered by institutional licensing, some academic publishers will quickly and easily grant this to you while you are signing your agreements just prior to the copyedit stage, but there is one academic publisher where this is a constant arm-wrestle leading to multiple emails being sent during copyedit stage, and significant time invested as you try to get the publisher to recognise the agreement that they already applied to another article a month before. This publisher has asked me multiple times to accept the raising of an invoice for between $4,000 and $5,000 which they then promise to cancel due to the existing agreement.

There has also been some contention around the use of AI for copyediting purposes emerging in recent times. Allegations that AI introduced significant errors sparked mass resignation from an Elsevier journal:

> In fall of 2023, for example, without consulting or informing the editors, Elsevier initiated the use of AI during production, creating article proofs devoid of capitalization of all proper nouns (e.g., formally recognized epochs, site names, countries, cities, genera, etc.) as well italics for genera and species. These AI changes reversed the accepted versions of papers that had already been properly formatted by the handling editors.
>
> (Former Editorial Board at the Journal of Human Evolution, 2024, p. 2)

It is pretty standard for my work to receive fewer than 10 author queries for me to attend to. In one instance in 2024 I received a copyedit that had a staggering *91 author queries* and so many errors introduced I was either dealing with an absolute novice or AI. Most of the suggested changes were pointless, and many of them were grammatically incorrect. Luckily, due to my experience, I knew that the situation was not even remotely normal, but I was very concerned that junior researchers may be exposed to this and think that it is standard practice, so I wrote to the editor to raise the issue. I was quickly sent a more 'standard' copyedit with far fewer suggested changes, but I'll probably never know whether my feedback made any difference, and whether there were any other 'victims' of this diabolical copyedit. As such, given that it is likely that academic journals will continue to experiment with AI, and given that AI can be notably flawed at this stage, if something feels off, speak to your supervisory team and get their support to request a standard copyedit done by a knowledgeable human.

Which is the easiest method to get over the line?

Which is the most reviewer-friendly research method?

As I've published in peer-reviewed journals across a wide range of methods, I often get asked this question, particularly given there's a lack of comparative research in this area, so what we are working with is typically anecdotal anyway.

I'm not sure why there seems to be a common perception that qualitative research will be easier to move through peer review than quantitative research. This has not been my experience at all; personally, purely quantitative research has been *far easier* to get over the line in peer review, even in higher impact journals, than qualitative or mixed methods research. Perhaps it is because as long as quantitative research follows a clearly articulated and rigorous method in its design, conduct and reporting, it's relatively hard to find fault with it. To be honest, I have found peer reviewers of my quantitative work vastly more reasonable in their expectations of what can be achieved through the peer-review process, as I explore further herein.

Recent research (which incidentally has a truly magnificent title!) on the challenges of getting qualitative papers through peer review focuses on perceived peer-reviewer deficiencies. Respondents felt that

> peer reviewers and editors universalized the assumptions and expectations of postpositivist research and reporting. Some also reported that peer reviewers and editors universalized the norms and values particular to specific qualitative approaches. Contributors were concerned that peer reviewers often accept review invitations when they lack relevant methodological expertise and editors often select peer reviewers without such expertise.
>
> (Clarke et al., 2024, p. 1)

The major thing that I have (anecdotally and personally) comparatively noticed while moving research through peer review is that qualitative researchers are far more likely to try to redirect your work towards *their own area of research interest*, even if it's only tangentially relevant to your research. While I can't think of a single instance where this has happened to me while attempting to publish quantitative data, it has happened many times while attempting to publish qualitative data. It's always really depressing to read these kinds of reviews because they are an unwarranted intrusion on your research work, demanding you magically transport yourself back in time to conduct research better aligned with their own personal research interests; in these instances, the problem isn't your work, it is that it isn't *their* work.

While we need actual research to confirm this, it's possible that the hardest research to move through peer review is actually mixed methods, as I've noted in our previous work:

> The revisions I find the hardest to accommodate are typically those on mixed-methods papers, where I keep getting reviews from people who are exclusively into quantitative or qualitative method. The quantitative people typically ask me to remove, deemphasize or quantise the qualitative data. The qualitative people sometimes don't understand what the quantitative data are saying, and again they ask me to remove or deemphasize the quantitative component.
>
> (Merga et al., 2018, p. 384)

However, I have anecdotally noticed (touch wood) that it is becoming a little easier to move mixed-methods research through peer review as familiarity with this kind of research grows.

Overall, while we have a notable research gap in this area, according to my anecdotal experience, quantitative research is the easiest to get through peer review in the fields where I have published it. While future research may prove my contention completely wrong and just a typical ungeneralisable 'sample of one' situation, in the meantime I strongly suggest that you do not use a perception that the qualitative peer-review experience will somehow be easier to inform the methodological choices relevant to your PhD. Just stick to using the methods that will best enable you to address your RQs, whatever they are.

## CHAPTER 7

Knowledge Mobilisation

When my friends and family asked me why I wanted to do a PhD, there were a lot of reasons, many associated with my family and child-rearing situation at that time, as the scholarship I won meant that I could afford to take time off full-time work to pursue it. However, personal circumstances aside, a key reason was that I simply thought that it would be great if we had a better understanding of how social influences can impact on young people's recreational book reading, with a view to empowering a range of social influences to support young people to read more often, and beyond the early years. Too often encouraging teenagers to maintain or develop an avid reading orientation was being put in the 'too hard basket', or deprioritised in my view. Given the range of benefits of an ongoing reading for pleasure habit that were emerging in the research, and lack of attention on this issue at that time in my context in Australia, I felt that I could really add value in this space.

Others also undertake a PhD in the hope that it will lead to some kind of real-world change, reaching end-user stakeholders beyond academia (Mason et al., 2020a). While there are practical and motivational reasons for this, increasing focus on real-world relevance is also an institutional and international research goal tied to funding:

> Society expects only research that offers the greatest social benefits in terms of economy, health, culture, etc., to receive funding, although there is considerable disagreement with regard to defining these 'greatest social benefits' and determining the criteria for allocation in a democratic society . . .
>
> (Schweiger et al., 2024, p. 1)

Of course, if we do research with high real-world relevance but only publish it in scholarly journals without sharing it beyond academia, it is unlikely to permeate. TBP students wanting to make this broader contribution will begin to grapple with the dimensions of KMb, which positions the sharing of research knowledge as an act of knowledge exchange between researchers and stakeholders who can contribute to, and gain from this exchange (Levin, 2013; Merga, 2021a). Note the focus on *sharing* here; KMb does not have to simply be a knowledge dump from a researcher to a receptive audience beyond academia, but rather a mutually beneficial sharing of knowledge, needs and experience.

Doctoral students and ECRs are already doing this KMb work. Research with ECRs in Australia and Japan found that they used many different avenues to promote their work to *both* the academic community and key stakeholders beyond it (Merga & Mason, 2020a). However, support was more typically found for the production of scholarly outputs rather than those designed for the consumption of audiences outside academia, and you can't necessarily assume that your supervisors or other academic mentors are well equipped to educate you in specific KMb skills and knowledge unless they have a track record in this space (Merga & Mason, 2021b). You may even find yourself educating them about the importance of KMb, and the ways in which to successfully achieve it. I'm also concerned that while expectations for KMb have ramped up in many institutions, recognition of the potential magnitude of this related workload may be poor (Merga, 2021a), and we badly need research that looks at the implications of undertaking high levels of KMb activities for doctoral completion.

We also need more research that looks at the impact of KMb on other outcomes within and beyond candidature, such as possible benefits for securing post-doctoral employment. While my reasons for wanting to be active in KMb through my TBP journey were lofty and ideological (naturally I wanted to change the world!), the possible career benefits could also warrant consideration for the more pragmatic, strategic student seeking to enhance their employment prospects. A growing volume of candidates pursuing a PhD do so in order to enhance their prospects in a professional field rather than as a bridge to academia, and this has influenced the nature of doctoral education in some contexts (McKenna & van Schalkwyk, 2024). While more research is needed, it is certainly likely that a TBP that includes published SOs can facilitate connection to professional or industry fields, increasing your visibility and acknowledged expertise in their spaces, while also being responsive to current real-world challenges and issues (García-Morante et al., 2024).

In this regard, it can be contended that a TBP might be the best option for PhD aspirants who are looking to use their degree to establish themselves within their professions, rather than to lever themselves into academia. They will finish their degree with multiple SOs rather than just one traditional thesis, and these SOs will have been exposed to a higher level of scrutiny, having gone through both peer review and thesis examination, but these SOs can also be used to enter into knowledge exchanges with stakeholders beyond academia during candidature when they are published. You might struggle to get industry and the professions to engage with a door-stop traditional monograph thesis, whereas they might be happier to look at and use the findings of SOs.

SOs may also be published in research journals with a wide professional readership, which was the case for some of the SOs in my own TBP. For example, see Merga, 2014b: the expected audience for this research journal is 'teachers of older learners', and it is available to all members of the International Literacy Association (Wiley, 2024b). When choosing this journal at the time, along with the relevant considerations outlined earlier in this book, I took into account the excellent reach outside academia. While more research is needed in this area, it is possible that a TBP may be more useful for bridging the gap between academic and real-world needs, as I explore subsequently in this section (e.g. Merga, 2015).

Opening up the conversation

One of the reasons that doctoral students may be hesitant to share their work during candidature in SOs and other related KMb outputs may be due to fears of inexperience and exposure, and I and other researchers have talked about marginally shifting our positions on some matters during the research process, perhaps dealing with some concepts in a less simplistic way, or adding further refinement to other aspects of our work (Mason et al., 2022). However, as long as you have the oversight of an experienced and knowledgeable supervisory team, these issues will be minimised, and indeed perhaps captured during the peer-review process, and as Mason found, being transparent about these shifts can actually be appreciated in examination:

> My supervisor stressed very clearly that is part of the process, and just because something is published doesn't make it [exempt] from critique or further development (by oneself or others), and so I came eventually to cherish it for the growth that it reveals – and was very transparent about this in my Prospective PhD by Publication. I worried it would work against me but one of the examiners actually said they loved the transparency.
>
> (Mason et al., 2022, p. 193)

Shifting, revising and refining will happen on your PhD project, but also across your research career; willingness to change your position in response to new research findings is a green flag, not a red flag. In the unlikely event that a retraction is needed as a substantial error has been made, while not ideal, this is not the end of the world: even 'some of the biggest names in scientific integrity' have faced retractions (Else, 2024, para. 1). While this issue of readiness and stability of insights is usually explored in relation to scholarly publishing, it is also very much worthy of consideration in relation to KMb.

Opening a conversation early with stakeholders beyond academia who will be potential consumers of your research can be a good idea as long as you do not anticipate your findings, misrepresent the stage of your research, or collect data from them outside ethics approvals. For example, introducing your project at a professional association conference while it is still in its relative infancy could have some positive effects for you, as I explored in the MOM university training I delivered in 2025.

Early KMb at conferences or other 'sharing' events can lead to:

- **Easier sample recruitment** when recruiting respondents from a professional area. If they are already familiar with your project, they may be more likely to invest the time to provide data for it.
- **Getting current feedback** on the fundamentals. Often a research proposal will be very heavily supported by academic research without necessarily considering the current needs of a professional or industry. You might find yourself getting feedback on an incredibly important consideration not yet captured by the relevant research.
- **Attracting funding/in-kind support.** For example, a professional or industry partner might have access to a resource that they can share with you so that you do not have to purchase that resource to conduct your research.
- **Attract the attention of field leaders beyond academia**. This is literally how I first became an invited keynote speaker; field leaders beyond academia saw the value of my work and then began to approach me with opportunities. The feedback and knowledge-sharing opportunities that have come out of the invited speaking engagements I have done have been *invaluable*, and at times played a huge role in shaping my research priorities. Comments during my presentations have been useful, but just as formative have been discussions I've had with attendees afterwards, when I had the opportunity to stop speaking and listen to their take on my research, and any gaps they would like me to investigate.

More on benefits of KMb on the TBP

The dissemination argument is one of the strongest justifications for the TBP, particularly given that research focused on some HASS fields has found that most PhD dissertation research may not achieve dissemination into the peer-reviewed literature (Evans et al., 2018). While this may be a stronger expectation in STEM, there is a growing desire that doctoral students will be actively involved in KMb, as described by a STEM researcher in Australia:

> . . . as PhD students, our whole team was very much encouraged to go out and do the public events. It wasn't just a case of only the senior academics have the knowledge and understanding to be able to go and tell the public that. It was very much made a point of that, 'Hey, actually, everyone can do that, everybody should do that'. It's something you should get used to right now because the way that the world is kind of moving, we are required to go out and tell the public on not a technical level, but we're required to go and tell the public what we're doing, because a lot of what we do is with public funds.
>
> (Merga & Mason, 2021a, p. 679)

As such, perhaps particularly in the case of public-funded research, this is increasingly a prerogative. It's a good idea to use your TBP journey to learn KMb skills; if you remain in research after your degree, you are almost certainly going to need them, given that 'many funders now require that researchers demonstrate clear commitment to sharing their findings in their funding applications', and you'll need to deliver on that (Merga & Mason, 2020b, para. 3). KMb skills can also be transferable communication skills relevant for use beyond academia. For example, if during or post-PhD you apply for a leadership position in a professional role outside academia that requires strong oral communication skills as part of the selection criteria, and you have recorded examples of your oral KMb activities, your response might link to a podcast you created for a professional audience, or a radio interview that you did to inform the public about your research. You can literally attach recordings of yourself speaking with the media to job applications to demonstrate that you are a persuasive communicator, in-demand and valued, and not overstating the broader societal value of your work.

We know we need to get better at sharing research, and a good place to start within universities is by building the skills needed into doctoral training, and encouraging and supporting the TBP as a thesis model. In their UK context, Robinson-Pant and Singal (2020) note that whilst concerns about dissemination, fuelled by discussions of impact (particularly as noted in the Research Excellence Framework, REF for UK higher education institutions), have become an important part of the reality of established academics, in our own experience over many years as doctoral supervisors and examiners this appears to be less reflected in doctoral training programmes. (p. 859)

They contend that 'it is essential for doctoral students to be more open in communicating and contributing within wider research networks' (p. 862).

Research with ECRs in Australia and Japan found that sharing research with non-academic stakeholders offered a range of benefits (Merga & Mason, 2021c), such as seeing the research used to drive innovation for 'specific occupations, industries or levels of governance' (p. 1487), contributing to social change, opening up avenues for future funding for further research, and fostering KMb exchanges with stakeholders, some of which led to enduring, ongoing partnerships (Merga & Mason, 2021c).

Thinking about connecting SOs with non-academic audiences

While many academics closely consider how their research can be used by end-users beyond academia and explicitly make these connections in their SOs, some papers do not include this detail even where this potential use exists. This can be a missed opportunity.

The longer the time I've spent in academia, the more attention I have paid to making these connections in my SOs where this works for the journal. For example, in our recent article reporting on mixed-methods data analysis from an international project, we were motivated to do the project by the needs of key external stakeholders, SLPs. As such, when we came to writing up our findings, their needs were foremost in our mind:

> . . . instead of delivering the traditional summative conclusion, given the urgency underpinning the findings and discussion, we have chosen to focus on five steps that could be beneficial for immediate enaction to address some of the serious issues raised in this article.
>
> (Merga & Mat Roni, 2025b, p. 12)

We then clearly explain five possible steps that can be taken and highlight some of the interrelationships between them. Given that we are fortunate enough to have open-access funding for this work, we then promoted it on social media with key professional associations tagged to ensure that this article could reach its professional readership. We then received some very interesting feedback from SLPs around the world. If your knowledge contribution for communities beyond academia is clear in your SOs, I am confident that you will see a lot more engagement with your work beyond academia. I will further discuss some of the benefits and risks of promoting work through social media subsequently in this chapter.

Open access and paywall workarounds

While SOs are typically less 'digestible' than knowledge translation works purposely created for non-academic audiences, we still want access to SOs to be as wide and far as possible, contributing to the scholarly community, and (hopefully) resonating beyond. For example, I know for a fact that one of my papers (Merga, 2020a) has regularly been used in discussions between SLPs and school leaders around negotiating their work role, and drawing attention to its complexity in a protective manner, as these professionals have told me that they've done this when I met them at conferences. I drew attention to this SO through a series of keynote presentations so that SLP awareness of its possibilities was raised, but the fact that this open-access 2020 paper has already been accessed more than 16,000 times through the journal website (and many other times where it is also hosted, such as through ResearchGate) is also an indicator that it is being consumed beyond academia. If this paper wasn't open access, this level of dissemination and use by professionals would not be possible.

If you are relatively new to academia, you might not be 100% sure about what is meant by *open access,* and like many promising phenomena in the space, you might be disappointed when you find out its limitations. As mentioned earlier, when we publish our research in academic journals, we have the option of selecting *open-access* availability. It is typical though not universal for academic publishers to charge for journal articles to be open access. Some universities are in the fortunate financial position of being able to sign agreements with academic publishers that enable their staff to publish open access in their journals. It is pretty disappointing that while there is a constant push for open access in research, only those at wealthy universities, or those who can afford to pay individually can publish their work in open access and enjoy the KMb and citation benefits of doing so.

If you are new to open access, it's useful to get your head around the differences in open access licensing. Some journals won't give you any choice in licence selection, whereas others will provide a range of options. I suggest heading over to the licensing page on the Creative Commons website, which at the time of this book publication was accessible here:

https://creativecommons.org/licenses. For example, where I'm allowed to select an agreement, I usually select the Creative Commons Attribution-NonCommercial licence (CC BY-NC 4.0) option. This means that others can reuse my content as long as they use correct attribution and don't use it for commercial gain.

How can I find out limitations on journal article sharing?

If you are at a university that does not hold an agreement to publish open access at the journal that you want to target, you need to go to Plan B for sharing options. Sadly, even though the journal is not going to pay you a single cent for your content, they usually have control over your legal right to share it. Every time you publish in an academic journal, you will almost certainly sign an agreement that will place limitations on your permission to share the published article, and perhaps also earlier iterations of the manuscript.

So if you want to share, but you don't have open access, the first place to check your sharing permissions is your author agreement. If for some reason that information is not available on the author agreement, check the website of the journal. If you can't find the information easily on the website of the journal, you can contact the journal directly.

Alternatively, you can use the Jisc Open policy finder (formerly SHERPA ROMEO): https://openpolicyfinder.jisc.ac.uk. The purpose of this website is 'helping authors and institutions to make informed and confident decisions in open access publication and compliance' (Jisc, 2025a, para. 1), and you can enter the journal name on the website to find out what restrictions apply.

Journals are very specific about which version of your manuscript can be shared with or without associated costs, and whether or not an embargo applies. For example, at one education journal, authors are required to pay open-access fees to share the published version in all instances. However, if you want to share the *accepted but not yet published version of the article* at a fixed range of locations (academic social network; institutional repository; named academic social network; named repository (PubMed Central); subject repository) in this journal, you need to wait 18 months and meet the following conditions:

- Published source must be acknowledged with citation
- Must link to publisher version
- Set statements to accompany deposits (see policy).

(Jisc, 2025b, para. 5)

I need to stress that you should check the conditions and options for each journal in which you publish, given that there is no norm in this space, and the situation doesn't necessarily remain static even at one journal, so you need to keep across changes to avoid accidentally stumbling into legal issues.

It is also worth noting that there are sometimes specific little loopholes that enable you to share the final version of your research with certain audiences even if you have not paid for open access. For example, Wiley (2025c) includes the following valuable information on this:

> You may share any version of your article with individual colleagues and students if you are asked for a copy, as part of teaching and training at your institution (excluding open online sharing), and as part of a grant application, submission of thesis, or doctorate. (para. 2)

You will note that there is some potential ambiguity around how this may apply.

Altmetrics and a few other non-traditional measures of SO impact

I benefit greatly when academics promote their work through social media, and quite a few of the most recent references in this book were included because I came across them on my LinkedIn feed, as either an author or a publisher promoted it in the space (e.g. McChesney et al., 2024). This book has already covered how research performance on SOs is measured through citation count and the h-index, among other measures. However, an SO's impact is often also measured by Altmetric, regardless of whether or not you or your institution is signed up (though if you are not a subscriber, your access to Altmetric analysis is comparatively sparse). When we share research work we encounter on social media, we're not only helping good research find a broader audience: we're also boosting the Altmetric performance of that paper for the benefit of our peers.

So what is Altmetric?

According to their website, 'Altmetric is a system that tracks the attention that research outputs such as scholarly articles and data sets receive online', drawing on data from social media pages, traditional media in English as well as many other languages, blogs, and online reference managers (Altmetric, 2023, para. 1). While it typically takes a while for you to amass citations to SOs, given the length of the peer-reviewing process, Altmetric impact occurs rapidly on publications if you quickly promote your work online, so you will see Altmetric impact well before you see impact on more traditional research measures.

This can be really handy if you are trying to use an SO as the basis of a grant submission that you are arguing is responsive to real-world relevance, as showing a strong Altmetric appeal can be part of your evidence for this contention. My former university (UNDA) wasn't a subscriber, but Figure 6 shows the information still available to me and therefore everyone with access to the internet.

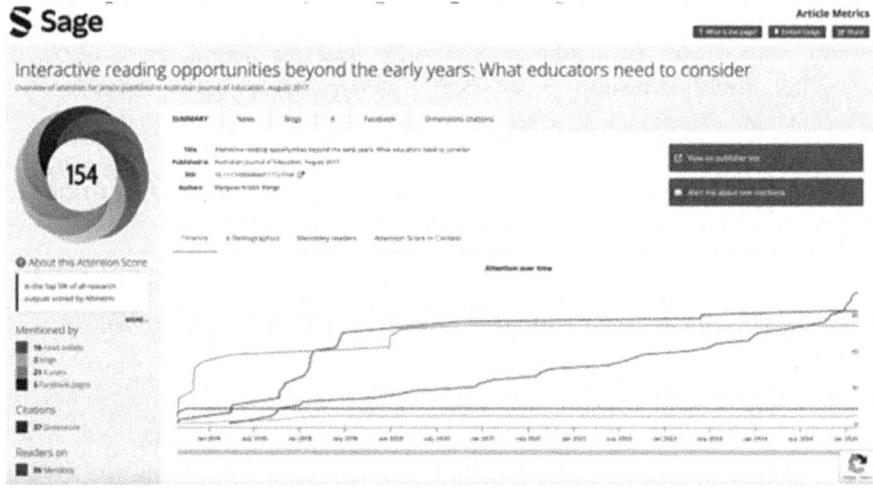

Figure 6 *Screenshot from Altmetric information on Merga, 2017a*

As such, I could link to this page in a grant application if I want to argue that this article is in the top 5% for attention online.

Journals also collect a wealth of information on exposure to your work that you can use to argue for impact beyond the traditional measures. If you are using journal-generated metrics on views or downloads of your open-access work that is available in final or pre-print form elsewhere, you should know that it is a limitation that these metrics will not include every access. For example, a journal might capture a viewing figure of 10,000 on an open-access article, but this article might also be available via ResearchGate, where it has an additional 2,000 views, as well as via an institutional repository, where it has 800 views, and other sources such as the pages of professional associations, where views *are not being counted at all*. As such, you can't claim that the journal figure is the all-encompassing figure.

This noted, I have still used both *most views* and *most downloads* status as a flex to apply for grants as well as academic positions as follows (also see Figures 7 and 8):

> **Most viewed**: Some of my research articles are the most read of all time in specific Q1-ranked scholarly journals. For example, one of my articles on struggling literacy learners is currently the most viewed article of all time in well-regarded UK literacy journal English in Education, with more than 40,000 views (as per image). I also authored the second-most viewed article of all time (with more than 29,000 views).

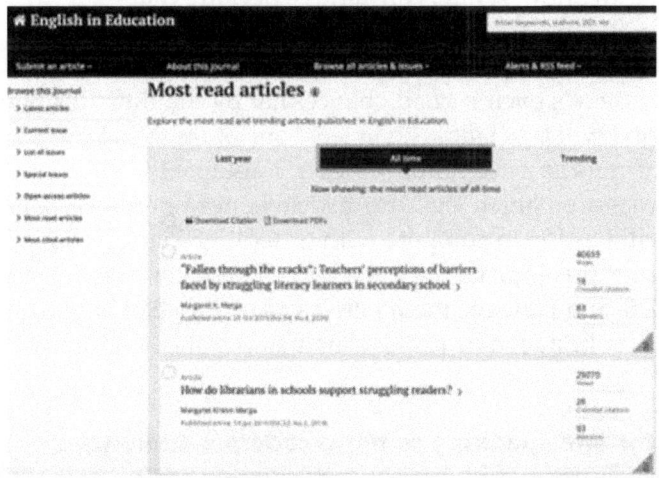

Figure 7 *Screenshot from English in Education*

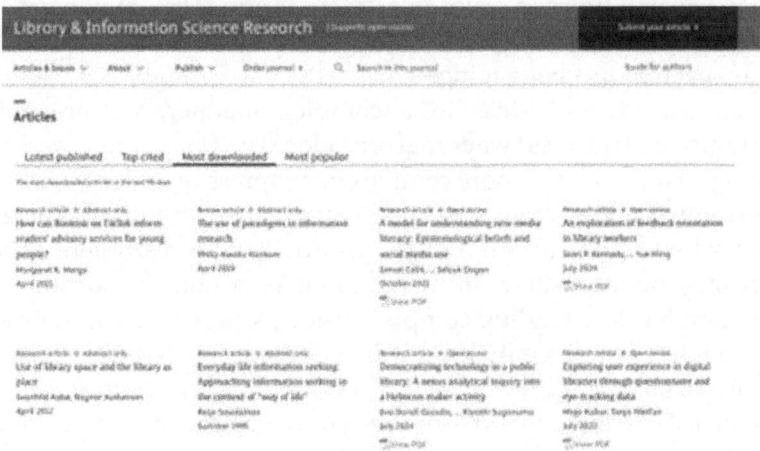

Figure 8 *Screenshot from* Library & Information Science Research

Most downloaded: Similarly, my article on BookTok on TikTok is the most downloaded in its cross-disciplinary and well-regarded US journal, which is pretty good as I didn't have funding to make it open access.

When I make these kinds of claims in funding applications, in addition to including a current image, I include a hyperlink so that my claim can be externally verified. This also comes in handy so that I can quickly check that my article is still the most viewed or most downloaded if I want to paste in the same content for a future application. I am like the evil stepmother in Snow White, constantly checking that I am the fairest one of all!

This is important as these figures are subject to *constant change*, and I know that there's even a good chance that by the time this book goes to publication I will lose status on at least one of these as I can't continually update during the publication process. I am most likely to lose the *most downloaded* status given that this article is not open access, and I don't think it will be able to compete with other high-performing open-access articles from this journal for very long. These statuses were current in March 2025, and I'll leave them here as an example of how to create your own research impact narratives drawing on some quantitative elements.

Writing for and speaking to non-academic audiences

Think back to the first time you read a dense research methods paper in English as a fledgling researcher. You may have needed to read the same sentence several times in order to extract meaning. You may have asked yourself, 'Is this even English?' Those from EAL backgrounds may have found it even more challenging.

When we express ideas in a complex manner, we are able to communicate in nuanced ways that are laden with both explicit and subtle meanings. However, the more complex our expression becomes, the more readers are excluded from what it attempts to communicate. This is the reason why some health messages produced by government organisations may be ineffective; in many contexts, a notable portion of the population has low reading comprehension skills, so written messaging that is pitched at university level will be inaccessible to these consumers (Ferguson et al., 2021).

As such, if we only share our research through academic journal articles and other SOs, our findings may have limited impact beyond academia. When we commit to writing and speaking for non-academic audiences, we break down this barrier, though this is a skill set that is often neglected in doctoral and ECR education. Taking complex ideas and presenting them in an accessible manner without changing or distorting their meaning is not easy, and compared with support for producing academic outputs, 'far less support for producing research outputs for non-academic users may be provided during doctoral candidature' (Merga & Mason, 2021a, p. 672). In our study of ECRs in Australia and Japan, we found that

> communication skill gaps emerged as a salient challenge. Japan-based STEM ECR Maya explained that 'to take some technical words and to explain the concept using simple words is quite difficult', a sentiment mirrored by Roc, who described difficulty translating academic jargon into accessible language. For Demelza, a greater challenge was finding 'the right outlet' for communication with non-academic end users, as 'it's hard to make that happen, you have to go and find it and figure out which channel and who and finding the right person'. As such, the concerns around communication related to use of appropriate voice (with close attention to complexity of terms), as well as identifying and utilising optimal outlets.
>
> (Merga & Mason, 2021c, p. 1492)

These skill gaps can have implications for those seeking to use their PhD beyond academia, as found by recent research on gaps in PhD training identified by PhD holders employed outside academia:

> Notably, among the critical skill gaps identified, the ability to effectively communicate with diverse audiences is particularly prominent. While the OECD (2013) report underscores the societal value of PhDs, emphasising both research conduct and information dissemination, recent evidence suggests a predominant emphasis on effective communication in many non-academic PhD careers (McAlpine and Castelló, 2024). This result accentuates the significance and often-overlooked nature of the prevalent communication modes and genres in such contexts. Our findings provide evidence – not present in previous studies – that PhD holders might perceive themselves as ill-prepared to engage with genres and audiences beyond academia.
>
> (García-Morante et al., 2024, p. 16)

If your university is not offering any support for developing a KMb skill set, you should request it, perhaps in the form of writing for Plain Language communication, or the more specialised request for media training supporting public speaking skills.

When I was completing my PhD, there was fortunately a strong emphasis on KMb at my university (ECU). This meant that I was exposed to free media training sessions led by experts on campus. The year after my PhD conferral, I wrote about how engaging in media opportunities during my PhD helped me to ensure my findings permeated:

> I found undertaking the process highly conducive to communicating my findings beyond academia, to reach teachers, adolescents and parents. The coverage of my work in the newspaper The *West Australian* (Hiatt, 2014; King, 2014) led to it being picked up by ABC online (Wynne, 2014), social networking pages and online blogs and websites (e.g. Byrne, 2015; Costa, 2014). This led to a trickle-down effect, with references to my work appearing in school newsletters both in Australia and in the UK, which was one of my ultimate translation goals. I was also interviewed for an audio podcast for JAAL and an audio/visual podcast for the *Australian Journal of Education*. The media opportunities have not only led to a dissemination of my findings; they have also increased opportunities for networking and collaboration in my field.
>
> (Merga, 2015, p. 294)

The media interest during my PhD was a real surprise, given that my topic wasn't one that I thought would exactly set the world on fire (book reading!), though it mattered a lot to me, and I believed it had an important educative purpose. Since that time, I have continued to be involved in KMb. Though in more recent times I've had to scale back the extent of my commitment due to time constraints I've outlined in previous work (Merga, 2021a), given that my research always has a pragmatic purpose, I'm always interested in amplifying it where possible.

If your university is not willing or able to provide this training and support, here are some self-directed learning possibilities so that you can start to upskill in this area on your own. One of the easiest areas to self-teach in terms of available free resourcing may be by grasping the role of *readability* in written communication, which I very briefly introduced earlier in this book. Readability refers to 'how accessible a text is to an intended audience' (Merga, 2023a, p. 101), and this can be calculated by drawing on a variety of different common formulas (Ferguson et al., 2021). For example, considering readability in relation to school-issued communication and implications for teachers, as a university-educated educator, you may find yourself inadvertently pitching your content to those with a similar level of literacy when in reality, the literacy levels in some aspects of your school community, such as linguistically diverse parents, may be far lower.

(Merga, 2023a, p. 101)

One of the biggest barriers to mastering readability comes from the fact that if you are reading this book, you probably have strong reading comprehension skills, and therefore there is a chance that you may not be able to understand the struggles of those with low reading comprehension unless you have a reading disorder, come from an EAL background, or you have attempted to learn another language.

So how can we know how 'readable' our writing is?

One really useful free online tool is the Health Literacy Editor created by the Sydney Health Literacy Lab (n.d.-a), currently found here: https://shell.techlab.works. You can simply paste some of your text into the field and get an assessment of its readability, as seen in Figure 9.

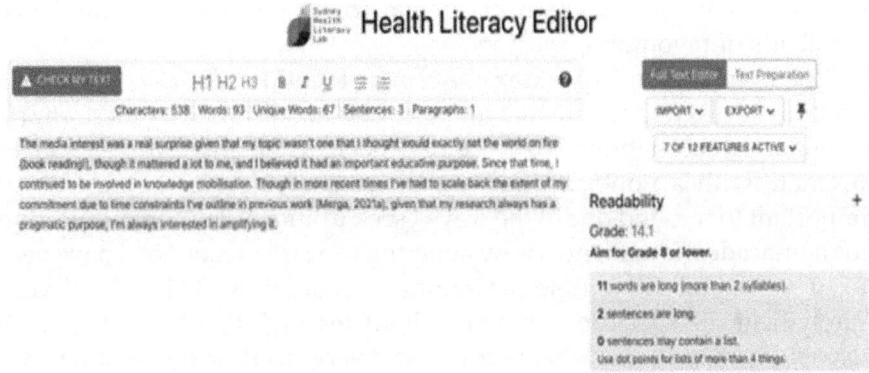

Figure 9 *Screenshot from Health Literacy Editor*

What is a 'good' level of readability to be understood by 'most'?

Given the widely varying levels of literacy in the general public, it simply is not possible to be accessible to all through the written medium without activating adjunct multimodal supports, such as read-aloud options for those at a very low level of English literacy. Furthermore, there is no universal consensus on readability levels for the general public. That said, to be understood by 'most', though there is no agreed universal target, the target has often been set at 'grade six in the US and year eight in Australia' (Ferguson et al., 2021, p. 117), and the Sydney Health Literacy Lab (n.d.-b) recommends Grade 8 as a target. What you aim for completely depends on the projected literacy level of your audience, whether they be industry CEOs or school-age children. As per Figure 6, the text I pasted in is at a level higher than high school, but the Health Literacy Editor shows me where to make changes to lower the complexity.

Another way of alienating your audience is through the use of jargon and unfamiliar acronyms which have not been clearly defined. I can think of several instances where I have gone into a conference presentation only to get completely lost early on due to overuse of these two elements. This is partly my own fault because I like to go to presentations that are somewhat tangential to my current research interests as I'm always interested in expanding my scope and learning about areas that I'm currently unfamiliar with. When presenting to audiences that may include non-expert members, briefly taking the time to define and/or introduce acronyms and concepts using clearly accessible language can do a lot to make sure the audience can travel with you. This is also an important consideration for where you are using concepts that have some controversy or ambiguity around their framing. If you don't pin down the exact dimensionality of your own working use of a concept, it is not uncommon at conferences in particular for this to trigger an audience member's unfavourable reaction.

When writing and speaking for non-academic audiences, great care needs to be taken to ensure that messages are not distorted by these efforts to enhance accessibility, or by a real need to be entertaining and to resonate with a non-academic audience. Credible messaging is very important to me, and one of the ways I seek to anchor my communication for non-academic audiences is by adhering to a strict sequence. I have very fixed views about credible messaging in relation to KMb. You'll very rarely hear me speak to the media about research that has *not yet gone through peer review*, and whenever I do so, I very clearly state this limitation regardless of my audience. In my opinion, media and social media spaces are crowded with pseudo experts and I don't want to add to the already huge volume of misinformation and disinformation, to be another opinion in a sea of opinions.

When I do research that I need to mobilise beyond academia, usually once it has been accepted having passed through a credible external process of peer review at a reputable journal, I start to think about the best way to share it, and the knowledge passes through *credible* to *readable* to *adapted* to *activated* outputs (further developed from Merga, 2021a). In Table 10, here's one example of what this looks like that does the double duty of also explaining what I mean by this.

Table 10 *Example of KMb and SO sequence*

Sequence stage and purpose	Example output	'Title' and description of output	Likely audience of output
1 *Credible:* Findings accepted SO through academic peer review. Authored by researcher, peer-reviewer input.	Merga, 2017a	'Interactive reading opportunities beyond the early years: What educators need to consider.' Peer-reviewed academic journal article.	Researchers and perhaps educators.
2 *Readable:* Based on SO but findings rewritten for a broader audience, still linked to original SO. Authored by researcher, editor input.	Merga, 2017b	'Research shows the importance of parents reading with children – even after children can read. 'Plain-language explainer article.	Parents, educators and the public.
3 *Adapted:* Merga 2017b triggers media interest, findings framed and communicated by media outlet based on radio interview with Merga. Authored by media (Wynne), researcher input.	Wynne, 2017	'Parents, teachers stop reading aloud too early and kids are missing out, researcher says' *Online news report* based on ABC radio interview (ABC Radio Perth, 2017) with Merga after the piece in *The Conversation* came out (Merga, 2017b)	Parents, educators and the public.
4 *Activated:* Department of Education Western Australia *Never Stop Reading* programme. Supported by hand-outs and resources, promoted through the media with researcher key political figure, promoted via school visits by key political figure. Written resources authored by Department of Education, researcher input.	Department of Education Western Australia	Multimodal *Never Stop Reading* programme	Parents, educators and the public.

(adapted from Merga, 2021a)

You will note from Table 10 that from a researcher perspective, I moved from having high control over the messaging at *credible* stage, to relatively low control when it is *activated* by the government department using the *credible* and *readable* outputs as their guide for new innovation. At activated stage,

> research is transformed into an intervention or framework by someone else, purposefully repositioned for a professional or other real-world purpose. In terms of sharing knowledge, at activated stage this involves the highest level of stakeholder influence in the sense that my work has become absorbed into theirs.
>
> (Merga, 2021a, p. 661)

While I still had input into this activated output, I certainly wasn't approving drafts or dictating the form that the messaging would take. As such, if you become active in KMb, there can be a time when your work is being transformed and championed by others, with the KMb labour passing out of your hands to some extent. I'll touch on some of the implications of losing control of your messaging in the later section on dealing with challenging end-users and the media.

While traditionally there has been far less focus on speaking skills in doctoral education, relatively recent initiatives such as the Three Minute Thesis (known as 3MT) have been launched to counter a perceived deficit in graduates' ability to 'communicate with non-specialist audiences', and 'widespread imbalance of privileging academic writing skills at the expense of spoken communication skills in higher degree programs and to better prepare graduate students for future academic or non-academic careers' (Hu & Liu, 2018, p. 17). If available in your context, signing up for the 3MT from early in your doctoral journey can help you develop the capacity to speak under pressure and share your findings in an accessible, audience-aligned manner.

Plain Language pieces

In Table 10, I introduced the idea of the readable output or Plain Language piece, which is a transformation of SO content into more simple language so that it can be comprehended by those with a broader range of reading comprehension skills. These pieces are often peppered with hyperlinks to the original peer-reviewed research so that interested readers can refer back to the more complex source to verify credibility and explore the original work. In my academic roles, and in my professional capacity as Lead Consultant for Merga Consulting, I have also created numerous

Plain Language resources on contract for international organisations, and I am really pleased with this body of work (e.g. Merga, 2022a; 2022b; 2022c; 2022d).

The main point of the Plain Language piece is to reach an audience beyond academia with a purposefully tailored version, making the original research more broadly accessible, and sometimes this is at least in part due to research funder requirements. Funding bodies increasingly seek connections and purpose of research beyond academia, requiring evidence of research dissemination planning, and responsibilities for publication and sharing of research are increasingly situated as an integral part of the process of conducting research (British Education Research Association (BERA), 2024):

> Educational researchers should communicate their findings, and the practical significance of their research, in a clear, straightforward fashion, and in language judged appropriate to the intended audience(s). Researchers have a responsibility to make the results of their research available for the benefit of educational professionals, policymakers and the wider public . . . (p. 30)

As such there is increasing expectation that researchers communicate their findings where relevant with a broad base of end-users, and for an array of purposes, and the inclusion of Plain Language pieces as a projected output on a funding submission may enhance its likelihood of success.

Careful attention is given during the construction of Plain Language pieces to ensure that they are at a readability level suitable for their audience as previously explored. These pieces are often available through accessible platforms such as *The Conversation*, enabling research to be readily consumed by educators and the general public.

As with SOs, Plain Language pieces are often produced by researchers for no publisher-related remuneration in order to ensure that their research has an impact on audiences beyond academia, but at least you (usually) don't need to (directly) pay for open access. The lines are getting more blurred on this, however, and I am increasingly receiving spam emails from new organisations promising to help me publicise my work for a fee, while also expecting me to provide free content. I can safely say that I will never agree to this. Given that you will be providing free content to the platform, I'm not a fan of models that require you to also pay for this opportunity.

In this vein, while the popular platform *The Conversation* does not pay its contributors, recent correspondence from them suggests that donating 'member' universities are given significant preferential treatment when pitches from academics to *The Conversation* are considered by the editorial team. See Figure 10 for their automated response to pitches in January 2025.

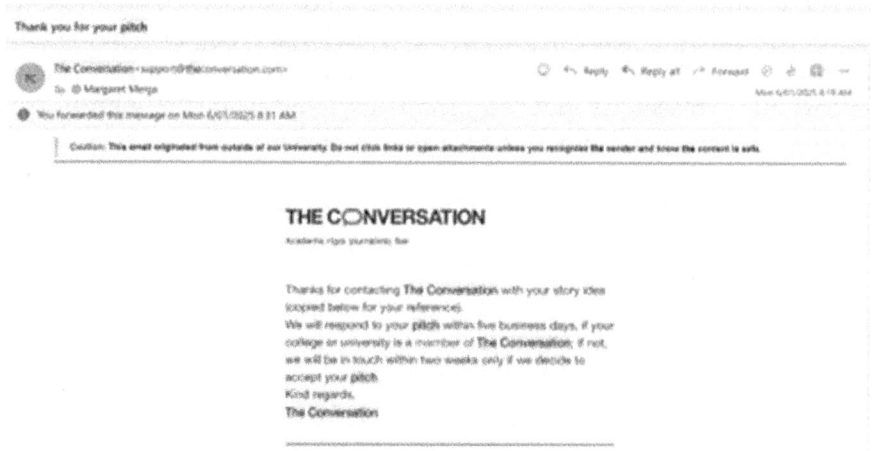

Figure 10 *Automated reply from* The Conversation, *2025*

In 2024, 39% of *The Conversation*'s Australian and New Zealand revenue was from 'Australian and New Zealand university members and research partners' (p. 18), listed on page 25 of this document. Despite Figure 10, *The Conversation* claims to be 'the world's leading independent publisher of research-based news and analysis' (2024, p. 24). However, it seems that wealthier universities in the position to hold member status may be more likely to have their research amplified through this mechanism and enjoy KMb advantages, further compounding their privilege described previously in relation to SOs and open access. There is not a level playing field for research communication and impact. It is not always the case that your university will have to pay a donation or subscription for your work to be given equal consideration, and remuneration is not out of the question; I would love to see a strong competitor to *The Conversation* emerge.

Finally, while I value these opportunities, I have found that my in-person, bi-directional interactions with stakeholders outside academia on my research have been more satisfying than written pieces. When we get to speak and interact, I have been able to find out possible translation needs of end-users and present my research accordingly, and listen closely to end-user needs. For example, the aspects of my research that I emphasise will differ if I am speaking with a father trying to encourage his teenage daughter to read more, or if I am speaking with a teacher librarian seeking to reinstate Silent Reading as a weekly practice for all students in their school. Platforms like *The Conversation* may not replace the importance of face-to-face opportunities to share knowledge, though they can bring attention to your work to connect you with these opportunities.

Dealing with challenging end-users and the media

While expectations that you share your research beyond academia continue to be ramped up by institutions and funders, the labour involved in actually doing this is often massively underestimated, and the complexity and risks of this kind of communication are often poorly recognised (Merga, 2021a). There is limited extant research exploring how the media presents or distorts academic findings in social sciences research, with Yettick (2015) noting (in relation to educational research) that 'little if any academic research has examined what kind of education-related studies, data, and experts are actually mentioned by the news media. In a sense, the issue has fallen through the cracks of the mass communication and education fields' (pp. 173–174). Her research found that peer-reviewed education research and the relevant professional organisation 'are barely a blip on the radar of American education reporting' (p. 181).

The media is ravenous for engaging content, and if your research is readily consumable and interesting, you might be able to get on the menu. These opportunities can be gold, promoting your work, deepening its impact, and bringing it to the attention of prospective future funders. I have been extremely grateful for the mutually beneficial opportunities I've had to share my work through the media. However, these experiences can also be like something out of your worst nightmares. You cannot assume that your priorities are aligned, or that the message that you want to share is what they are interested in. In the worst-case scenario, you may find yourself being positioned for controversy value at the expense of your reputation:

> For example, different formats have mechanisms for filtering who phones into a radio programme, for inviting live members of an audience, for designing talk for clapping or laughter or even using 'tracks' put such apparent audience responses where they want them; guests on programmes may know the agenda or even specific questions they will be asked ahead of time – or conversely, they may be deliberately lulled into a specific situation that will include surprises in order to capture 'authentic' responses . . .
>
> (Robles & Xie, 2024, p. 2)

You may also become the target of members of the public with extreme views in live media coverage.

I cannot sufficiently stress that once your research moves into the hands of media, to some extent, you certainly will not have total control of the messaging, and you may have surprisingly little. Dealing with the media may be an even greater challenge given the exposure risks involved:

> Henry's research had significant implications, for both industry and the public, so he had to employ great caution in the messages he used, and how he involved the media as a vehicle, noting that 'we want the press involved in our work because it's good publicity, but we're always cognisant that we don't want to create something that's blown out of proportion. That does happen sometimes.'
>
> (Merga & Mason, 2021c, p. 1493)

Live media offers no retake if you accidentally misrepresent your research, lose your chain of thought, or get confronted with a line of questioning that takes you into the realm of the highly controversial: sometimes it can feel like being gently boiled over a stove.

Some research has sought to capture the potential for message distortion. As contended by Haber et al. (2018), in the context of health-related scientific research,

> the pathway from research generation to consumption begins with academic research production, followed by publication, then media reporting, and ultimately leading to distribution on social and traditional media. Each step contains many mechanisms which could yield inaccurate and/or overstated evidence at the point of media consumption. Because each step of this pathway builds upon the previous one, issues with systematic selection, spin, overstatement, inaccuracy, and weak evidence are likely to accumulate by the time scientific research reaches the consumer. (p. 2)

Their research found that media articles reporting on health-related academic studies 'were likely to overstate strength of causal inference and inaccurately report key study characteristics and/or results' (p. 22). The misrepresentation may begin with academics themselves, as noted in the medical research context, where 'researchers and their funders, and even medical journals, often court media attention through press releases. The strategy works: Press releases increase the chance of getting media coverage' (Woloshin et al., 2009, p. 613). The researchers found that as a result of this impetus to feed the media with the findings it demands, 'press releases issued by 20 academic medical centers frequently promoted preliminary research or inherently limited human studies without providing basic details or cautions needed to judge the meaning, relevance, or validity of the science' (p. 616). As such, engaging with the media is a complex process that risks compromising the integrity of the research and researcher.

In recent times, there is the added risk of distortion through AI assistants that further misrepresent media reporting (British Broadcasting Corporation (BBC), 2025):

> The answers produced by the AI assistants contained significant inaccuracies and distorted content from the BBC. In particular:
>
> - 51% of all AI answers to questions about the news were judged to have significant issues of some form.
> - 19% of AI answers which cited BBC content introduced factual errors – incorrect factual statements, numbers and dates.
> - 13% of the quotes sourced from BBC articles were either altered from the original source or not present in the article cited. (p. 2)

Research on the possible role of AI assistants in distorting KMb work by academic researchers is badly needed at this juncture.

In some instances, the media will literally be chasing the most controversial take possible on your work, and they want you to deliver your findings in the most engaging manner possible. You are possibly going to feel aggressively steered to come into conflict with ethical guidelines for KMb such as those articulated by BERA in 2024:

> Researchers must not bring research into disrepute by in any way falsifying, distorting, suppressing, selectively reporting or sensationalising their research evidence or findings, either in publications based on that material, or as part of efforts to disseminate or promote that work. (p. 31)

Similarly, guidelines to support researchers' engagement with the media encourage them to 'be up front and honest about any uncertainties in your work, and explain the limitations of your research' (Science Media Centre, 2019, p. 5), assuming that the media will allow time and deliver aligned questioning for limitations to be outlined.

What these and similar documents fail to acknowledge is that the media is all about selective reporting and sensationalisation. The reporting will *inevitably* be selective, and even if you spend hours preparing messaging and memorising it, there's no guarantee that you will be asked a question that will allow you to articulate it as sometimes the interviewer is only interested in a micro-tangent relevant to your work. And if you try to pivot on live radio questioning (also bearing in mind that the questions are not usually provided in advance) to discuss all of the limitations on your project, I can't imagine that working well for you *unless these limitations are juicy*. You can go into live media with the best intentions, but the high pressure of immediacy and scrutiny coupled with low control can pose a significant challenge to even the most seasoned media communicator, which is one reason why politicians still record huge gaffes despite a wealth of relevant training and experience.

For example, if you are given 10 minutes of live radio air time answering questions, you don't control the questioning, and the questioning is going to take the most sensational angle on your work as possible to keep listeners engaged. If we add public talk back to this, even the presenter may have no idea what direction we might wind up taking, and I've been in this position many times now. It's very exciting, but I had no illusions about my level of control in this situation, and had to carefully consider before moving into this situation *where my boundaries were*, and *how to deflect* from moving into comment on areas *tangential to my expertise*, or *provoking unnecessary controversy*. Even then, when your work is subsequently remixed for other forms of media, such as where a radio piece is then selectively edited and developed for an online news article, you have no control over how your work is presented. They can take block quotes of your words and present them out of context, juxtaposed with events that have occurred *after* your initial media appearance. As soon as spoken words move into text, a lot of nuance is lost: for example, *sarcasm becomes a literal statement*. On the other hand, if you spend the entire time in the radio interview self-consciously measuring the potential impact of every single word that you utter, you're going to fall short of being entertaining and engaging, putting a line through future media opportunities.

I would love to see guidelines such as those articulated by BERA being more responsive to the realities of working with the media; ignoring or misrepresenting them doesn't help anyone. While there are increasingly articulated expectations for the ethics of KMb in this space, these also may not necessarily be supported by institutional training that takes into account the challenges in this space.

If you are good at speaking with the media, you may get a lot of opportunities. 'Good' in this instance means passionate, articulate, and able to tell a compelling story about research that is relatable, interesting, and responsive to the audience. Unfortunately, while we need more research on this, it's likely that certain demographics may be privileged voices possibly more likely to get a callback, and presenters have experienced racist attacks while on air (Xie & Durrheim, 2025), so the media do not necessarily provide a safe or equal opportunity platform for all speakers.

Speaking to the media can be incredibly stressful. The toll that the stress of live media can take on those who are not necessarily super keen on dealing with high-pressure situations can be notable, and depending on how comfortable you are with this, you may need to factor in recovery time. If you get a lot of engagements, the engagement time coupled with recovery commitment can seriously interfere with your ability to do the other parts of your job, and different strata in your university may not agree about what you should prioritise:

> One piece in particular involved multiple live media engagements per day, which was more than I could handle around my teaching load, so I declined many media engagement opportunities. There was also an instance where my School wanted me to teach, but at higher University level, they wanted me to do a live international television program at the same time, and I felt torn between expectations that were poorly resolved between these levels of governance over myself and my time. I followed the School's directive, and then had to face the University's disappointment with me, which made the balancing act of meeting a high volume of media commitments around teaching even more stressful to manage.
>
> (Merga, 2021a, p. 659)

Where a piece has generated broader media interest, I have felt pressure to overstate my findings in radio and television pieces, pressure which I have resisted to the best of my ability. As I have become more experienced, I have increasingly specified what I will discuss on air. For example, before a previous television experience, I explained to the producer that my research did not exactly align with the research brief that they sought to pursue, and I was clear about what I would be willing to talk about in advance, giving them plenty of time to find an alternative respondent if desired. They were satisfied with my parameters in that instance. I would not have been as confident or knowledgeable in defining these earlier in my career. Despite my sense that I have grown in my capacity to deal with the media, given the pressures of questions without notice and the sensationalist agenda, I still have ongoing concerns that under pressure, I will make a significant error that I will fail to notice or not be given time to rectify, and I know that such an error could have a detrimental impact on my career. Risk of such errors can be significantly heightened when the research falls in a high-risk category (see the next section).

Some people can just front up and talk about their research with no preparation or recovery needed. I am not one of those people. I usually do the following for radio (I've done a lot) and television work (I've done a little bit):

1 Sort out some key messages that I want to share from the research that I think will be of interest, taking direction from the production staff that I speak to when I am approached to do the gig to try to get good alignment.
2 Be prepared for the interviewer to completely ignore what the production staff suggested would be prioritised in the interview and go with the flow, while bringing the conversation back to key messages where this can be managed without it seeming too contrived (if you want to know what I mean by too contrived, I'm thinking about politicians who 'stay on messaging' and completely refuse to sincerely engage with interviewers).
3 Prepare/refresh some safe responses to interviewers wanting to explore tangents that go beyond the scope of my work, and have a brief 'go to' response for common criticisms of my work if applicable (Science Media Centre, 2019).
4 Front up to the interview remotely (preferred as I can keep my slippers on) or in person. If it's in person, check that I do not have lipstick on my teeth, and in both instances, try to manage anxiety using some simple techniques I've learned over the years.
5 Leave the interview allowing for an hour or so to recover because my brain is completely useless after such high-intensity engagement, and try to avoid finding fault with literally everything I said while at the same time considering if there is anything I could improve for the future, as every single one of these engagements is a learning opportunity and a chance for me to improve my skills.

Of course, the media aren't the only entity that can be challenging to communicate with beyond academia. Our research with ECRs in Australia and Japan found that working with bureaucratic organisations such as government could involve some notable issues:

Atticus described deep frustration working with government to lead to positive change.

... there's still that much back and forth because there's three or four different government departments that are involved in the process and it goes to different people. Some people don't want it to be changed because they're vested in the old way of doing things, and then they've got to bring Ministers up to speed, and then all of a sudden you're got a new state government that comes in so that all changes, the advisors change. So, yeah, that can definitely be frustrating, but at the end of the day, all we can do is keep producing that research and be consistent with the messages.

Similarly, Alice talked about frustrations in attempting to challenge the status quo for professionals working in a specific field, with research contradicting 'ingrained practice, and people who are stubborn in their belief that what they learned 30 or 40 years ago, what they've been doing for the length of their career is right and valid'.

(Merga & Mason, 2021c, p. 1492)

As your experience grows, your resources for dealing with challenging end-users beyond academia will become more extensive; in the interim, draw on advice from experienced colleagues within and beyond your university so that you can navigate the often significant challenges that you may face in these interactions.

Interactive media: managing response to online comments

Some Plain Language pieces and media forms have comments enabled so that readers, viewers, and/or listeners can interact in relation to the content. In my experience, managing responses to comments to support KMb has been challenging at times, and there is growing analysis of comments on similar kinds of online news and opinion sites. Diakopoulos and Naaman (2011) noted that 'the *quality* of the discussion anchored around online news stories is of paramount importance to news organizations wishing to stimulate public criticism, debate, and discussion while maintaining a credible community profile' (p. 1). They contend that the unique aspects of online news commenting spaces 'include often-volatile participation patterns, imbalance between professional and amateur content, and interaction between regular users and other actors in various official capacities' (p. 9). Implications around the reach and impact of user comments should also be considered:

Firstly, user comments are usually presented beneath the articles and therefore distributed via mass media, thus potentially reaching the same audience as journalistic items. Secondly, due to the interchange of the roles of addressee and speaker, the commenting feature creates conditions for deliberative interactions. Thus, regardless of how many readers actually notice user comments, comments have an effect on the process and structure of public communication.

(Springer et al., 2015, p. 798)

As such, comments provide opportunities for interactions between the article author and reader, and between readers, and they may wield their own persuasive power. Commenters' motivations to contribute can be 'influenced by cognitive motives and the desire to interact with the authors of news pieces' (p. 810), and thus commenters may be typically open to participation in knowledge exchange with the author. While I enjoy critical debate and am robust enough to be comfortable with lively but valid challenges to my work, everyone who uses the internet knows that commenters do not always engage in good faith, and trolling, misinformation, disinformation and straw-man arguments may all feature in comments.

So how can we manage such comments? I have drawn on teacherly strategies of providing *early positive reinforcement responses* on some logical and thoughtful comments, while often ignoring some comments that would be deleted by the moderator due to inappropriate or unrelated content. I have also responded to some comments that I disagree with, citing supporting evidence for my position.

My articles in *The Conversation* have been commented on by the following kinds of respondents:

Anecdotal reflector. The anecdotal reflector would take the findings and apply them to their own experiences, giving me insight into further applications of the research. In many cases their responses were consciously subjective. Their responses provided rich texture around the findings.

Unequivocal endorser. This commenter would support my findings and promote them.

Equivocal endorser. This commenter would endorse my findings, but also suggest future avenues for consideration, or challenging aspects of my research. While some of these further avenues were already explored in the linked articles, suggesting that comment engagement often occurs before the provided links are closely read, in some instances these commenters were really useful in highlighting interesting areas that I might consider in subsequent research.

Information seeker. This commenter would be attracted by a tangent or minor area within the research, or related research, and would comment to get direction for their own self-directed learning.

Uninformed challenger. This respondent either challenged my original post, or posts of other commenters, on uninformed, often anecdotal grounds. Sometimes they would read one or two sources and quote them, but typically showed a lack of understanding around the area. These were often also what I term 'sample of one respondents', where their view was dictated by their own experience, or on the experience of their child. In this regard, they could be quite similar to the anecdotal reflector, but they could be difficult to manage as they were often disinterested in deeply engaging in the area. These respondents often began arguing among themselves, often drawing an anecdotal reflector or unequivocal endorser into their discussion.

Tangential chatter. This respondent came to chat with another respondent, and they would take the discussion into an area with limited relevance to the original piece.

Tangential challenger. This respondent came to my comment section with what I imagine to be a pre-existing anger with something that was only very tangentially related to my research (like me existing on Earth as a woman). For example, the piece I did about supporting boys as readers attracted tangential challengers who were angry about women brainwashing men. These comments were usually deleted by the moderator.

While time to respond to commenters was a notable challenge, the biggest challenge for me was *knowing when not to engage*. Writing for *The Conversation*, where KMb is the goal, I felt there must be reciprocal engagement to some extent. However, I am still learning how to manage these interactions. I felt uncomfortable contesting strident contentions of 'sample of one' uninformed challengers, as they seemed fully committed to a view based on this sample, and personally invested in their opinions while being research resistant. This discomfort was greatest in the very rare instances where the challenger was also an academic. Diakopoulos and Naaman (2011) have explored 'the extent of the impact of low quality comments on both users and journalists' and 'how individual differences in reading motivations can impact perceptions of quality' (p. 9), and both of these issues had currency in my engagement with, and internal reactions towards, the public commentary on my work.

The tone and research basis of the commentary is usually far removed from that received in academic peer review, where criticism is ostensibly directed from a position of knowledge, and typically (but not always) impersonal. This must also relate to textual differences, as the peer reviewer is expected to make an informed contribution to the final shaping of a work, whereas a piece in *The Conversation* is a finished piece in its own right, and while some comments could deepen reader understandings of the issues in play, others showed that the commenter had not read the article, let alone any of the hyperlinks. I would love to share the optimism expressed by Wojcieszak and Mutz (2009), that online spaces can encourage 'discourse among those of opposing views, one where the status of participants is less important, and where ideas sink or swim by virtue of the strength of their arguments' (p. 40), a kind of 'deliberative digital democracy' (Weber, 2014, p. 942). However, I also know from my own research that inexpert voices often thrive in online spaces (e.g. Merga, 2024d).

Reading comments where there was little to no understanding of my work led to occasional feelings of a loss of control, and a sense of dismay and frustration. In academic communities, I have been able to rely on mutual respect, even where disagreements around approach or theory may exist. In the comments section, there can be little regard for my expertise, and commenters' opinions on the subject can be intractable, despite the research evidence challenging their views. While some academics may hold fixed viewpoints, I am a researcher who constantly seeks to learn and adapt to new knowledge, and the fixed mindset in some comments, drawing on an extremely shallow or non-existent knowledge base, posed a unique challenge. However, once I developed my own kind of informal triage around my responses, developing my skills in determining which uninformed challengers were worth engaging with, my emotional reaction diminished somewhat.

Ethics, high-risk projects and knowledge mobilisation

I have made a special section around ethics, high-risk projects and KMb, as I know there will be some TBP students reading this book on high-risk projects wanting to share their work beyond academia. I am very concerned by the lack of support that these students sometimes receive to perform a role that can benefit the university, but that is also frankly so incredibly risky I would have serious misgivings about undertaking it without training and support (and even then, I'd be moving carefully).

So what is high-risk research?

Risk related to data

While there are many kinds of possible risks involved in research, I'll first focus on projects that work with data collected from or produced by human beings. The current National Statement on Ethical Conduct in Human Research 2023 is produced by the NHMRC, and it is supposed to guide research ethics conduct across Australian universities:

> Low risk research describes research, including some types of clinical trials, in which the only foreseeable risk is no greater than discomfort. Accordingly, research in which the risk for participants or others is greater than discomfort is not low risk research. Research in this category is considered higher risk research and carries risk of harm.

(NHMRC, 2023, p. 13)

Now let's imagine that your project is on a very important topic but also high risk, such as one that analyses qualitative focus group data reporting on first-hand traumatic accounts of workplace bullying in the higher education workforce. This can be considered high-risk for multiple reasons, but perhaps most notably because:

1 if participant comment and identity are leaked and/or discerned in reporting, a person could lose their job, and/or be subject to defamation proceedings if the alleged bully learns of this work and wishes to challenge representation of their behaviour;
2 it may also have a negative impact on the wellbeing of participants who have to 'relive' assaults through disclosure.

These possibilities clearly involve more than 'foreseeable risk' that is 'greater than discomfort', because even if you get every focus group member to declare that they will preserve the confidentiality of all participants, your respondents *may not be researchers*, and if the 'tea' is compelling, they may forget/ignore their declaration and succumb to the temptation to tell a friend or partner. With humans being human, such leaks are possible. And unless you are going to have qualified mental health professionals to hand to support disclosure on assaults, mitigating the wellbeing risk will be challenging.

So how could this play out?

Let's imagine that the last time your principal supervisor published in a high-risk area was in the 1990s, but they've taken a close look at your project and they are confident that the risks involved are manageable; they were able to conduct a similar project in the 1990s with no issues. They are also confident that any risks will be identified when you submit your project for ethics approval from your HREC.

It's already a high-risk project in that recalling these events can have an adverse impact on your participants, so you are careful to address this in your ethics application. You put your project through your institution's HREC and it gets through with minor revisions. You are aware that there has been considerable recent turnover of staff in the HREC, with new staff still being trained in their roles, but your supervisor isn't worried, so neither are you.

You plan to do a TBP, and you are really keen to connect your findings with stakeholders at the earliest possible opportunity so that your project can lead to real-world change.

One respondent in your focus group makes a disclosure about being physically assaulted by their immediate line manager in higher education while at an international conference. The assault was not reported. You are very careful in your transcription and analysis of these data to ensure that none of your participants can be identified, particularly given your commitment to KMb. However, a minor descriptive detail that is included in relation to this respondent in a journal article that you publish makes them identifiable.

You were inadvertently the source of the leak.

In the 1990s, this may have gone under the radar, but you've amplified your research through online opinion pieces that you've written for three media outlets, and the line manager has been identified and is the subject of vilification in the comments section on two of these publications. This is not going to end well for any of the concerned parties.

Engaging in KMb can amplify risk. While 'maintaining confidentiality has always been a fraught enterprise, it is substantially magnified in an era of Google and social media' (Jerolmack & Murphy, 2019):

> ... it no longer takes a determined journalist willing to commit hours or days of shoe leather investigation for our subjects and field sites to be unmasked. Instead, in a matter of minutes and in the comfort of one's home or office, lay readers can easily perform key word searches based on information or events depicted in the ethnography to hone in on our subjects or research settings. Or they can scour the web in search of publicly available information on the researcher's whereabouts and affiliations that might reveal the people and organizations to which her research is connected ... (p. 806)

While it's a given that you need to protect the confidentiality of your respondents by compliance with institutional ethics requirements, *even greater care and scrutiny is warranted in current times* (Merga, 2024c). If you have any doubt about the sufficiency of your supervisory and HREC safeguards, your own diligence in this space absolutely needs to be heightened. *Do not proceed without advice from an expert with current experience.*

Risk related to topic

In addition to risks around project design, in this day and age in particular, topic can bring its own risks. A project that deals with controversial issues can amplify the risk that you are targeted by individuals with questionable motives and ideologies once this research spreads beyond academia.

Unlike in the previous instance, this risk can extend to *any research on a controversial topic,* and it is also important to note that what counts as a controversial topic changes over time as the world sees shifts in ideological norms (writing this section early in 2025 with an eye on US politics is an interesting experience!), so even work that you have done in the past that was somewhat neutral at the time might slide into a higher risk category over time (which is obviously outside your control, but worth noting in case you suddenly start receiving weird emails and friend requests based on past work).

While there are many topic-related risks, one of the most prominent relevant to this chapter occurs where important media work needed for research impact inadvertently leads to the researcher becoming a target:

> All researchers should expect their work to be scrutinised by the public, policy makers and campaigners. However, some researchers working on high-profile subjects that attract controversy, such as radiation, climate change, animal research, chronic fatigue syndrome/ME, or gender studies, have also found themselves targeted by people who have extreme views about their research . . . in contrast to healthy debate about research, this harassment could include abusive emails, social media 'trolling', threats to personal safety, malicious complaints to institutions or regulatory bodies, bombardment with Freedom of Information (FOI) requests or libelous online posts about researchers. Not only can this hold up research and present a risk to the reputation of the researchers involved, it can also prevent researchers engaging effectively with the media, the public and other stakeholders.
>
> (Science Media Centre, 2019, p. 2)

Research is lagging on the risks and possibilities of media engagement during the doctoral journey, with reports on this often not yet subject to peer review (e.g. Borkowski et al., 2023). While we wait for the research to catch up, we can consider findings from research with more senior academics and university administrators, which suggests that:

- university policies and practices may be inadequate to support you if you experience online abuse (Gosse et al., 2024), with online abuse seen as 'beyond the scope of institutional responsibility' (O'Meara et al., 2024, p. 1), despite it occurring as a result of work-related research promotion activities.
- online abuse is most likely to be experienced by already marginalised faculty, further compounding disadvantage (O'Meara et al., 2024).
- online abuse may be underreported due to issues relating to 'individual reputation or safety, the lack of action from the workplace, subjective norms regarding marginalized populations, and lack of clarity around process and procedure'.

(Hodson et al., 2024, p. 6)

As such, before going public with research findings on risky topics, I strongly urge you to find out what, if any, institutional support mechanisms will be available to you. If there are none, determine whether it is safe to proceed in actively promoting your research in the public domain; you will need to endeavour to understand and weigh the risks as foreseeable and relevant in your context, and you may need external advice to make safe decisions.

Managing KMb workload within the doctorate

Like many areas in life, competence in KMb may be rewarded with more work, and while engaging in KMb activities is important, your first priority needs to be PhD completion. As I've explored previously elsewhere, media activities can be hugely time-consuming and they can certainly interfere with your ability to focus on your work (Merga, 2021a).

While the benefits and risks for amplifying your research can be notable as I've outlined herein, KMb activities are 'not always rewarded through the universities' metrics systems such as REF' in the UK (Silverwood, 2023, p. 153). In my own experience, at one university I was given the university-wide Deputy Vice Chancellor (Research) Outstanding Public Engagement Award for the high-level media promotion of my research, which the university had determined reached a total audience of more than 1.8 million people in one year. There was no associated workload or financial award associated with this award, but I did hope that it would be recognised when I applied for academic promotion. However, I discovered that this work was poorly valued by the promotions committee; basically, I was left with the impression that this university would've preferred me to do a greater volume of low-skill internal service instead of spending my time speaking to national and international news outlets about my research. KMb labour being outside the realm of their own experience, they didn't seem to understand the commitment involved. In short, if KMb activities really take off and threaten your ability to meet milestones on your doctorate, there is no guarantee that your university will show any lenience despite your status as an ambassador generating positive public exposure for their work.

I'm not the only one who has lost sleep and felt the squeeze of KMb workload pressures – one of the reasons I do far less media work now than I've done in the past. ECRs have also commented on how these activities are crowded out due to workload and related time limitations:

> Alice and Mary both felt that their opportunities to share with the non-academic community were crowded out by their demanding and diverse workloads. Similarly, Niki explained that 'even though I've seen lots of opportunities to build partnerships with (practitioners)', 'I just cannot do that, because I'm doing other things that, in my work, are a priority'. As such, both time and workload limitations could inhibit ECRs' potential to share their research with both academic and non-academic communities.
>
> (Merga & Mason, 2021c, p. 1491)

This may seem like a minor consideration if you have never experienced your research absolutely blowing up in the media, but if that happens, you may find your KMb activities taking over your whole life. The first time this happened to me I was utterly unprepared for it, given that I am a human embodiment of a hermit crab who prefers to just work away inside my shell with singular focus.

For example, in 2017 one of our pieces in *The Conversation* became very popular with the media (Merga & Mat Roni, 2017), with more than 256,000 people reading this piece to date.

The problem was that I had a significant teaching and research workload, there was no one advising me on how to manage/prioritise media requests, my co-author was (understandably) not keen to speak with the media, I was still very new to media and terrified that I was going to kill my career by getting my messaging wrong, and I was receiving more media requests than I could possibly manage. On one hand, it was amazing to be able to do justice to my research respondents, our work as a research team, and to justify the funder's investment (the Ian Potter

Foundation). On the other, the stress of constant live media engagements and being bombarded by missed media calls while teaching was overwhelming.

My point is that at this stage, the KMb commitments that you make may be poorly valued by your university, so don't imagine that you are doing this for your university unless is it truly supported and valued. Do this for your stakeholders, your communities, your research respondents, and so that you can enjoy the satisfaction of knowing that your research is leading to real-world change, but don't let your doctorate suffer unless you are sure that your university supports your activities (and get this in writing).

Finally, maintaining a commitment to KMb both during my TBP and throughout my academic career has been super helpful for times when I have wanted to step out of academia. Investing time and energy in ensuring that your research connects with communities outside academia can help you to keep your options open.

## CHAPTER 8

Conclusions, Future Research and Policy Directions

Often when you ask people about their experience doing a PhD, the face they make tells a tale of trauma before they even open their lips.

I was fortunate, and I loved almost every moment of my TBP experience. It was a chance to make a meaningful contribution to the knowledge and professional space and to truly extend myself, and I often think nostalgically of a time when I was expected to be leading *just one project at a time*, balanced among the paid and unpaid labour and other issues in my life.

The PhD journey I describe in this book may not be possible, or desirable, in your unique case. As I've already mentioned previously, you should read this book bearing in mind that the decisions you make on your TBP need to be informed by your own context, circumstances, and perhaps above all, institutional expectations as detailed in relevant policy documents.

None of the research areas that I've touched upon are static, and universities and educational and social systems are also constantly evolving in their norms, expectations and internal and external drivers, meaning that parts of this book will be incorrect or irrelevant probably by the time it moves out of press. I'm writing this section in February 2025 and on a large scale, we're seeing an erosion and redirection of norms that I imagined would be universal and enduring.

Experts in specific areas within higher education, such as journal impact evaluation, will probably be highly frustrated by the cursory manner in which I've dealt with many key topics. Given that many of the areas covered could warrant books in their own right, my ice-skating over the surface of these areas was to just give you an overview and hopefully inspire further reading where warranted. I tried to focus on the gaps that I personally encountered and that others have reportedly encountered on their TBP journeys, rather than aspects extensively covered elsewhere, such as the mechanics of academic writing. I will be the first to admit that I have been perhaps ridiculously ambitious in what I have hoped to achieve with this book in terms of complexity, and hopefully it has not been too overwhelming.

While it is a bonus to be writing this book as someone who personally completed a TBP, I'm not for a moment suggesting that my own TBP is some kind of perfect exemplar, even though I draw on it heavily. For example, at that stage as a novice researcher, my understanding of integration in mixed methods was poor, and therefore I believe that overall, my TBP project would've been greatly enhanced had my methods knowledge been more developed. I do try not to fixate on the deficiencies of my TBP, given that it was the best I could do at the time with the knowledge and resources that I had, and after all, I am committed to being a lifelong learner; finding fault with my former work is going to be an inevitable part of being an academic as both my own knowledge and norms in methods continue to advance.

Finally, I must note that where research has been cited in languages other than English (e.g. Pozniak et al., 2023), Google Translate was used to machine generate a translation. This technology is imperfect, so the potential for error must be acknowledged.

Now I'd like to briefly touch on some of the things I'd like to know more about.

Hidden voices and experiences

As we've touched upon in previous research (Mason, Morris & Merga, 2021), higher education research is dominated by certain privileged voices from a subset of contexts not representative of the whole world, and depending on where you are reading this book, parts of this book may be laughably irrelevant, so I apologise for that. We need more research that looks at the experiences of TBP for all groups of marginalised scholars.

Extant TBP research including our own is strongly focused on those who 'made it' on the TBP journey, rather than those who left the journey or reverted to a traditional monograph; we need to capture and hone in on the factors triggering attrition if we are to develop a full picture of how to support a TBP from an institutional perspective.

Personally, despite trying on multiple occasions to secure research funding to explore these kinds of projects, I have only ever been successful in achieving internal funding. I do not know why the appetite for funding TBP-related research projects is so low with external funders given the benefits they offer for institutions as well as society, professions, industry and other applicable audiences; it would be great to see substantial research investment in this space.

Media risk

As you have probably grasped from the book, one of the areas I am most worried about is actually the KMb part of the TBP, as it is clear to me that activities and expectations in this space may be poorly supported by policy, resourcing and research-informed models of safe and best practice, exposing TBP students engaging with the media to real risk.

Brave research

Too many people will be reading this in contexts and supervisory scenarios where pervasive academic norms that no longer align with ethical principles are still being enacted, even when they contravene institutional policy. While there is a growing body of research in this area, I would love to see institutions develop more aggressive policies for stamping out toxic dated norms, so maybe we need even more research about their impact, risks and costs in order to spur change.

Fit for purpose policy

I'd also like to see more attention given to creating high-quality TBP policies that actually align with what we know from the available research. This policy needs to be fit for purpose and consider its own aims so that it supports rather than inhibits the production of high-quality TBPs and SOs. I'm going to go out on a limb here and suggest that the people involved in the writing of this policy should have some first-hand familiarity with TBP as well as the extant research so that they understand its dimensionality, forms that it can take, and the realities of the workload involved; while this isn't an outrageous ask, this is clearly not always happening in universities.

Ethics beyond compliance

In my experience, it seems that doctoral training around ethics may in some contexts exclusively focus on compliance with required frameworks, policies and related structures, rarely inviting doctoral students to think about how their work fits into bigger-picture debates and evolving understandings of what it means to conduct ethical research in the contemporary context. I feel that this can result in research ethics being seen by students (and let's be honest, also by many more senior researchers) as a box-ticking exercise rather than an orientation towards ensuring that research is carried out and reported in a manner that is sound and just. I would love for research leaders to provide more dynamic and responsive contexts for debates and discussions around research ethics involving TBP students and junior scholars, perhaps drawing on cases from COPE so that research ethics are seen as something integral to, and interwoven in, all considerations of research rather than just a compliance mechanism that it is subject to.

Attention to environments

Many universities make sound strategic use of their resources, creating and continually adapting policies to underpin supportive environments for conducting the PhD. They use ongoing needs analysis and other feedback mechanisms to inform fair and logical decisions in this space, and they enjoy the fruits of their investment evidenced in strong PhD completion rates and student satisfaction.

In other institutions, it's honestly surprising that any students manage to graduate, given the lack of support they experience, and it's amazing how long an institution may get away with providing a hostile environment without taking serious measures to address this.

I would suggest that in this day and age, given the level of external scrutiny faced by many institutions, *even if providing a supportive environment can't be understood as an ethical and moral imperative, we can* at the very least attempt to provide a supportive environment *to protect a university's reputational and related financial interests*. It's not surprising how often a toxic environment is under the diligence of leadership lacking qualifications and related research literacy to support students' research attainment. What is surprising is that the upper ranks at some institutions continue to be bloated by unqualified leadership with limited appetite or capacity to upskill to meet the needs of their role.

This is why I encourage you, where safe and viable, to speak up if your environment is falling short of norms and needs to support the TBP. Now that you've read this book you know what can be possible. I hate that this onus gets shifted onto students to generate dissent to hopefully trigger change, but if you're working in an unsupportive environment and can reasonably advocate to improve your conditions and those of your peers, please do so.

Final note

As the TBP continues to evolve and our understanding of its limitations and potential further develops, I hope to be in some way involved. If you have feedback on this book, want to collaborate on TBP research, or want to see if I can do some training or policy consulting for your institution, the best place to find me is at merga.consulting@gmail.com or on LinkedIn.

Appendix

Social sciences disciplines: breadth of author

My research is usually concerned with the social influences on learning, engagement, communication, wellbeing and workforce in education, library and health-related contexts.

I wanted to briefly show that I have published across a range of areas relevant to social sciences to highlight my experience relevant to this book. The Academy of the Social Sciences in Australia (2023) has created a list of divisions and (sub)groups that are recognised as 'being within the scope of social science' (para. 1). In Table 11, I list a publication as an example of where I've published with relevance to a division and subgroup as per this list.

Table 11 *Relevant example publications across social sciences*

Division	Group within division	Publication
Commerce, management, tourism, and services	Strategy, management and organisational behaviour	Merga, 2023b
	Human resources and industrial relations	Merga & Mat Roni, 2025b
Economics	Econometric and statistical methods	Mat Roni et al., 2020
Education	Curriculum and pedagogy	Merga, 2017a
	Education policy, sociology and philosophy	Merga, 2022e
	Education systems	Merga et al., 2021
	Specialist studies in education	Merga, 2020a
Health sciences	Health services and systems	Merga, 2016b
	Nursing	Merga, Hays & Coventry, 2020
	Public health	McManus et al., 2011
Human society	Gender studies	Merga, Mat Roni & Mason, 2020
Indigenous Studies	Aboriginal and Torres Strait Islander peoples, society and community	Merga & Booth, 2017
Language, Communication and Culture	Communication and media studies	Merga, 2021c
	Language studies	Ferguson et al., 2021
Law and legal studies	Law in context	Merga, 2024c

References

ABC Radio Perth (2017). Interview with Dr Margaret Merga. Radio interview with Gillian O'Shaughnessy on *Perth Afternoons*.

Academy of the Social Sciences in Australia (2021). State of the Social Sciences 2021. https://stateofthesocialsciences.org.au/wp-content/uploads/sites/4/2021/11/State-of-the-Social-Sciences-2021.pdf

Academy of the Social Sciences in Australia (2023). Social sciences disciplines (fields of research). https://socialsciences.org.au/social-science-fields-of-research

Albert, T., & Wager, E. (2003). How to handle authorship disputes: A guide for new researchers. *The COPE Report 2003*.
https://publicationethics.org/files/2003pdf12_0.pdf

Allington, R. L., & McGill-Franzen, A. M. (2021). Reading volume and reading achievement: A review of recent research. *Reading Research Quarterly, 56*, S231–S238.

Altmetric (2023). What is Altmetric and what does it provide?
https://help.altmetric.com/support/solutions/articles/6000232837-what-is-altmetric-and-what-does-it-provide

American Economic Association (2024). Author randomization tool.
www.aeaweb.org/journals/policies/random-author-order/generator

American Psychological Association (2022). Plagiarism.
https://apastyle.apa.org/style-grammar-guidelines/citations/plagiarism

American Psychological Association (2023). Using psychological science to understand and fight health misinformation.
www.apa.org/pubs/reports/misinformation-consensus-statement.pdf

Arrieta, G. S., Chung, W. C., & Ancho, I. V. (2024). To publish or not: Philippine graduate students' motivation, experiences, and needs in research publication. *International Journal of Education, 17*(1), 39–50.

Asanov, A. M., Asanov, I., Buenstorf, G., Kadriu, V., & Schoch, P. (2024). Patterns of dissertation dissemination: Publication-based outcomes of doctoral theses in the social sciences. *Scientometrics, 129*(4), 2389–2405.

Asante, L. A., & Abubakari, Z. (2021). Pursuing PhD by publication in geography: A collaborative autoethnography of two African doctoral researchers. *Journal of Geography in Higher Education, 45*(1), 87–107.

Australian Government (2016). Comparative analysis of the Australian Qualifications Framework and the European Qualifications Framework for lifelong learning: Joint technical report. https://internationaleducation.gov.au/News/Latest-News/Documents/ED16-0165%20-%20693040%20-%20Joint%20Technical%20Report_ACC.pdf

Australian Government (n.d.). Research funding and expenditure. Transparency portal. www.transparency.gov.au/publications/health/national-health-and-medical-research-council-nhmrc/national-health-and-medical-research-council-annual-report-2021-22/part-1-overview/research-funding-and-expenditure

Australian Qualifications Framework (AQF) (n.d.). AQF level 10 criteria. www.aqf.edu.au/framework/aqf-levels#aqf-level-10-criteria

Bahji, A., Acion, L., Laslett, A. M., & Adinoff, B. (2023). Exclusion of the non-English-speaking world from the scientific literature: Recommendations for change for addiction journals and publishers. *Nordic Studies on Alcohol and Drugs, 40*(1), 6–13.

Bahtilla, M., & Huang, X. (2024). Engagement in research: Doctoral students' reasons for not engaging in research activities in universities in Cameroon. *Higher Education Research & Development.* https://doi.org/10.1080/07294360.2024.2439860

Banerjee, A. (2022). The story of writing and publishing a research article: An autoethnographic account of an early career researcher (ECR) in India. *Qualitative Report, 27*(8), 1445–1461.

Baptista, A., Frick, L., Holley, K., Remmik, M., Tesch, J., & Åkerlind, G. (2015). The doctorate as an original contribution to knowledge: Considering relationships between originality, creativity, and innovation. *Frontline Learning Research, 3*(3), 5–67.

BBC (2025). Representation of BBC News content in AI Assistants. www.bbc.co.uk/aboutthebbc/documents/bbc-research-into-ai-assistants.pdf

Bedenlier, S., Buntins, K., Bond, M., Händel, M., & Marín, V. I. (2025). Evidence syntheses in educational technology research: What is not published in English is not visible? A tertiary mapping review. *Review of Education, 13*, e70022. https://doi.org/10.1002/rev3.70022

Billsberry, J. (2014). Desk-rejects: 10 top tips to avoid the cull. *Journal of Management Education, 38*(1), 3–9.

Boell, S. K., & Cecez-Kecmanovic, D. (2015). On being 'systematic' in literature reviews in IS. *Journal of Information Technology, 30*(2), 161–173.

Bøgelund, P. (2015). How supervisors perceive PhD supervision – and how they practice it. *International Journal of Doctoral Studies, 10*, 39–55.

Booth, S., Merga, M. K., & Mat Roni, S. (2016). Peer-mentors reflect on the benefits of mentoring: An autoethnography. *International Journal of Doctoral Studies, 11*, 383–402.

Borkowski, A., Grant, M. T., & Coulter, N. (2023). Trolling and doxxing: Graduate students sharing their research online speak out about hate. *The Conversation.* https://theconversation.com/trolling-and-doxxing-graduate-students-sharing-their- research-online-speak-out-about-hate-210874

Brien, D. (2008). Publish or perish: Investigating the doctorate by publication in writing. In *Proceedings of the 13th Annual Australasian Association of Writing Programs [AAWP] Conference* (pp. 1–16). Sydney.

British Education Research Association (BERA) (2024). Ethical guidelines for educational research (5th ed.). www.bera.ac.uk/wp-content/uploads/2024/04/Ethical-Guidelines-for-Educational-Research-5th-edition.pdf

Brownlow, C., Eacersall, D. C., Martin, N., & Parsons-Smith, R. (2023). The higher degree research student experience in Australian universities: A systematic literature review. *Higher Education Research & Development, 42*(7), 1608–1623.

Buirski, N. (2022). 'Ways of being': A model for supportive doctoral supervisory relationships and supervision. *Higher Education Research & Development, 41*(5), 1387–1401.

Burford, J., Henderson, E. F., Dahl, S., Bajwa-Patel, M., McKee, F., Moody, J., Branch, D., & Martyn, R. (2024). *Mitigation and adjustment for doctoral education (MADE): Final project report.* University of Warwick.

Button, K. S., Bal, L., Clark, A., & Shipley, T. (2016). Preventing the ends from justifying the means: Withholding results to address publication bias in peer-review. *BMC Psychology, 4*, 1–7.

Byrne, M. (2015). Reading for the fun of it. Blog posting, *The Royal Children's Hospital Melbourne*, 7 May. http://blogs.rch.org.au/education/2015/05/07/young-people-love-reading-fun

Cabells (2025). Predatory reports. https://cabells.com/solutions/predatory-reports

Campbell, K. (2022). The retrospective PhD by publication: A lesser Doctorate? In S. W. Chong & N. H. Johnson (Eds.), *Landscapes and narratives of PhD by publication: Demystifying students' and supervisors' perspectives* (pp. 95–117). Springer International.

Carless, D., Jung, J., & Li, Y. (2024). Feedback as socialization in doctoral education: Towards the enactment of authentic feedback. *Studies in Higher Education, 49*(3), 534–545.

Cash, B. (2023). The good, the bad and the ugly of completing a thesis by publication. In D. L. Mulligan, N. Ryan & P. A. Danaher (Eds.), *Deconstructing doctoral discourses: Stories and strategies for success* (pp. 145–160). Springer International.

Castelao-Huerta, I. (2025). Violence in doctoral education: Uncaring/uncareful practices of supervisors, co-supervisors, professors, and institutional authorities. *Pedagogy, Culture & Society.* https://doi.org/10.1080/14681366.2025.2463452

Christianson, B., Elliott, M., & Massey, B. (2015). *The role of publications and other artefacts in submissions for the UK PhD.* UK Council for Graduate Education.

Churchill, M. P., Lindsay, D., Mendez, D. H., Crowe, M., Emtage, N., & Jones, R. (2021). Does publishing during the doctorate influence completion time? A quantitative study of doctoral candidates in Australia. *International Journal of Doctoral Studies, 16*, 689–713.

Clarke, V., Braun, V., Adams, J., Callaghan, J. E., LaMarre, A., & Semlyen, J. (2024). 'Being really confidently wrong': Qualitative researchers' experiences of methodologically incongruent peer review feedback. *Qualitative Psychology*. https://doi.org/10.1037/qup0000322

Committee on Publication Ethics (COPE) (2017). Authorship dispute regarding author order. https://publicationethics.org/guidance/case/authorship-dispute-regarding-author-order

Connoway, I. J. L., & Malherbe, J. (2024). Time to tame the tome: Motivating the Thesis by Publication as a mode of study for a PhD in the Humanities. *South African Journal of Higher Education, 38*(2), 63–80.

Conversation, The (2024). The Conversation stakeholder report 2024. https://cdn.theconversation.com/static_files/files/3573/2024_Stakeholder_Report_AU_NZ__%2810%29.pdf?1734410202

Costa, S. (2014). Evolving to eReading: Is it time? Blog posting, *Sam Costa: Youth, popular culture and texts*, 20 October. https://samcrn600blog.wordpress.com/tag/prensky

Dai, K., Doi, K., & Oladipo, O. A. (2025). *The motivation and research experiences of international doctoral students in China: Navigating the PhD journey*. Taylor & Francis.

Davies, R. E., & Rolfe, G. (2009). PhD by publication: A prospective as well as retrospective award? Some subversive thoughts. *Nurse Education Today, 29*(6), 590–594.

Deakin University (2021). PhD by Folio. www.deakin.edu.au/__data/assets/pdf_file/0011/1449596/PhD_by_folio_mar_2021.pdf

Diakopoulos, N., & Naaman, M. (2011). Towards quality discourse in online news comments. In *Proceedings of the ACM 2011 conference on computer supported cooperative work*. https://doi.org/10.1145/1958824.1958844

DORA. (n.d.). San Francisco Declaration on Research Assessment. https://sfdora.org/read

Douglas Research Centre (n.d.). Persistent identifiers. https://douglas.research.mcgill.ca/persistent-identifiers

Dowling, R., Gorman-Murray, A., Power, E., & Luzia, K. (2012). Critical reflections on doctoral research and supervision in human geography: The 'PhD by publication'. *Journal of Geography in Higher Education, 36*(2), 293–305.

Doyle, M., & Caissie, C. (2024). Doctoral student reading and writing: Making our processes visible. *Discourse and Writing/Rédactologie, 34*, 1–23.

Dryden, S. K. (2024). *Understanding the impact of translingual discrimination on migrants' linguistic integration and emotional wellbeing in Australia* [Doctoral dissertation, Curtin University]. Espace. https://espace.curtin.edu.au/handle/20.500.11937/96146

Dwivedi, Y. K., Hughes, L., Cheung, C. M., Conboy, K., Duan, Y., Dubey, R., . . . & Viglia, G. (2022). How to develop a quality research article and avoid a journal desk rejection. *International Journal of Information Management, 62*, e102426.

Ellis, C., & Bochner, A. (2000). Autoethnography, personal narrative, reflexivity: Researcher as subject. In N. Denzin & Y. Lincoln (Eds.), *Handbook of qualitative research* (pp. 733–768). Sage.

Else, H. (2024). 'Doing good science is hard': Retraction of high-profile reproducibility study prompts soul-searching. *Nature.* www.nature.com/articles/d41586-024-03178-8

Elsevier (2017). Salami slicing. https://researcheracademy.elsevier.com/uploads/2018-02/2017_ETHICS_SS02.pdf

Europass (n.d.). Description of the eight EQF levels. https://europass.europa.eu/en/description-eight-eqf-levels

Evans, A. B., Clay, G., Fahlén, J., Hoekman, R., Lenneis, V., Smith, M., . . . & Wilcock, L. (2021). Why do some papers get desk rejected from the European Journal for Sport and Society? *European Journal for Sport and Society, 18*(4), 287–292.

Evans, S. C., Amaro, C. M., Herbert, R., Blossom, J. B., & Roberts, M. C. (2018). 'Are you gonna publish that?' Peer-reviewed publication outcomes of doctoral dissertations in psychology. *PloS one, 13*(2), e0192219.

Ferguson, C., Merga, M., & Winn, S. (2021). Communications in the time of a pandemic: The readability of documents for public consumption. *Australian and New Zealand Journal of Public Health, 45*(2), 116–121.

Ford, E., Curlewis, K., Wongkoblap, A., & Curcin, V. (2019). Public opinions on using social media content to identify users with depression and target mental health care advertising: Mixed methods survey. *JMIR Mental Health, 6*(11), e12942.

Former Editorial Board at the Journal of Human Evolution (2024). Journal of Human Evolution: Resignation of the editorial board. https://retractionwatch.com/2025/01/06/elsevier-denies-ai-use-in-response-to-evolution-journal-board-resignations

Forsyth, A. (2022). A chance to try again: The soft rejection. *Journal of the American Planning Association, 88*(2), 147–148.

Frick, L. (2019). PhD by publication – Panacea or paralysis? *Africa Education Review, 16*(5), 47–59.

García-Morante, M., Weise, C., Diaz Villalba, L. K., & Castelló, M. (2024). Strengths and weaknesses of PhD training to develop alternative careers: Insights from PhD holders working beyond academia. *Studies in Graduate and Postdoctoral Education.* https://doi.org/10.1108/SGPE-12-2023-0115

Goddiksen, M. P., Johansen, M. W., Armond, A. C., Clavien, C., Hogan, L., Kovács, N., . . . & Lund, T. B. (2023). 'The person in power told me to': European PhD students' perspectives on guest authorship and good authorship practice. *PLoS One, 18*(1), e0280018.

Gosse, C., O'Meara, V., Hodson, J., & Veletsianos, G. (2024). Too rigid, too big, and too slow: Institutional readiness to protect and support faculty from technology facilitated violence and abuse. *Higher Education, 87*(4), 923–941.

Griffith University (2019). Resource paper: Supervision and HDR candidate research outputs. www.griffith.edu.au/__data/assets/pdf_file/0032/442949/HDR-Super-publication-v1-6.pdf

Grudniewicz, A., Moher, D., Cobey, K. D., Bryson, G. L., Cukier, S., Allen, K., Ardern, C., Balcom, L., Barros, T., Berger, M., Ciro, J. B., Cugusi, L., Donaldson, M. R., Egger, M., Graham, I. D., Hodgkinson, M., Khan, K. M., Mabizela, M., Manca, A., . . . Lalu, M. M. (2019). Predatory journals: No definition, no defence. *Nature, 576*(7786), 210–212.

Guerin, C. (2016). Connecting the dots: Writing a doctoral thesis by publication. In C. Badenhorst & C. Guerin (Eds.), *Research literacies and writing pedagogies for masters and doctoral writers* (pp. 31–50). Brill.

Gulbrandsen, M., & Smeby, J. C. (2005). Industry funding and university professors' research performance. *Research Policy, 34*(6), 932–950.

Gülen, S., Fonnes, S., Andresen, K., & Rosenberg, J. (2020). More than one-third of Cochrane reviews had gift authors, whereas ghost authorship was rare. *Journal of Clinical Epidemiology, 128*, 13–19.

Haber, N., Smith, E. R., Moscoe, E., Andrews, K., Audy, R., Bell, W., . . . & McClure, E. S. (2018). Causal language and strength of inference in academic and media articles shared in social media (CLAIMS): A systematic review. *PloS one, 13*(5), e0196346.

Hardouin, S., Cheng, T. W., Mitchell, E. L., Raulli, S. J., Jones, D. W., Siracuse, J. J., & Farber, A. (2020). RETRACTED: Prevalence of unprofessional social media content among young vascular surgeons. *Journal of Vascular Surgery, 69*(3), e31.

Hemant, A. (2022). UGC withdraws mandatory research publication before PhD thesis submission to enhance quality. *The Times of India.* https://timesofindia.indiatimes.com/education/news/ugc-withdraws-mandatory-research-publication-before-phd-thesis-submission-to-enhance-quality/articleshow/94619260.cms

Hiatt, B. (2014). Only one in five teens reads books. *The West Australian*, 9 October. https://au.news.yahoo.com/thewest/a/25216032/only-one-in-five-teens-reads-books

Hidayat, N., Setiawan, S., & Anam, S. (2024). Publishing a research paper in reputable journals: Doctoral students' perspectives. *International Journal of Evaluation and Research in Education, 13*(2), 1227–1234.

Hodson, J., O'Meara, V., Owen, J., Veletsianos, G., & Morales, E. (2024). Why don't faculty members report incidents of online abuse and what can be done about it? *Computers in Human Behavior Reports, 15*, e100469.

Hu, G., & Liu, Y. (2018). Three minute thesis presentations as an academic genre: A cross-disciplinary study of genre moves. *Journal of English for Academic Purposes, 35*, 16–30.

Hu, X. (2023). Prejudice, interests, jealousy: Inappropriate peer reviewers may be exacerbating inequality in academic publication in health research. *Journal of Korean Medical Science, 38*(33), 1–5.

Huang, Y. (2021). Doctoral writing for publication. *Higher Education Research & Development, 40*(4), 753–766.

Indrayadi, T. (2024). The long journey to my first publication in a reputable international journal: An autoethnographic account. *Issues in Educational Research*, 34(4), 1332–1349.

Inouye, K., & Bengtsen, S. (2023). New spaces for agency in doctoral education: An ecological approach. In Y. I. Oldac, L. Yang & S. Lee (Eds.), *Student agency and self-formation in higher education* (pp. 217–239). Palgrave Macmillan.

International Committee of Medical Journal Editors (ICMJE). (2024). Recommendations for the conduct, reporting, editing, and publication of scholarly work in medical journals. www.icmje.org/icmje-recommendations.pdf

Jackson, D. (2013). Completing a PhD by publication: A review of Australian policy and implications for practice. *Higher Education Research & Development*, 32(3), 355–368.

Jalongo, M. R. (2024). Scholarly publication during doctoral candidature: Obstacles, benefits, and strategies for success. *Early Childhood Education Journal*. https://doi.org/10.1007/s10643-024-01724-7

Jerolmack, C., & Murphy, A. K. (2019). The ethical dilemmas and social scientific trade-offs of masking in ethnography. *Sociological Methods & Research*, 48(4), 801–827.

Jisc (2025a). Welcome to open policy finder. https://openpolicyfinder.jisc.ac.uk

Jisc (2025b). English in Education. https://openpolicyfinder.jisc.ac.uk/id/publication/7659

Johnson, L.M., & Ebrahimiji, A. (2020). A medical journal apologized after an article prompted health professionals to post images of themselves in bikinis. *CNN*. https://edition.cnn.com/2020/07/25/cnn10/medbikini-backlash-and-apologies-trnd/index.html

Kamler, B. (2008). Rethinking doctoral publication practices: Writing from and beyond the thesis. *Studies in Higher Education*, 33(3), 283–294.

Kamler, B., & Thomson, P. (2008). The failure of dissertation advice books: Toward alternative pedagogies for doctoral writing. *Educational Researcher*, 37(8), 507–514.

Khan, K. S., Kunz, R., Kleijnen, J., & Antes, G. (2003). Five steps to conducting a systematic review. *Journal of the Royal Society of Medicine*, 96(3), 118–121.

Khodakarami, M., Mohammad Rezaei, F., Sarlak, A., Garg, M., & Rezaee, Z. (2025). Free-riding in academic co-authorship: The marginalization of research students. *Research Policy*, 54(2), e105165

Kiley, M., Holbrook, A., Lovat, T., Fairbairn, H., Starfield, S., & Paltridge, B. (2018). An oral component in PhD examination in Australia: Issues and considerations. *Australian Universities' Review*, 60(1), 25–34.

King, R. (2014). Books still cool for teens. *The West Australian*, 13 March. https://thewest.com.au/news/australia/books-still-cool-for-teens-ng-ya-367405

Kis, A., Tur, E. M., Lakens, D., Vaesen, K., & Houkes, W. (2022). Leaving academia: PhD attrition and unhealthy research environments. *Plos One*, 17(10), e0274976.

Kitano, N., & Lane, M. (2024). Alone, together: How a strategy of writing, reflecting and relating helped research students deal with isolation. *Journal of Applied Research in Higher Education*. https://doi.org/10.1108/JARHE-10-2023-0485.

Klein, G., & Müller, R. (2022). Getting past the editor's desk. *Project Management Journal, 53*(6), 543–546.

Kousha, K., & Thelwall, M. (2020). Google Books, Scopus, Microsoft Academic, and Mendeley for impact assessment of doctoral dissertations: A multidisciplinary analysis of the UK. *Quantitative Science Studies, 1*(2), 479–504.

Kubota, F. I., Cauchick-Miguel, P. A., Tortorella, G., & Amorim, M. (2021). Paper-based thesis and dissertations: Analysis of fundamental characteristics for achieving a robust structure. *Production, 31*, e20200100.

Kumar, S., Roumell, E. A., & Bolliger, D. U. (2023). Faculty perceptions of e-mentoring doctoral dissertations: Challenges, strategies, and institutional support. *American Journal of Distance Education.* https://doi.org/10.1080/08923647.2023.2213137

Kuper, A., O'Sullivan, P., & Cleland, J. (2023). How should I determine author order for this paper? *Advances in Health Sciences Education, 28*(5), 1367–1369.

Kuzhabekova, A. (2025). Ph.D. publication requirement and its effects on research productivity trends in Kazakhstan. *Higher Education Quarterly, 79*, e12590.

Larivière, V. (2012). On the shoulders of students? The contribution of PhD students to the advancement of knowledge. *Scientometrics, 90*(2), 463–481.

Larivière, V., Zuccala, A., & Archambault, É. (2008). The declining scientific impact of theses: Implications for electronic thesis and dissertation repositories and graduate studies. *Scientometrics, 74*, 109–121.

Laudel, G., & Gläser, J. (2008). From apprentice to colleague: The metamorphosis of early career researchers. *Higher Education, 55*, 387–406.

Lee, A., & Kamler, B. (2008). Bringing pedagogy to doctoral publishing. *Teaching in Higher Education, 13*(5), 511–523.

Lee, I., Xu, Y., & Jha, P. (2025). From 'all-but-dissertation' to doctorate: The dissertation experiences of doctoral candidates with extended time to degree. *Journal of Counselor Leadership and Advocacy.* https://doi.org/10.1080/2326716X.2024.2449358

Lei, J., & Hu, G. (2015). Apprenticeship in scholarly publishing: A student perspective on doctoral supervisors' roles. *Publications, 3*(1), 27–42.

Levin, B. (2013). To know is not enough: Research knowledge and its use. *Review of Education, 1*(1), 2–31.

Light, R., Gullickson, A., & Harrison, J. A. (2025). Inequality in measuring scholarly success: Variation in the h-index within and between disciplines. *PloS one, 20*(1), e0316913.

Martins, R. S., Mustafa, M. A., Fatimi, A. S., Nasir, N., Pervez, A., & Nadeem, S. (2023). The CalculAuthor: Determining authorship using a simple-to-use, fair, objective, and transparent process. *BMC Research Notes, 16*(1), e329.

Mason, S. (2018). Publications in the doctoral thesis: Challenges for doctoral candidates, supervisors, examiners and administrators. *Higher Education Research & Development, 37*(6), 1231–1244.

Mason, S., Frick, L., Castelló, M., Cheng, W., Chong, S. W., Díaz Villalba, L., . . . & Weise, C. (2024a). Prominence, promotion and positioning of the 'Thesis by

Publication' in six countries. *Higher Education Policy*.
https://doi.org/10.1057/s41307-024-00350-7

Mason, S., Frick, L., Castelló, M., Cheng, W., Chong, S. W., Díaz Villalba, L., . . . & Weise, C. (2024b). What makes a Thesis by Publication? An international study of policy requirements and restrictions. *Journal of Higher Education Policy and Management*. https://doi.org/10.1080/1360080X.2024.2389357

Mason, S., & Merga, M. K. (2018a). A current view of the thesis by publication in the humanities and social sciences. *International Journal of Doctoral Studies*, *13*, 139–154.

Mason, S., & Merga, M. K. (2018b). Integrating publications in the social science doctoral thesis by publication. *Higher Education Research & Development*, *37*(7), 1454–1471.

Mason, S., & Merga, M. K. (2021). Less 'prestigious' journals can contain more diverse research, by citing them we can shape a more just politics of citation. *London School of Economics Impact Blog*. https://blogs.lse.ac.uk/impactofsocialsciences/2021/10/11/less-prestigious-journals-can-contain-more-diverse-research-by-citing-them-we-can-shape-a-more-just-politics-of-citation

Mason, S., Merga, M. K., & Bond, M. (2022). From PhD by publication to full-time academic: Narratives of three women. In S. Chong & N. Johnson (Eds.), *PhD by publication: Landscapes and narratives* (pp. 185–198). Springer Cham.

Mason, S., Merga, M. K., Canche, M. S. G., & Mat Roni, S. (2021). The internationality of published higher education scholarship: How do the 'top' journals compare? *Journal of Informetrics*, *15*(2), e101155.

Mason, S., Merga, M. K., & Morris, J. E. (2020a). Choosing the thesis by publication approach: Motivations and influencers for doctoral candidates. *The Australian Educational Researcher*, *47*(5), 857–871.

Mason, S., Merga, M. K., & Morris, J. E. (2020b). Typical scope of time commitment and research outputs of thesis by publication in Australia. *Higher Education Research & Development*, *39*(2), 244–258.

Mason, S., Morris, J. E., & Merga, M. K. (2021). Institutional and supervisory support for the Thesis by Publication. *Australian Journal of Education*, *65*(1), 55–72.

Mat Roni, S., & Merga, M. K. (2019). The influence of extrinsic and intrinsic variables on children's reading frequency and attitudes: An exploration using an artificial neural network. *Australian Journal of Education*, *63*(3), 270–291.

Mat Roni, S., Merga, M. K., & Morris, J. (2020). *Conducting quantitative research in education*. Springer.

Mattoon, E. R., Miles, M., Broderick, N. A., & Casadevall, A. (2024). Analysis of justification for author order and gender bias in author order among those contributing equally. *Mbio*, *15*(5), e00646-24.

McAlpine, L., & Castelló, M. (2024). What do PhD graduates in non-academic careers actually do? Interaction between organisation mission, job specifications and graduate lived experience. *Learning and Teaching*, *17*(1), 77–106.

McChesney, K., Burford, J., & Frick, L. (2024). Living the best way possible: Distance doctoral students navigating care for others and themselves. *Access: Critical Explorations of Equity in Higher Education, 12*(1), 106–125.

McKenna, S., & van Schalkwyk, S. (2024). A scoping review of the changing landscape of doctoral education. *Compare: A Journal of Comparative and International Education, 54*(6), 984–1001.

McManus A., Merga, M. K., & Newton W. (2011). What consumers need to know about omega 3 fatty acids. *Appetite, 57*(1), 80–83.

Merga, M. K. (2013). Should Silent Reading feature in a secondary school English programme? West Australian students' perspectives on Silent Reading. *English in Education, 47*(3), 229–244.

Merga, M. K. (2014a). The influence of parents, English teachers, friends & peer group on West Australian Adolescents' Recreational Book Reading: Findings from the West Australian Study in Adolescent Book Reading (WASABR). [Unpublished doctoral thesis]. Edith Cowan University. https://ro.ecu.edu.au/theses/1909

Merga, M. K. (2014b). Peer group and friend influences on the social acceptability of adolescent book reading. *Journal of Adolescent & Adult Literacy, 57*(6), 472–482.

Merga, M. K. (2014c). Exploring the role of parents in supporting recreational book reading beyond primary school. *English in Education, 48*(2), 149–163.

Merga, M. K. (2015). Thesis by publication in education: An autoethnographic perspective for educational researchers. *Issues in Educational Research, 25*(3), 291–308.

Merga, M. K. (2016a). What would make them read more? Insights from Western Australian adolescents. *Asia Pacific Journal of Education, 36*(3), 409–424.

Merga, M. K. (2016b). Gaps in work readiness of graduate health professionals and their impact on early practice: Possibilities for future interprofessional learning. *Focus on Health Professional Education, 17*(3), 14–29.

Merga, M. K. (2017a). Interactive reading opportunities beyond the early years: What educators need to consider. *Australian Journal of Education, 61*(3), 328–343.

Merga, M. K. (2017b). Research shows the importance of parents reading with children – even after children can read. *The Conversation.* https://theconversation.com/research-shows-the-importance-of-parents-reading-with-children-even-after-children-can-read-82756

Merga, M. K. (2020a). School librarians as literacy educators within a complex role. *Journal of Library Administration, 60*(8), 889–908.

Merga, M. K. (2020b). How can school libraries support student wellbeing? Evidence and implications for further research. *Journal of Library Administration, 60*(6), 660–673.

Merga, M. K. (2021a). The academic labour of knowledge mobilization: What scholarly publishers need to know. *Learned Publishing, 34*(4), 655–665.

Merga, M. K. (2021b). What is the literacy supportive role of the school librarian in the United Kingdom? *Journal of Librarianship and Information Science, 53*(4), 601–614.

Merga, M. K. (2021c). How can TikTok inform readers' advisory services for young people? *Library & Information Science Research, 43*(2), e101091.

Merga , M. K. (2022a). How to encourage teens to read. *The Education Hub.* https://theeducationhub.org.nz/how-to-encourage-teens-to-read

Merga, M. K. (2022b). How to plan for whole-school literacy. *The Education Hub.* https://theeducationhub.org.nz/how-to-plan-for-whole-school-literacy

Merga, M. K. (2022c). School libraries as safe spaces promoting literacy and wellbeing. *The Education Hub.* https://theeducationhub.org.nz/school-libraries-as-safe-spaces-promoting-literacy-and-wellbeing

Merga, M. K. (2022d). Turning boys of all ages into life-long readers. *The Education Hub.* https://theeducationhub.org.nz/turning-boys-of-all-ages-into-life-long-readers

Merga, M. K. (2022e). The role of the library within school-level literacy policies and plans in Australia and the United Kingdom. *Journal of Librarianship and Information Science, 54*(3), 469–481.

Merga, M. K. (2023a). *Creating a reading culture in primary and secondary schools: A practical guide.* Facet Publishing.

Merga, M. K. (2023b). *Creating an Australian school literacy policy.* Amba Press.

Merga, M. K. (2024a). Understanding 'predatory' journals and implications for guiding student and client information seeking. *Journal of Library Administration, 64*(6), 682–694.

Merga, M. K. (2024b). Is your thesis by publication policy hostile to students? *London School of Economics Impact Blog.* https://blogs.lse.ac.uk/impactofsocialsciences/2024/09/18/is-your-thesis-by-publication-policy-hostile-to-students

Merga, M. K. (2024c). Working on scorched earth: Contemporary risks of higher education leadership critique through autoethnography. *Higher Education Research & Development.* https://doi.org/10.1080/07294360.2024.2416394

Merga, M. K. (2024d). TikTok and digital health literacy: A systematic review. *IFLA Journal.* https://doi.org/10.1177/03400352241286175

Merga, M. K. (2025). The library as a safe space in contemporary schools: An international study. *IFLA Journal,* https://doi.org/10.1177/03400352251318368

Merga, M. K., & Booth, S. (2017). Investigating debates around racism in sport to facilitate perspective transformation in the secondary English classroom. *Journal of Transformative Education, 15*(3), 184–202.

Merga, M. K., Hays, A., & Coventry, T. (2020). Nurse managers' perceptions of barriers to the mentoring of early career nurses. *Mentoring & Tutoring: Partnership in Learning, 28*(1), 60–77.

Merga, M. K., & Mason, S. (2020a). Sharing research with academia and beyond: Insights from early career researchers in Australia and Japan. *Learned Publishing, 33*(3), 277–286.

Merga, M. K., & Mason, S. (2020b). Researchers are expected to share their research beyond academia but they need support from universities to do so. *London School of Economics Impact Blog.*

https://blogs.lse.ac.uk/impactofsocialsciences/2020/10/07/researchers-are-expected-to-share-their-research-beyond-academia-but-they-need-support-from-universities-to-do-so

Merga, M. K., & Mason, S. (2021a). Doctoral education and early career researcher preparedness for diverse research output production. *Journal of Further and Higher Education, 45*(5), 672–687.

Merga, M. K., & Mason, S. (2021b). Mentor and peer support for early career researchers sharing research with academia and beyond. *Heliyon, 7*(2), e06172.

Merga, M. K., & Mason, S. (2021c). Early career researchers' perceptions of the benefits and challenges of sharing research with academic and non-academic end-users. *Higher Education Research & Development, 40*(7), 1482–1496.

Merga, M. K., Mason, S., & Morris, J. (2018). Early career experiences of navigating journal article publication: Lessons learned using an autoethnographic approach. *Learned Publishing, 31*(4), 381–389.

Merga, M. K., Mason, S., & Morris, J. E. (2019). 'The constant rejections hurt': Skills and personal attributes needed to successfully complete a thesis by publication. *Learned Publishing, 32*(3), 271–281.

Merga, M. K., Mason, S., & Morris, J. E. (2020). 'What do I even call this?' Challenges and possibilities of undertaking a thesis by publication. *Journal of Further and Higher Education, 44*(9), 1245–1261.

Merga, M. K., Mason, S., & Morris, J. E. (2025). 'I really try to model good practices': Reflecting on journal article publication from mid-career. *Learned Publishing, 38*, e1668.

Merga, M. K., & Mat Roni, S. (2017). Children prefer to read books on paper rather than screens. *The Conversation*. https://theconversation.com/children-prefer-to-read-books-on-paper-rather-than-screens-74171

Merga, M. K., & Mat Roni, S. (2018). Children's perceptions of the importance and value of reading. *Australian Journal of Education, 62*(2), 135–153.

Merga, M. K., & Mat Roni, S. (2025a). 'An uphill battle': School library professionals fostering student reading engagement. *English in Education*. https://doi.org/10.1080/04250494.2025.2456718

Merga, M. K., & Mat Roni, S. (2025b). School library professionals' perspectives on current and future workforce challenges. *Journal of Librarianship & Information Science*. https://doi.org/10.1177/09610006241309104

Merga, M. K., & Mat Roni, S. (2025c). School library professionals' perceptions of students' digital information literacy. *Journal of Library Administration, 65*(4), 397–411.

Merga, M. K., Mat Roni, S., & Malpique, A. (2021). Do secondary English teachers have adequate time and resourcing to meet the needs of struggling literacy learners? *English in Education, 55*(4), 351–367.

Merga, M. K., Mat Roni, S., & Mason, S. (2020). Should Google Scholar be used for benchmarking against the professoriate in education? *Scientometrics, 125*, 2505–2522.

Merga, M. K., & Oddone, K. (2025). 'This review is useful': The novel knowledge mobilisation contributions of narrative reviews in higher education. *Issues in Educational Research, 35*(2), 698–715.

Mertkan, S., Onurkan Aliusta, G., & Suphi, N. (2021). Profile of authors publishing in 'predatory' journals and causal factors behind their decision: A systematic review. *Research Evaluation, 30*(4), 470–483.

Mills, D., & Inouye, K. (2021). Problematizing 'predatory publishing': A systematic review of factors shaping publishing motives, decisions, and experiences. *Learned Publishing, 34*(2), 89–104.

Mills, L., Read, G. J., Bragg, J. E., Hutchinson, B. T., & Cox, J. A. (2024). A study into the mental health of PhD students in Australia: Investigating the determinants of depression, anxiety, and suicidality. *Scientific Reports, 14*(1), e22636.

Miranda, R., & Garcia-Carpintero, E. (2019). Comparison of the share of documents and citations from different quartile journals in 25 research areas. *Scientometrics, 121*(1), 479–501.

Mullins, G., & Kiley, M. (2002). 'It's a PhD, not a Nobel Prize': How experienced examiners assess research theses. *Studies in Higher Education, 27*(4), 369–386.

Muñoz-Carpena, R., Batelaan, O., Willems, P., & Hughes, D. A. (2020). Why it is a blessing to be rejected: Improving science with quality publications. *Journal of Hydrology: Regional Studies, 31*, 1–5.

National Health and Medical Research Council (NHMRC) (2019). *Authorship: A guide supporting the Australian Code for the Responsible Conduct of Research.* www.nhmrc.gov.au/file/14358/download?token=jrA-2qrR

National Health and Medical Research Council (NHMRC) (2023). *National Statement on Ethical Conduct in Human Research 2023.* www.nhmrc.gov.au/file/19531/download?token=rpY3-bU5

Neumann, C. B., & Neumann, I. B. (2015). Uses of the self: Two ways of thinking about scholarly situatedness and method. *Millennium, 43*(3), 798–819.

Niazi, S. (2022). Regulator scraps publication requirement for PhD hopefuls. *University World News.* www.universityworldnews.com/post.php?story=20221117150116915#:~:text=As%20part%20of%20far%2Dreaching,qualify%20for%20a%20doctoral%20degree

Nicholas, J., Onie, S., & Larsen, M. E. (2020). Ethics and privacy in social media research for mental health. *Current Psychiatry Reports, 22*, 1–7.

Nygaard, L. P., & Solli, K. (2021). *Strategies for writing a thesis by publication in the social sciences and humanities.* Routledge.

Oboirien, B. (2024). Supporting doctoral candidates to disseminate their research. In K. Luneta, J. Golding, H. M. Kapenda, & P. Phiri Nalube (Eds.), *Doctoral Supervision in Southern Africa: From Theory to Practice* (pp. 159–171). Springer.

OECD (2013). *Education at a glance 2013: OECD indicators.* Paris. https://doi.org/10.1787/eag-2013-en

O'Keeffe, P. (2020). PhD by publication: Innovative approach to social science research, or operationalisation of the doctoral student . . . or both? *Higher Education Research & Development, 39*(2), 288–301.

O'Keeffe, P. (2022). The PhD by publication as preparation for work in the 'performative university'. In S. W. Chong & N. H. Johnson (Eds.), *Landscapes and narratives of PhD by publication: Demystifying students' and supervisors' perspectives* (pp. 199–213). Springer International.

O'Meara, V., Hodson, J., Gosse, C., & Veletsianos, G. (2024). Invisible, unmanageable, and inevitable: Online abuse as inequality in the academic workplace. *Journal of Diversity in Higher Education.* https://doi.org/10.1037/dhe0000545

Osterloh, M., & Frey, B. S. (2015). Ranking games. *Evaluation Review, 39*(1), 102–129.

Palmer, K. (2025). As NIH grant reviews resume, NSF hunts for flagged terms. *Inside Higher Ed.* www.insidehighered.com/news/quick-takes/2025/02/05/nsf-hunts-female-other-flagged-terms

Paltridge, B., & Starfield, S. (2023). The PhD by publication in the humanities and social sciences: A cross-country analysis. *Journal of Further and Higher Education, 47*(7), 863–874.

Parray, U. Y., Loan, F. A., & Khan, A. M. (2024). The dark side of publishing: Unveiling the deceptive tactics of cloned journals in India. *Journal of Librarianship and Information Science.* https://doi.org/10.1177/09610006241256392

Patience, G. S., Patience, C. A., Blais, B., & Bertrand, F. (2017). Citation analysis of scientific categories. *Heliyon, 3*(5), 1–2.

Perlin, M. S., Imasato, T., & Borenstein, D. (2018). Is predatory publishing a real threat? Evidence from a large database study. *Scientometrics, 116*(1), 255–273.

Pfleegor, A. G., Katz, M., & Bowers, M. T. (2019). Publish, perish, or salami slice? Authorship ethics in an emerging field. *Journal of Business Ethics, 156*, 189–208.

Pfost, M., & Heyne, N. (2023). Fostering children's reading comprehension: The importance of fiction reading. *Zeitschrift für Bildungsforschung, 13*(1), 127–137.

Poli, M., Russotto, S., Fornaro, M., Gonda, X., Lopez-Castroman, J., Madeddu, F., . . . & Calati, R. (2025). Suicide risk among residents and PhD students: A systematic review of the literature. *Journal of Psychiatric Research, 181*, 432–462.

Pozniak, L., Luckerhoff, J., & Guillemette, F. (2023). Rédiger une thèse par insertion d'articles dans une démarche générale de méthodologie de la théorisation enracinée. *Enjeux et Société, 10*(2), 17–47.

Pruschak, G. (2021). What constitutes authorship in the social sciences? *Frontiers in Research Metrics and Analytics, 6*, e655350.

Pruschak, G., & Hopp, C. (2022). And the credit goes to . . . Ghost and honorary authorship among social scientists. *PloS one, 17*(5), e0267312.

Pyhältö, K., Tikkanen, L., & Anttila, H. (2024). Relationship between doctoral supervisors' competencies, engagement in supervisory development and experienced support from research community. *Innovations in Education and Teaching International, 61*(3), 555–569.

Pyne, D. (2017). The rewards of predatory publications at a small business school. *Journal of Scholarly Publishing, 48*(3), 137–160.

Razoumova, O., & Hooley, N. (2024). Formations of new knowledge in doctoral supervision and examination in Australia: A preliminary investigation of the adequacy of the written thesis. *Higher Education Research & Development*, 43(8), 1846–1861.

Remenyi, D. (2015). The monograph dissertation versus the papers approach. *Alternation Journal*, 22(1), 327–335.

Retraction Watch (2017). Dispute over author order torpedoes paper on syndrome linked to autism. https://retractionwatch.com/2017/10/11/dispute-author-order-torpedoes-paper-syndrome-linked-autism

Retraction Watch (2025a). The Retraction Watch Hijacked Journal Checker. https://retractionwatch.com/the-retraction-watch-hijacked-journal-checker

Retraction Watch (2025b). His manuscript was rejected. Then he saw it published by other authors. https://retractionwatch.com/2025/03/06/peer-reviewer-publishes-mistake-manuscript-rejected

Rigby, J., & Jones, B. (2020). Bringing the doctoral thesis by published papers to the Social Sciences and the Humanities: A quantitative easing? A small study of doctoral thesis submission rules and practice in two disciplines in the UK. *Scientometrics*, 124(2), 1387–1409.

Robins, L., & Kanowski, P. (2008). PhD by publication: A student's perspective. *Journal of Research Practice*, 4(2), M3.

Robinson, C. (2023). Mainstreaming the alternative format thesis in UK higher education: A systematic narrative review of institutional policies. *Perspectives: Policy and Practice in Higher Education*, 27(4), 140–149.

Robinson-Pant, A., & Singal, N. (2020). Beyond authorship and accountability? The ethics of doctoral research dissemination in a changing world. *British Educational Research Journal*, 46(4), 859–877.

Robles, J. S., & Xie, Y. (2024). Managing blame for racism in broadcast media. *Discourse, Context & Media*, 59, e100785.

Rousseau, S., & Daraio, C. (2025). Research evaluation reform and the heterogeneity of researchers' metric-wiseness. *Journal of Data and Information Science*, 10(1), 1–27.

Royal Melbourne Institute of Technology (2019). *Practice and evidence guide for research*. www.rmit.edu.au/content/dam/rmit/rmit-images/staff-site/my-employment/documents/academic-promotions/2019/Practice_and_Evidence_Guide_for_Research_2019.pdf

Sage (2025). Manuscript preparation for double-anonymized journals. https://us.sagepub.com/en-us/nam/Manuscript-preparation-for-double-anonymized-journal

Sammon, D., Nagle, T., McAvoy, J., Heavin, C., Fitzgerald, C., McCarthy, S., ... & Alhassan, I. (2024). Exploring the PhD supervisor/candidate relationship for a 'publication-based thesis': A metaphor-driven approach. *Journal of Decision Systems*. https://doi.org/10.1080/12460125.2024.2363036

Saragih, E., Saddhono, K., Yannuar, N., & Sumbayak, D. M. (2024). Scholarly manuscript assessment: Scientific journal editor desk evaluation. *Malaysian Journal of Library and Information Science*, 29(2), 1–18.

Scarcella, M. (2024). Academic publishers face class action over 'peer review' pay, other restrictions. *Reuters*. www.reuters.com/legal/litigation/academic-publishers-face-class-action-over-peer-review-pay-other-restrictions-2024-09-13

Schmidt, M., & Hansson, E. (2021). 'I didn't want to be a troublemaker' – doctoral students' experiences of change in supervisory arrangements. *Studies in Graduate and Postdoctoral Education*, 13(1), 54–73.

Schneider, A., & Gur-Arie, R. (2017). Negotiating co-authorship, ethically and successfully. *International Journal of Contemporary Education Research*, 5, 71–82.

Scholars at Risk (2024). *Free to think 2024: Report of the scholars at risk academic freedom monitoring project*. www.scholarsatrisk.org/download-the-free-to-think-2024-pdf/#!

Schweiger, G., Barnett, A., van den Besselaar, P., Bornmann, L., De Block, A., Ioannidis, J. P., . . . & Conix, S. (2024). The costs of competition in distributing scarce research funds. *Proceedings of the National Academy of Sciences*, 121(50), e2407644121.

Scicluna, K. (2024). The academic publishing rort. *The Australia Institute*. https://australiainstitute.org.au/post/the-academic-publishing-rort

Science Media Centre (2019). Advice for researchers experiencing harassment. www.sciencemediacentre.org/wp-content/uploads/2019/10/Advice-for-Researchers-Experiencing-Harrasment-2019.pdf

Sellers, C., Samuel, G., & Derrick, G. (2020). Reasoning 'uncharted territory': Notions of expertise within ethics review panels assessing research use of social media. *Journal of Empirical Research on Human Research Ethics*, 15(1–2), 28–39.

Sharmini, S., Spronken-Smith, R., Golding, C., & Harland, T. (2015). Assessing the doctoral thesis when it includes published work. *Assessment & Evaluation in Higher Education*, 40(1), 89–102.

Shrestha, A. (2023). Incorporating agile principles in completing and supervising a thesis by publication. In D. L. Mulligan, N. Ryan & P. A. Danaher (Eds.), *Deconstructing doctoral discourses: Stories and strategies for success* (pp. 161–176). Springer International.

Silverwood, V. (2023). True dissemination of knowledge doesn't gather dust on a library shelf. In D. Jones, M. Jones, K. Strudwick & A. Charles (Eds.), *Public criminology: Reimagining public education and research practice* (pp. 147–165). Springer.

Solli, K., & Nygaard, L. P. (2023). The doctorate in pieces: A scoping review of research on the PhD thesis by publication. *Higher Education Research & Development*, 42(4), 984–999.

Sparkes, A. C. (2018). Autoethnography comes of age: Consequences, comforts, and concerns. In D. Beach, C. Bagley, & S. Marques da Silva (Eds.), *Handbook of Ethnography of Education* (pp. 479–499). Wiley.

Springer, N., Engelmann, I., & Pfaffinger, C. (2015). User comments: Motives and inhibitors to write and read. *Information, Communication & Society*, 18(7), 798–815.

Springer Nature (2023). Duplicate submission/publication and redundant publication. www.springer.com/gp/authors-editors/editors/duplicate-submission-publication-and-redundant-publication/4224

Springer Nature (2024). Springer Nature unveils two new AI tools to protect research integrity. https://group.springernature.com/gp/group/media/press-releases/new-research-integrity-tools-using-ai/27200740

Stewart, S., Willmott, D., Murphy, A., & Phillips, C. (2024). 'I thought I'm better off just trying to put this behind me': A contemporary approach to understanding why women decide not to report sexual violence. *Journal of Forensic Psychiatry & Psychology, 35*(1), 85–101.

Stolowy, H. (2017). Letter from the editor: Why are papers desk rejected at European Accounting Review? *European Accounting Review, 26*(3), 411–418.

Stracke, E., & Kumar, V. (2020). Encouraging dialogue in doctoral supervision: The development of the feedback expectation tool. *International Journal of Doctoral Studies, 15*, 265–284.

Sullivan, A., & Brown, M. (2015). Reading for pleasure and progress in vocabulary and mathematics. *British Educational Research Journal, 41*(6), 971–991.

Sydney Health Literacy Lab (n.d.-a). Health Literacy Editor. https://shell.techlab.works

Sydney Health Literacy Lab (n.d.-b). Readability. www.sydneyhealthliteracylab.org.au/the-shell-editor#readability

Taylor, S. (2023). The changing landscape of doctoral education: A framework for analysis and introduction to the special issue. *Innovations in Education and Teaching International, 60*(5), 606–622.

Taylor and Francis (2025). Anonymous authorship and researchers at risk. https://authorservices.taylorandfrancis.com/editorial-policies/defining-authorship-research-paper

Taylor, S. J., Pinnock, H., Epiphaniou, E., Pearce, G., Parke, H. L., Schwappach, A., Purushotham, N., Jacob, S., Griffiths, C., Greenhalgh, T., & Sheikh, A. (2014). A rapid synthesis of the evidence on interventions supporting self-management for people with long-term conditions. *Health Services and Delivery Research, 2*(53), 1–580.

Taylor, S., & Whisker, G. (2025). The changing landscape of doctoral education in the UK. In S. Taylor, K. Holley & M. Kiley (Eds.), *Global perspectives on graduate and doctoral education: International case studies* (pp. 156–171). Taylor & Francis.

Tertiary Education and Quality Standards Agency (TEQSA) (2023). Australian Qualifications Framework. www.teqsa.gov.au/how-we-regulate/acts-and-standards/australian-qualifications-framework

Tertiary Education and Quality Standards Agency (TEQSA) (2024). Predatory conferences: A to Z elements. www.teqsa.gov.au/sites/default/files/2024-09/predatory-conferences-A-to-Z-elements.pdf

Think Check Submit (2023). Checklist. https://thinkchecksubmit.org/wp-content/uploads/2023/06/ThinkCheckSubmit-Journals-English.pdf

Thomson, P., & Kamler, B. (2012). *Writing for peer reviewed journals: Strategies for getting published*. Taylor & Francis.

Tomaselli, K. G. (2019). Humanities, citations and currency: Hierarchies of value and enabled recolonisation. *Critical Arts, 33*(3), 16–29.

Torppa, M., Niemi, P., Vasalampi, K., Lerkkanen, M. K., Tolvanen, A., & Poikkeus, A. M. (2020). Leisure reading (but not any kind) and reading comprehension support each other: A longitudinal study across grades 1 and 9. *Child Development, 91*(3), 876–900.

Trahar, S. (2009). Beyond the story itself: Narrative inquiry and autoethnography in intercultural research in higher education. *Forum Qualitative Sozialforschung/Forum: Qualitative Social Research, 10*(1), 1–20.

Tseng, F. C., Huang, M. H., & Chen, D. Z. (2020). Factors of university–industry collaboration affecting university innovation performance. *The Journal of Technology Transfer, 45*(2), 560–577.

UK Council for Graduate Education (2024). UK Research Supervision Survey 2024. https://ukcge.ac.uk/resources/resource-library/ukrss2024#heading424824

Universities Australia (2024). Investing in PhD candidates in Australia. https://universitiesaustralia.edu.au/wp-content/uploads/2024/12/Investing-in-PHD-Candidates-in-Australia.pdf

University of Bath (2025). A checklist of topics for doctoral researchers and supervisors to consider over their initial meetings. www.bath.ac.uk/publications/checklist-for-first-meetings-between-supervisor-and-doctoral-student/attachments/Initial_meetings_checklist_for_supervisory_teams_and_doctoral_researchers(2).pdf

University of Notre Dame Australia (2024). Guideline: Authorship, peer review and dissemination of research. www.notredame.edu.au/__data/assets/pdf_file/0018/216261/Guideline-Authorship,-Peer-Review-and-Dissemination.pdf

University of Newcastle (2021). Academic promotion information for candidates 2021. www.newcastle.edu.au/__data/assets/pdf_file/0008/749735/2021-Academic-Promotions-Information_Session_Candidate_circulation.pdf

University of Queensland (n.d.). Structuring your thesis. https://my.uq.edu.au/information-and-services/higher-degree-research/hdr-candidature-support/how-write-thesis/structuring-your-thesis

Vanderbilt University Centre for Teaching (n.d.). Bloom's Taxonomy. www.flickr.com/photos/vandycft/29428436431

Wall, S. (2006). An autoethnography on learning about autoethnography. *International Journal of Qualitative Methods, 5*(2), 146–160.

Walters, W. H. (2022). The citation impact of the Open Access accounting journals that appear on Beall's List of potentially predatory publishers and journals. *Journal of Academic Librarianship, 48*(1), e102484.

Weber, P. (2014). Discussions in the comments section: Factors influencing participation and interactivity in online newspapers' reader comments. *New Media & Society, 16*(6), 941–957.

Wiley (2024a). Peer review. https://authorservices.wiley.com/author-resources/Journal-Authors/submission-peer-review/peer-review.html

Wiley (2024b). *Journal of Adolescent & Adult Literacy*. https://ila.onlinelibrary.wiley.com/journal/19362706

Wiley (2025a). Types of peer review. https://authorservices.wiley.com/Reviewers/journal-reviewers/what-is-peer-review/types-of-peer-review.html

Wiley (2025b). *The Journal of Adolescent & Adult Literacy*. https://ila.onlinelibrary.wiley.com/journal/19362706

Wiley (2025c). Article Sharing Policy. https://authorservices.wiley.com/author-resources/Journal-Authors/Promotion/article-sharing-policy.html

Wojcieszak, M. E., & Mutz, D. C. (2009). Online groups and political discourse: Do online discussion spaces facilitate exposure to political disagreement? *Journal of Communication, 59*(1), 40–56.

Woloshin, S., Schwartz, L. M., Casella, S. L., Kennedy, A. T., & Larson, R. J. (2009). Press releases by academic medical centers: Not so academic? *Annals of Internal Medicine, 150*(9), 613–618.

Wu, J., Sanchez-Diaz, I., Yang, Y., & Qu, X. (2024). Why is your paper rejected? Lessons learned from over 5000 rejected transportation papers. *Communications in Transportation Research, 4*, 100129.

Wynne, E. (2014). The key to encouraging teen reading is finding the right story. *ABC News Perth*, 13 October. www.abc.net.au/news/2014-1013/encouraging-teen-reading-with-the-right-story/5805122

Wynne, E. (2017). Parents, teachers stop reading aloud too early and kids are missing out, researcher says. *ABC News online*. www.abc.net.au/news/2017-08-29/reading-to-kids-ending-too-early-study-says/8849622

Xie, Y., & Durrheim, K. (2025). Handling racism in a radio phone-in programme: Telling it like it is. *Journalism, 26*(3), 656–675.

Xu, Y., Fatemi, G., & Saito, E. (2024). Reflection on publishing experiences of taught master's course students with their faculty member: Actor-network theoretic discussion. *Journal of Applied Research in Higher Education, 16*(3), 804–819.

Xu, X., Sit, H. H. W., Chen, S., Xu, X., Sit, H. H. W., & Chen, S. (2020). Surviving and thriving: Navigating the doctoral trajectory. In H. H. W. Sit, S. Chen & X. Xu (Eds.), *The eastern train on the western track: An Australian case of Chinese doctoral students' adaptation* (pp. 87–116). Springer.

Yettick, H. (2015). One small droplet: News media coverage of peer-reviewed and university-based education research and academic expertise. *Educational Researcher, 44*(3), 173–184.

Zhao, H. (2025). PhD terminated after 6 years with excellent work done: Retaliation from Prof. Zofia Lukszo, TU Delft. *YouTube*. www.youtube.com/watch?v=ChS0eT683bA

Index